Learning English and Chinese as Foreign Languages

NEW PERSPECTIVES ON LANGUAGE AND EDUCATION
Founding Editor: Viv Edwards, *University of Reading, UK*

Series Editors: Phan Le Ha, *University of Hawaii at Manoa, USA* and Joel Windle, *Monash University, Australia.*

Two decades of research and development in language and literacy education have yielded a broad, multidisciplinary focus. Yet education systems face constant economic and technological change, with attendant issues of identity and power, community and culture. This series will feature critical and interpretive, disciplinary and multidisciplinary perspectives on teaching and learning, language and literacy in new times.

All books in this series are externally peer-reviewed.

Full details of all the books in this series and of all our other publications can be found on http://www.multilingual-matters.com, or by writing to Multilingual Matters, St Nicholas House, 31-34 High Street, Bristol BS1 2AW, UK.

NEW PERSPECTIVES ON LANGUAGE AND EDUCATION: 74

Learning English and Chinese as Foreign Languages

Sociocultural and Comparative Perspectives

Wen-Chuan Lin

MULTILINGUAL MATTERS
Bristol • Blue Ridge Summit

DOI https://doi.org/10.21832/LIN5143
Library of Congress Cataloging in Publication Data
A catalog record for this book is available from the Library of Congress.
Names: Lin, Wen-Chuan, 1966- author.
Title: Learning English and Chinese as Foreign Languages: Sociocultural and Comparative Perspectives/Wen-Chuan Lin.
Description: Bristol; Blue Ridge Summit: Multilingual Matters, [2019] | Series: New Perspectives on Language and Education: 74 | Includes bibliographical references and index. | Summary: "This book compares English as a Foreign Language teaching in Taiwan with Chinese as a Foreign Language education in England and highlights how classroom activities are embedded within ethnic or social group cultures, family resources and school visions or goals, and it highlights the potential for a perpetuation of social inequality as a result"—Provided by publisher.
Identifiers: LCCN 2019018873 (print) | LCCN 2019022396 (ebook) | ISBN 9781788925143 (hbk : alk. paper) | ISBN 9781788925136 (pbk : alk. paper)
Subjects: LCSH: Language and languages—Study and teaching—Social aspects. | English language—Study and teaching—Taiwan—Chinese speakers. | Chinese language—Study and teaching—England—English speakers.
Classification: LCC P53.8 .L55 2019 (print) | LCC P53.8 (ebook) | DDC 495.180071/042—dc23
LC record available at https://lccn.loc.gov/2019018873
LC ebook record available at https://lccn.loc.gov/2019022396

British Library Cataloguing in Publication Data
A catalogue entry for this book is available from the British Library.

ISBN-13: 978-1-78892-514-3 (hbk)
ISBN-13: 978-1-78892-513-6 (pbk)

Multilingual Matters
UK: St Nicholas House, 31-34 High Street, Bristol BS1 2AW, UK.
USA: NBN, Blue Ridge Summit, PA, USA.

Website: www.multilingual-matters.com
Twitter: Multi_Ling_Mat
Facebook: https://www.facebook.com/multilingualmatters
Blog: www.channelviewpublications.wordpress.com

Copyright © 2019 Wen-Chuan Lin.

All rights reserved. No part of this work may be reproduced in any form or by any means without permission in writing from the publisher.

The policy of Multilingual Matters/Channel View Publications is to use papers that are natural, renewable and recyclable products, made from wood grown in sustainable forests. In the manufacturing process of our books, and to further support our policy, preference is given to printers that have FSC and PEFC Chain of Custody certification. The FSC and/or PEFC logos will appear on those books where full certification has been granted to the printer concerned.

Typeset by Deanta Global Publishing Services Limited.
Printed and bound in the UK by Short Run Press Ltd.
Printed and bound in the US by NBN.

Contents

	Abbreviations	vi
	Acknowledgements	vii
	Foreword *Michael Byram*	ix
	Preface	xi
1	Introduction	1
2	A Theoretical Insight: Sociocultural Views on Language Learning	30
3	Learning English/Chinese as Foreign Languages: The Contexts	39
4	Getting Access to English and Chinese: Everyday Practice	71
5	Classroom Life and Pedagogical Comparisons	90
6	Language Learning and Identity: Communities of Practice	129
7	Synthesis and Cross-Cultural Comparisons	173
8	Conclusion	196
	Appendix	206
	References	207
	Index	213

Abbreviations

CfBT	Centre for British Teachers, UK
CFL	Chinese as a foreign language
CiLT	National Centre for Languages, UK
DPP	Democratic Progressive Party, Taiwan
EDT	Education Development Trust
ESOL	English as a second language for speakers of other languages
EFL	English as a foreign language
GCE	General Certificate of Education
GCSE	General Certificate of Secondary Education
GEPT	General English Proficiency Test, Taiwan
HNCs	Higher National Certificate
HNDs	Higher National Diplomas
ICU	Intensive Care Unit
IMF	International Monetary Fund
IRE	Initiation (question)-response-evaluation
KK	Kenyon and Knott phonetic symbols
KMT	Kuo-Ming Tang (former Chinese Nationalist Government)
LEA	Local Education Authority
MFL	Modern foreign languages
MOE	Ministry of Education, Taiwan
OECD	The Organisation for Economic Cooperation and Development
PGCE	Postgraduate Certificate in Education
PISA	Programme for International Student Assessment
RDEC	Research, Development and Evaluation Commission, Taiwan
RE	Religious Education
RMB	Renminbi
SDR	Special drawing right
SLA	Second language acquisition
UCLA	University of California, Los Angeles
WTO	World Trade Organisation

Acknowledgements

This book could not have been written without the loving support and enthusiastic participation of many individuals and academic scholars. I am grateful to all the students, parents, teachers and school heads in Taiwan and England who took part in the different periods of fieldwork throughout this book project. Without their enthusiastic participation, assistance and warmth, this book would not have been possible.

I am deeply indebted to many academic scholars who scaffolded my intellectual growth in the niche of sociocultural theory, language education which eventually led to the writing of this book. Professor Gabrielle Ivinson and Professor Brian Davies provided me with invaluable guidance throughout my PhD phase in Cardiff University, UK. Professor Harry Daniels helped with vital consultation as my mentor during my ESRC postdoctoral phase in Bath University and, in particular, Professor Michael Byram shared every step with me during fieldwork in England and throughout the book writing phase. Moreover and again, I am particularly indebted to Professor Brian Davies whose caring support with proofreading and critiquing significantly informed the analysis of the English fieldwork data. It would not have been possible to complete this social scientific adventure or the writing of this book without their enduring encouragement and support.

Special thanks are offered to those participating English teachers in Taiwan and the Chinese language teachers in England – Dr Theresa Munford, Mrs Yalun Ellen Yilmaz (吳亞倫), Mr Thomas Godber (高峰) and Ms Xia Feng (冯霞), for their support in allowing me to intrude in their classrooms; and to school administrators, Ms Laura Waters, Ms Cathy Shail and Mr Alan Bird. Several institutions have facilitated this work including the Department of Education at Bath University and the School of Education at Durham University in England through the support of visiting scholarships in 2013 and 2015, respectively. In particular, I am grateful to Dr Trevor Grimshaw from Bath University and Dr Prue Holmes from Durham University for their support.

I would like to give special recognition to the Ministry of Science and Technology (MOST) and Wenzao Ursuline University of Languages,

Taiwan, for their continuing support for this book project. Funding from MOST (NSC102-2918-1-160-002 / NSC102-2410-H-160-001-MY2) enabled me to travel to England to conduct sociocultural fieldwork in five schools in two different cities. Lastly, I am very grateful to Multilingual Matters for their vision, support and guidance in publishing this book.

Foreword

Some 50 years ago, my director of undergraduate studies, Robert Bolgar, said that anything one wrote should be put in a drawer for a couple of years, and then reread. If one still thought it was worthwhile, then one should seek to publish. Although I have not always been able to follow this advice, I remember it as a warning about the rush to publication which bedevils current academic life.

One striking feature of this book is its long period of gestation. Work and thought over a decade and more is published here. In today's academic world, which mirrors the world in general, this devotion to writing is an admirable endeavour, and one which has met the quality test Dr Bolgar recommended to us.

I have known Wen-Chuan Lin for only a part of the period covered by his book. In fact I know him as 'Richard' Lin because that is how he introduced himself, and this English name-identity has stuck in my mind. Richard's Chinese and English names reflect his professional identification with the two phenomena of Chinese and English as foreign languages. This places him in an ideal position to reflect on both. He is, I am sure he would agree, not bicultural, although he is certainly bilingual to a very high degree. He is, on the contrary, an intercultural person who has used his experience and perspectives to analyse two language teaching and learning situations. Studying the Taiwan context while being a researcher in British universities has given him new insights into the familiar, into the pedagogical world in which he grew up as a learner and teacher. Seeking in-depth experience of situations of Chinese as a foreign language in British schools has made him familiar with a new and strange educational world. Using both perspectives, he has made the strange familiar and the familiar strange – to use that old ethnographer's phrase – for himself and his readers, whether in Taiwan, Britain or beyond.

Using an analytical framework from comparative education is an additional and very valuable dimension. As Richard/Wen-Chuan says, comparison is inherent in our modes of understanding. He himself no doubt used comparison, inevitably if not always consciously, in his fieldwork and analysis. His readers will do the same. It is therefore important that he has provided a systematic and theoretically well-founded way of doing so, since comparison can be of two kinds. Comparison can lead to evaluation – X is better than Y – and it can lead to new insights – seeing X makes us see Y differently and vice versa. It is the second which we should pursue, and a systematic comparative methodology ensures we do so. Comparison as evaluation is seldom if ever productive, as Richard's quote from Michael Sadler and his famous garden analogy reminds us.

It is now a commonplace to refer to the globalised world and the significance of language learning, and therefore of language teaching of a specific, intercultural kind. I need not add to the usual remarks. Richard's book is written in that context and *inter alia* is a response to it. Readers will find a book with this general, wide scope but also – and this is less common and the particular value of this work – a deep focus on specific issues raised from the decade-long work to which I alluded above. I am sure readers will enjoy and learn, just as Richard himself has done. I can only congratulate the latter on his achievement and encourage the former to delve into this substantial and innovative work.

Michael Byram
Professor Emeritus
Durham University, UK

Preface

This book is derived from sociocultural fieldwork carried out in Taiwan and England between 2004 and 2015. The first phase was carried out mainly in 2004 and 2005 in four Taiwanese secondary schools, the second between 2013 and 2016, when I travelled to England for fieldwork. In order to maintain methodological continuity between these two research phases as cross-cultural comparative investigations of young people's foreign language learning, both followed a Vygotsky-inspired sociocultural framework. Sociocultural perspectives have grown in influence on the development of the field of second language acquisition (SLA), arguing that language learning does not take place in a social vacuum. It involves the engagement of ideas among people, developed in everyday practice and shaped by social and cultural factors. Work from the first phase generated very rich findings which have been disseminated to the academic world through several journal articles over the past few years. However, since a single paper has to focus on relatively narrow aspects in limited journal space, findings from these separate articles inevitably failed to provide a sufficiently holistic view of English as a foreign language (EFL) learning in Taiwanese schools, homes and communities. I kept feeling that there was a need to disseminate these findings in full and in book format, providing more complete pictures of EFL learning and teaching practices with readers both in Taiwan and abroad.

In addition, three timely inspirations propelled me to write this book. In 2014, the first came with the call for book projects from the Ministry of Science and Technology (MOST) in Taiwan, part of an attempt to broaden and prolong the impact of social scientific research because 'books tend to last longer'. The next lay in the increasing interest in learning Mandarin Chinese worldwide. Chinese, my mother tongue, appears to be growing in popularity with learners, young and old, including those in English-speaking countries such as Britain, Australia and the USA. The third grew from a realisation that very little is known about differences in students' choices, experiences and difficulties in learning Chinese as a foreign language (CFL) in secondary schools in countries where it has been a recent addition to the school curricula.

With these considerations in mind, the ultimate purpose of this book is to enhance our understanding of the processes whereby young people in Taiwan and England recognise, access and value English or Chinese as foreign languages at school, home or in the community. Hopefully, by comparing schools within the distinctive social and cultural settings of Taiwan and England, we are able to use another culture's 'lens' to see things from new analytical angles and improve our understanding of the limitations and strengths of our own educational practice and challenge our taken-for-granted viewpoints towards the familiar everyday practices of foreign language teaching and learning within our own cultures.

Wen-Chuan Lin
September 2019

1 Introduction

More than half a century ago, the American sociologist C. Wright Mills (1959/2000) argued in his influential book *The Sociological Imagination* that in order to propose a feasible answer or explanation to the sociological problems we encounter, we usually need to undertake 'comparison'. He suggested that we have to observe social phenomena through comparison of different social situations in order to transcend the limits of 'flat description' of the social situations under study. C. Wright Mills (1959/2000) suggested that

> Comparisons are required in order to understand what may be the essential conditions of whatever we are trying to understand.... We must observe whatever we are interested in under a variety of circumstances. Otherwise we are limited to flat description. To go beyond that, we must study the available range of social structures, including the historical as well as the contemporary.... If we limit ourselves to one national unit of one contemporary (usually Western) society, we cannot possibly hope to catch many really fundamental differences among human types and social situations. (Mills, 1959/2000: 147)

Standing on Wright Mill's shoulders, contemporary research studies in comparative education suggest that it is beneficial to undertake comparative studies of education research because we can use another culture's 'lens' to better understand the limitations and strengths of our own practice. In an era of rapid globalisation, the educational world is constantly becoming 'smaller' and interaction between people within the same or different cultures is happening with greater intensity. English, the traditional lingua franca, and Chinese, the new emergent foreign language, are increasingly used in the 'flattened' (Friedman, 2005) business world. As Mason (2014) rightly reminds us, comparative studies of foreign language education research cannot ignore globalised cultural contexts, including ways in which local identities may have been strengthened in resistance to globalisation processes.

With Mills' words in mind, the prime purposes of this book are to enhance our critical understanding of processes in which young people in Taiwan and Britain recognise, access and value English or Mandarin Chinese as foreign languages at school, home or in the community and to enable us as educational practitioners to improve our understanding of the limitations and strengths of our own educational practices, to challenge our taken-for-granted viewpoints on familiar everyday practices of foreign language teaching and learning within our own culture.

This introduction seeks to outline the benefits and potential interest of cross-cultural and cross-national comparisons of two foreign languages learnt by secondary students from different sociocultural backgrounds. It provides an introduction to and an explanation of the selection of English as a foreign language (EFL) in Taiwan and Chinese as a foreign language (CFL) in England, and begins by addressing why young people in these two nations believe that they need to learn them. It delineates current issues involved in the rise in importance of EFL learning in Taiwan and CFL learning in England in relation to recent, national economic growth and concern about future global markets. Concern has also been raised about substantial gaps in English academic achievement between different social groups in Taiwan and there are related emerging issues of learning Chinese in Britain. These issues are framed in a discussion of the sociocultural, theoretical and methodological approach used and the benefits of comparison.

The Study of English in Taiwan and Chinese in England: Current Issues

Learning English in Taiwan: A national movement

Globally, the history of teaching and learning EFL has deep economic and political roots. The popularity of EFL learning is increasing among many Asian countries, including China, Japan, Korea and Taiwan. Teaching English in China stretches back 150 years to the opening of the first English language school in 1861 during the Qing dynasty. Following its overthrow in 1911, the government of the Republic of China announced in 1912 that English had been chosen as the foreign language in secondary school education. In 1937, following the Japanese invasion, the English language reverted to non-compulsory status in the secondary curriculum, though when the Chinese Nationalist government (KMT) retreated to Taiwan in 1949, English was still its major foreign language (Lin & Byram, 2016). Since the 1980s, Taiwanese society has undergone far reaching, rapid, economic change, becoming the world's 15th largest trading country in 2004. Learning English in Taiwan has become a primary economic concern as industries have recognised the need to compete within global markets in which trade is predominantly carried out in English. People in Taiwan now tend to assume that anything involving English must be good. English-speaking ability carries considerable prestige, and it is strongly believed that speaking English more fluently fuels upward mobility, in terms of both occupational and social status (Lin, 2007, 2012a).

Taiwan's entry into the World Trade Organisation (WTO) in 2002 led to increased economic cooperation and trade exchange between Taiwan and the other countries in the global community. Growth in the demand for and supply of English language education in business and public sectors and in school settings is increasing. For example, in the public sector a plan to establish a bilingual environment was incorporated in the Challenge 2008 National Development Plan. A Chinese–English signage system was provided for roadways, public places and tourist sites, and bilingual websites were created. English news programmes were produced and laws and regulations were translated into English. In education, the extension of EFL to younger ages of Year 3 in 2005 in the national curriculum was a response to a dramatic sense of sociopolitical change and consciousness of global economic trends (Ministry of Education – MOE Taiwan, 2015). Given this seemingly 'national movement' (*quán-mín yùn-dòng* 全民運動) of learning English in Taiwan, problems exist, such as substantial gaps in English academic achievement between students of differing geographical regions and social groups, that have led to emerging educational inequalities.

A gap in EFL academic achievement in secondary schools

Although English has gained in prestige in Taiwan, students from different geographical regions and various social groups seem to have unequal access to it in their everyday learning activities, both in and out of school. Despite the official downward extension of English education to Year 3 of schooling in 2005, which highlighted its economic and political significance, it was nevertheless already a matter of concern that national longitudinal achievement data had consistently demonstrated substantial gaps in English ability, one that is known locally as the 'urban–rural divide' (*chéng-xiāng chā-jù* 城鄉差距) in learning English among junior high school candidates (age 13) living in different locales (Lin, 2007, 2012a). In addition, there is yet another divide in English language achievement that concerns local scholars and educators. For example, the first National Basic Competence Test for junior high school students in 2002 indicated that English was the only subject that had a statistically bimodal or 'double skewed distribution' (*shuāng-fēng xiàn-xiàng* 雙峰現象) of scale scores, leading local scholars and educational authorities to recognise that approximately half of junior high students (out of a total number of 299,714 nationwide) participating in the test were either low achievers or appeared to have given up learning English. In fact, this urban–rural ability divide in English is a long-standing problem in Taiwan. English has always been the only school subject among all five main subjects (Chinese, English, Math, Social Sciences and Natural Sciences) that revealed 'double skewed' in statistical distribution in the last two decades regardless of region or gender differences (Lin, 2007). Official endeavours to rectify the situation have tended to focus on macro aspects, such as urban–rural resource discrepancies. This overly simplified interpretation and examination of the gap in EFL learning fails to provide micro views of language learning processes, which examine the complexities of social and psychological forces affecting language learning and teaching. One of these social forces is Taiwan's multilingual social reality, which arises from its hybrid population.

Emerging educational inequality among social groups

Before we move on to see how EFL learning may have any impact on multilingual and intercultural education in Taiwan and vice versa, it is helpful to detail the historical and cultural roots of the four Taiwanese social groups and their geographical settlements. Taiwan, with a population of approximately 23 million, is an island with a diverse population, composed mainly of Holo (also named Hokkien) (69%), Hakka (15%), Chinese Mainlanders (14%) and indigenous people (2%) (Ministry of Foreign Affairs, Taiwan, 2019). These four social groups have different geographical and historical roots, as well as specific group cultural and linguistic variations.

Holo and Hakka arrived in Taiwan from China to join Taiwan's indigenous inhabitants at the beginning of the 17th century. Most migrants were fleeing social turmoil or hardship in the south-eastern provinces of China, namely, the southern Fujian and eastern Guangdong areas. The descendants of these two major migratory groups now make up the two largest population groups in Taiwan. In the post-war era, mainly in 1949, an influx of Chinese Mainlanders (i.e. the Chinese Nationalist government led by Chiang Kai-Shek) fleeing the communist advance in Mainland China replaced the Japanese colonial government (1895–1945) and came to comprise some 14% of the population. For thousands of years before any Han Chinese migrants arrived, however, aboriginal footprints could be found all over Taiwan.

Each of the three immigrant groups speaks different language varieties that have various linguistic roots. Those from the Fujian province, who constituted the majority of immigrants before Japanese colonialism, spoke the Holo dialect, currently termed 'Taiwanese language' (*tái-yǔ* 台語) or 'Southern Min language' (*mǐn-nán yǔ* 閩南語), while those from the Guangdong province spoke the Hakka language (*kè-jiā huà* 客家話). The Chinese Mainlanders who took over control of the Taiwanese state from the Japanese colonists mainly spoke Mandarin Chinese, officially called the 'national language' (*guó-yǔ* 國語), which is identical to the official language of China. By 2014, the indigenous people had 16 officially recognised 'tribes' (*zú* 族) island-wide, each with its own tribal language whose characteristics are mainly Austronesian (Malayo-Polynesian) (Thompson, 1984).

Geographically, the Holo people settled in the plains, developing the sea and river ports, particularly in Taipei (to the north) and Kaohsiung (to the south), which provided good living conditions and close networks for trade with the mother country (China) (see Figure 1.1). The Hakka people, who originated from the eastern part of Guangdong province, settled in Taiwan somewhat later than the Holo; they inhabited marginal areas, living on rough and less lucrative farmland. The later-arriving Mainlanders were primarily soldiers and Chinese Nationalist government (KMT) officials, who lived mainly in military camps and urban areas. As Greenhalgh (1984: 537) argued, the Mainlanders were largely concentrated in Taiwan's cities, and 'the larger the city, the higher the proportion of mainlanders'. Urbanisation and modernity were the features that distinguished the Mainlanders from other groups. The indigenous peoples were, and are, the only group living mainly in the mountains and along the rivers, practicing traditional hunting and farming lifestyles. Though many of them had originally been plains dwellers, they were forced to leave and head inland, becoming labelled 'mountain people' (*shān-dì rén* 山地人) by the Chinese migrants (Thompson, 1984) and, later, 'high mountain people' during the Japanese occupation from 1895. The current terms 'aborigines' and 'indigenous people' (*yuán zhù-mín* 原住民) were not officially used to describe these groups until 1995.

Political tension among the four social groups has existed for the past 200 years, centring primarily on limited land resources. Before the arrival of the Chinese Mainlanders in 1949, feuds between Holo land occupants and later Hakka incomers were widely documented, the latter tending to cluster together for self-protection in the foothills or allying themselves with other Hakka communities 'against the numerically superior Holo-speakers and, occasionally, against the aborigines located further into the mountains', thus giving rise to the stereotypical notion of the Hakka people's 'ethnic cliquishness' (Thompson, 1984: 555). Due

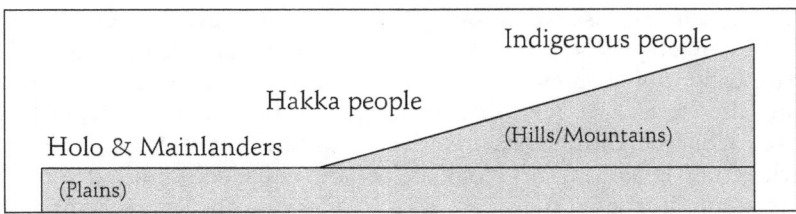

Figure 1.1 Geographical distribution of social groups in Taiwan

to their inferior social, political and economic position to that of other social groups, many Hakka people tend to avoid speaking the Hakka language in public to hide what was known locally as 'Hakka humble identity' (Lin, 2007, 2012a).

Political rivalry between Chinese Mainlanders and other social groups in Taiwan in the post-war era also led to a language hierarchy and political conflict, although, in recent years, multiculturalism has become the official policy. To ensure national monolingualism and to justify its perceived role as legally representing China, the Chinese Nationalist government promoted Mandarin Chinese as Taiwan's 'national language', from 1949 until 1987, enforcing a Chinese language policy in schools, whereby pupils were not permitted to speak their mother tongues (Sandel, 2003). This declaration of Chinese as the national language gave it 'high language' political status (Huang, 1993), ostensibly denying the legitimacy of other languages, undergirding a language hierarchy that Giles and Johnson (1981) term 'ethnic speech markers', which has been a constant source of antagonism among social groups within Taiwanese society for decades. Given the fact that language suppression has impaired social group identity within minority groups, including causing a diminution of the Hakka language, successive Taiwanese governments have intended to pursue multilingualism and mother tongue education policies as a means to promote local identities and social equality.

However, since English language competence has been reinforced and recognised at official, community and institutional levels as a key to success, it has become a new form of 'high language' (Huang, 1993), muddying the water of local multilingual and intercultural education and provoking further linguistic identity, conflict and competition. In addressing what he referred to as 'the world crisis in education', Coombs (1985) insightfully suggested that:

> Language differences are inextricably tied to ethnic, religious, tribal, and other differences... Any nation that encompasses various ethnic linguistic groups... inevitably faces the serious difficulties in achieving a binding sense of nationhood among its different peoples. These internal language difficulties are compounded by each country's need for linguistic bridges to the rest of the world. (Coombs, 1985: 256)

Indeed, political tension and conflict due to linguistic divisions and the suppression of languages in Taiwan has emerged in relation to the substantial, historically rooted gap in English achievement between learners from the four different groups. Five different languages, including the national language (Chinese), the high-status foreign language (English) and three other social group languages (i.e. Holo, Hakka and indigenous, the latter a complex group in its own right), are used in Taiwan. They are schematically compared in Table 1.1, which highlights a hierarchical linguistic order

Table 1.1 Ranking of language status among Taiwanese ethnic groups

Language	Holo	Mainlander	Hakka	Indigenous	Feature
English	2	2	2	2	International
Chinese	1	1	1	1	National
Holo	3	3	3	3	Neo-political
Hakka	N/A	N/A	4	N/A	Local dialect
Indigenous	N/A	N/A	N/A	4	Ethnic dialects

Note: N/A indicates that the language is not used or taught in the social group.

beneath which there are growing tensions. The values (1 through 4) do not suggest a rank order based on empirical research; however, this ranking of language status is widely held in Taiwan (Lin, 2012b: 11).

Although oversimplified, this ranking points to the reality that learning either English or local languages, for some students from certain social groups, may not be perceived to offer equal benefits, even if students are provided with standardised national or school curricula. For example, the Hakka language is embedded in the school curriculum in local Hakka village schools since the implementation of mother tongue education or locally termed 'home-soil education' (*xiāng-tǔ jiào-yù* 鄉土教育) aimed at celebrating social group identities and preserving minority languages from extinction. However, this language is in conflict with Chinese as the official, or national, language (ranking No. 1) and English (ranking No. 2), a robust competitor, especially as Taiwan moves towards further engagement in international trade and politics. The Hakka participant village school which I observed failed to provide lessons on Hakka ethnic, cultural or linguistic matters in the one-hour weekly home-soil education class, the session often being 'lent' to teachers of the five main subjects (e.g. English) for remedial purpose or for quizzes. The unique, low-status identity of the Hakka language and culture was mirrored by this absence of ethnic and cultural subject matters in schools.

As Huang (2000: 146) noted, in Taiwan, 'local languages are facing stiff competition on two fronts', from Chinese and English. However, with the increasing political status of the Holo people, comprising more than two thirds of the population, and the Taiwanese language (*tái-yǔ* 台語) following the local Taiwanese Democratic Progressive Party's (DPP) first ever presidential win in 2000, the Hakka local language is now encountering a third front of competition, rather than two. Even more generally, tensions concerning social identities among Chinese, English, Taiwanese and various native languages place students, some more than other social groups, in a quandary over how to allocate their language priorities. Unfortunately, there has been very little recognition of the impact of such linguistic identity clashes, emerging language competition and social inequality at institutional and political level within Taiwanese society.

Learning Chinese in England: A growing trend

Before considering how learning Chinese is slowly becoming a trend, it is helpful to capture the historical context of foreign language learning in the UK, which may serve as a basis for our understanding of why some young people have access to or value the Chinese language, but not others. As a preliminary comment, we need to note that within the political entity which is the United Kingdom of Great Britain and Northern Ireland, there are four separate education systems. In general, education is a devolved responsibility in Scotland, Wales and Northern Ireland. In Scotland, there is a long educationally independent system; Northern Ireland clings to formal secondary school selection and a predominantly sectarian provision; and England and Wales are becoming increasingly divergent as England pursues policies of removing schools from local government control which the Welsh devolved government rejects, while pursuing a policy of steady expansion of Welsh medium schooling which must, effectively, be taken up at nursery or infant stage.

In terms of languages in Wales there is a substantial Welsh medium sector and Welsh is compulsory as a second language in all English medium state schools. Gaelic is taught as a second language in very limited parts of Scotland and there is currently a political crisis in Northern Ireland about the status of Erse in schools and public life. It could be said that the state of modern foreign languages (MFLs) in each of these three regions is in even poorer shape than in England though Scotland seems to have the systems in place to develop better capacity in Chinese (Tinsley & Board, 2014). It is also the case of course, that substantial numbers of British children – with wide regional and class variation – have first languages other than indigenous British ones. It is worth noting that in the following analysis and discussion of MFL learning situations in the UK, distinctions have to be made, according to circumstances and themes, between England and other parts of the UK.

The historical situation of MFL learning in the UK, in fact, suggests a 'reluctance' of the British to learn a foreign language (e.g. Wikeley & Stables, 1999). There is a widespread view that, historically, foreign language learning and teaching in the UK has had limited success (e.g. Jones, 2007). National data from the National Centre for Languages (CiLT, 2006) demonstrate that the situation in England has deteriorated with a consistent decline in the numbers of students pursuing MFLs at various levels, as witnessed by the concern set out in the National Languages Strategy of the early 2000s which aimed explicitly to tackle 'a cycle of national underperformance in languages... low take up of languages beyond schooling and a workforce unable to meet the demands of a globalised economy' (DfES, 2002: 10). More recently, a consistent decline in the numbers of students pursuing MFLs at various levels (British Council, 2014; CiLT, 2006) appeared to exacerbate the 'cycle'. French, despite its conventional popularity, was among the worst 'hit', with a disappointing decline in uptake at secondary level.

The learning of French, for instance, has been seen as poor along with other MFLs (e.g. Bartram, 2006). Although almost all state schools in England offer French at Key Stage 4,[1] it is not obligatory and 'French and German have seen decreases in pupil numbers over the past three years' (CiLT, 2006: 1–2). Similar declines in student numbers both for French and German were also reported by one third of schools in the independent sector (British Council, 2014). Many attribute this cycle of national underperformance and decline in languages either to the ending of compulsory language study at the end of Key Stage 3 in 2004 (e.g. Jones, 2007) or the gap between curriculum content and students' perceptions of the impact on their career choices. Others pinpoint issues of a gender gap in foreign language learning, attributing boys' 'opting-out' or 'underachieving' to a negative identity of French as a 'feminised' language (e.g. Bartram, 2006). Unfortunately, very few of these accounts provide a holistic view of language learning that helps to chart students' choices and experiences of learning foreign languages at different educational levels in the UK in general or England in particular.

In fact, if we are to understand the historically limited success of foreign language learning in the UK, we should not ignore the influences from the broader level of national curriculum or language policy changes. For example, in his book *Modern Languages in the Curriculum*, Hawkins (1987) argued that there was a major change when universities stopped requiring all students to have a General Certificate of Education (GCE) pass in a foreign language in order to enter university. This policy change apparently undermined the status of languages. Another indication of government policy in England withdrawing support for languages was the merger of CiLT with the Centre for British Teachers (CfBT) Education Trust in 2011. Whether or not this merger may have had a direct impact on the decline of learning languages is not certain. Unfortunately, there is little space in this book for a full study of the decline.

As a way of concentrating our main focus, I shall turn to an examination of a recent government-commissioned survey to map the picture of the current foreign language learning situation in England (British Council, 2014). This survey titled *Language Trends 2013/14: The State of Language Learning in Primary and Secondary Schools in England* reveals a general picture of foreign language intake in England:

> In secondary schools French, Spanish and German are easily the most widely taught languages. Arabic, Italian, Japanese, Chinese and Russian are offered much less frequently and often only as extra-curricular subjects. The range of languages offered is much richer in the independent sector. (British Council, 2014: 10)

The national data highlighted that the 'big three' (French, Spanish and German) are most commonly taught within the secondary curriculum. Nevertheless, there are interesting differences in foreign language intake between state and independent schools, in particular among the less frequently taught languages such as Chinese. For example, Italian, Latin and Chinese are offered by more than 10% of state schools outside curriculum time. These and other less frequently taught languages such as Arabic, Japanese and Russian are often taught as extra-curricular subjects. However, in the independent/public school[2] sector, although one third of schools report declines for both French and German, there are more opportunities to learn a second foreign language than there are in state schools (British Council, 2014). As indicated in Figure 1.2, the recent national data (EDT, 2016) reveal that Chinese language provision has been approximately four times higher in independent secondary schools than state schools for a decade, giving rise to issues of inequality of language resources.

Among those less frequently taught languages in the secondary sector, Chinese seems to have gained in popularity. Evidence from national data has indicated that even though 'there are no strong indications that lesser taught languages are gaining ground in the school system. ...the study of Chinese is increasing slowly from a small base, with ...six per cent of state secondary schools and ten per cent of independent schools offering pupils the opportunity to learn Chinese as a curriculum subject' (British Council, 2014: 8). However, as highlighted in this survey report by the British Council, the sustainability of Chinese as a new emergent foreign language is not assured, and this is worthy of our attention and further investigation.

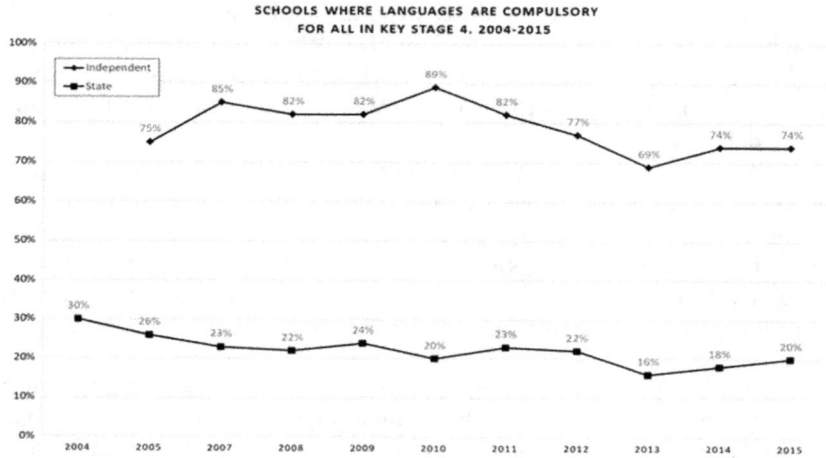

Figure 1.2 Schools where languages are compulsory for all in Key Stage 4 (Reprinted with permission from the Education Development Trust)

Learning Chinese: The beginning of success?

In 2015, the International Monetary Fund (IMF) recognised the elite status of the renminbi – RMB (*rén-mín-bì*) – as one of the major world currencies alongside others, such as the US dollar and the Euro. The IMF executive board determined that the RMB is freely usable and decided to include the RMB in the special drawing right (SDR) basket, which took effect in 2016. According to the IMF, this inclusion has three significant meanings for China (IMF News, 2016):

- The RMB becomes the fifth currency making up the SDR basket.
- Its inclusion is an important milestone in China's global financial integration.
- The decision reflects growing international use and trading of the RMB.

This economic inclusion means the Chinese government and people are able to use their own currency to undertake direct trade with the world. The 'green light' from the IMF for China to trade directly in the business world not only signifies the upcoming economic power of China, but has also fuelled the learning of Chinese globally including Britain. Learning Chinese is becoming an economic concern as the British government recognises the importance of future economic relations with China, in particular after the decision to leave the European Union in 2016. In 2015, the bilateral relationship between Britain and China reached a new height when Chinese President Xi Jinping, the Chinese leader since 2005, paid a state visit to Britain. Although the main purpose of the visit was perhaps the controversial Chinese involvement in the British nuclear industry which created a big division in public debate between 'the money men and the security side' (BBC News, 2015), the visit further demonstrated the considerable and highly valued economic ties between the two countries, whose status might become even more important under some of the possible outcomes of the UK decision to leave the European Union.

In addition, the growing number of Confucius Institutes worldwide reveals the increasing influences of the Chinese language and culture. Confucius Institutes are administered by the Confucius Institute Headquarters (or Hanban), a non-government agency reporting directly to the Ministry of Education, China. Although the growth of Confucius Institutes has not been without controversy, given concerns about academic freedom and the right to free speech (e.g. BBC News, 2014a), 'Confucius had positive associations with teaching in particular, and culture more generally, and the name offered global brand recognition' (Starr, 2009: 69). Therefore, many believe that Confucius Institutes are designed to support the growth of the Chinese language and culture worldwide, as

Table 1.2 Number of Confucius Institutes/Classrooms

Regions	Countries	Year			
		2014	2015	2016	2017
European	UK	134	156	177	186
Asian-Pacific	Australia	60	69	81	83
America	USA	542	603	611	629

well as the training of Chinese language teachers. Recent shifts in geopolitical and language education priorities worldwide reveal a growing popularity for learning CFL and an increasing number of Confucius Institutes around the globe, including Anglophone countries such as the UK, Australia and the USA (see Table 1.2).

According to the annual development report of the Confucius Institute 2017 (Hanban, 2018), there are 219 Confucius Institutes/Classrooms in 34 countries (regions) in Asia. By 2017, as many as 83 Confucius Institutes/Classrooms had been established in Australia. In America, there are 735 Confucius Institutes/Classrooms in 22 countries with the USA claiming the largest number of 629. In Africa, there are 84 Confucius Institutes/Classrooms in 41 countries. Lastly, in Europe, there are 480 Confucius Institutes/Classrooms in 43 European countries with Britain claiming the largest number of 186 (Figure 1.3). In Britain, for example, a new Confucius Institute was set up in London in 2015, aiming to increase the number of Mandarin teachers to 1200 by 2019, with the hope that many will head to state schools due to their shortage of qualified Mandarin teachers (BBC News, 2014b).

It is not clear if the growing economic, political and cultural ties with China in recent years will have a positive impact on young people

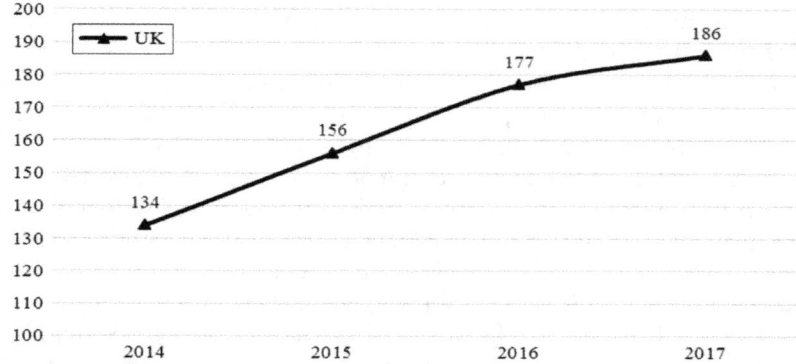

Figure 1.3 Increase in the number of Confucius Institutes/Classrooms in the UK

in England learning Chinese. However, empirical evidence from national data has suggested a growing trend for learning Chinese. For instance:

- A rising number of both state and independent schools are introducing Chinese into the school curriculum (CiLT, 2006, 2007).
- Among the top 10 languages which emerged as the most important for Britain, Chinese ranked number four (Spanish, Arabic, French and Chinese) according to the British Council (2013) commissioned survey in 2013.
- Of the lesser-taught languages (Chinese, Urdu and Russian), only Chinese is showing any tendency to increase, in terms of schools' provision in Key Stage 3 (British Council, 2014).
- Chinese appears as the strongest of the lesser-taught languages in Key Stage 3 (EDT, 2016).

The national data from CiLT and the British Council for the years 2006–2014 suggest a growing trend for learning Chinese. However, data from the British Council (2014) caution that the sustainability of Chinese is 'not assured'. The national data from the Education Development Trust (EDT, 2016: 124) also caution that 'although it appears as the strongest of the lesser-taught languages, being taught in more schools, in the state sector, it is most commonly offered as an enrichment subject in Key Stage 3'. Research shows that there are particular problems associated with learning this new, emergent language in countries such as Britain (CiLT, 2007; Clegg, 2003; Wang, 2009) and Australia (Orton, 2008; Singh & Han, 2014), which are worthy of our attention.

Emerging issues in teaching and learning Chinese

More than a decade ago, Clegg (2003) identified several factors that constrain the development of Chinese language provision in educational sectors in Britain, namely, teaching materials and exam syllabus; staffing and teacher supply; organisation of teacher training; curriculum time constraints; perceptions of the Chinese language; and inadequate advisory support. He further suggested that Britain should carry out a full-scale review of the school curriculum to ensure coverage of China and the provision of both the Chinese language and culture studies. In addition, there is an urgent need for teacher training in Chinese as a MFL, with provision for student funding. In fact, recent studies have shown that some of the above-mentioned problems that Clegg identified have been solved or at least partly solved (Wang, 2009). For example, more schools are starting to offer Chinese (e.g. British Council, 2014), have link schools in China and organise summer immersion courses in China (e.g. CiLT, 2007; Wang, 2009). Nevertheless, there seems to be several recurring issues associated with teaching and learning Chinese not only in Britain but also elsewhere such as Australia. These issues are, for instance, concerns about the quality of existing teachers and the high dropout rates of students.

In England, CiLT launched a national survey in 2007 – Mandarin Language Learning: Research Study – and revealed significant insights into the incidence and patterns of the provision of Chinese language teaching in secondary schools. Emerging issues of concern were

- *High dropout rates*: The reasons for the high dropout rates from Year 7 (3427) to Year 11 (430) in pupil numbers remain unclear.
- *Gender gap*: A gender gap in achievements emerged in learning Chinese, similar to other foreign languages (e.g. French), although a more nuanced exploration is needed.
- *Inequality of offer*: The tendency in some schools to offer Chinese to high achieving students which might deter their peers, thereby engendering social inequality.
- *Inequality of language resources*: Chinese language provision was four times higher in independent secondary schools than state schools. Whereas link-ups with partner schools in China were identified as having a positive impact on pupil motivation to learn Chinese.

In particular, the unequal access to Chinese, as a lesser-taught language, between state and independent schools has been a long-existing social phenomenon in England. For example, according to the most recent national data from the British Council (2016: 124), 'Chinese is offered by 13% of state schools and 46% of independent schools in Key Stage 3', indicating that Chinese language provision[3] – four times higher in independent secondary schools than state schools – is still true.

In their research report *The Teaching of Chinese in the UK*, Tinsley and Board (2014) presented a general picture of how Chinese was taught and the strategic challenges that existed for each of the four nations in the UK. They noted that

> in English speaking countries the position of English as a lingua franca gives rise to particular challenges for the learning of other languages. …because there is no obvious single language which everyone should learn. Previous research into the development of Chinese teaching in the UK has highlighted the challenges in moving from an 'enrichment' to a 'mainstream' subject and the lack of a centrally-directed vision. Previous studies both in the UK and in Australia have highlighted the importance of adequate curriculum time, appropriate teacher training and smooth transition between educational phases. The motivations of pupils and the attitudes of their parents are also identified as important considerations. (Tinsley & Board, 2014: 5)

Indeed, despite the fact that there is a 'fertile context' for the development of Chinese in the UK, the position of English as a lingua franca poses challenges to English-speaking countries such as the four nations in the UK and Australia for learning other languages, including Chinese. The key challenge areas of learning Chinese both in the UK and Australia are identified – inadequate curriculum time, lack of appropriate teacher training, smooth transition between educational phases and the motivation of pupils, which worth our attention.

For example, in other English-speaking countries such as Australia, there is a similar trend of increasing interest in learning Chinese due to Australia's geographical location in the Pacific realm and its growing economic ties with China. According to Orton:

> Chinese is a language of unique and continuing significance to Australia in the twenty-first century: we cannot afford not to have a significant percentage of the community workforce with a degree of competence in the language. (Orton, 2008: 8)

However, the high dropout rates in Chinese learning, as in the UK (Tinsley & Board, 2014), also concern many researchers and educationalists in Australia. Orton (2008: 8) argues that, '94% of those who begin Chinese at school quit before Year 10; and beginners at university drop out at rates close to 75%'. To confront this challenge of high dropout rates, the Australian government's target is for at least 20% of learners to study an Asian language through to the end of Year 12 (Singh & Han, 2014). Singh and Ballantyne (2014) further point out the vulnerability of Chinese learning situations for English-speaking learners in Australia. They argue that:

> In New South Wales there is a major problem in the retention of second-language (L2) learners studying Chinese from primary to the end of secondary school. The learning of Chinese by English-speaking learners in Australia is as fragile as fine bone china. Facilitating the learning of Chinese by beginning second-language learners in English-speaking school communities in a multilingual country such as Australia is a challenge. (Singh & Ballantyne, 2014: 200)

Although the situation of Chinese learning in Australia is not our foci in this book, the foregoing issues of concern over Chinese learning reveal that although there is a growing trend to learn this language, it does not appear to be consistently popular with students or have equal access in secondary schools. Nor do those students who choose to study Chinese as part of their curriculum appear to perform in line with expectations.

In fact, the foregoing concerns in EFL and CFL only provide us with a general view of emerging issues. Further investigation is needed to explore the various sociocultural resources provided by locales, such as parental engagement, pedagogical practice and differences in state and independent sector school aims, which are a matter of discussion in the following chapters. With the complexities of a multilingual reality within Taiwanese society in mind and the potential gap in EFL learning between different social groups, the question of social advantage and 'cultural capital' (Bourdieu, 1986), which is raised in respect of EFL in Taiwan and CFL in England, is at issue. The popularity of learning CFL in England is growing, albeit not itself without problems regarding who has access to the opportunity to learn Chinese, not unlike the question of who has access to English learning in Taiwan. Given the similarities and differences of the current issues in learning the two MFLs in Taiwan and England, Wright Mills' insightful suggestion to undertake comparisons should be borne in mind in order to enhance critical understanding of different social situations. This is also one of the main reasons why carrying out a comparative study can be beneficial and will be argued further in the next section.

The Value of a Comparative Perspective

Why comparison? A critical view from comparative education research

As previously mentioned, contemporary research studies in comparative education suggest that it is beneficial to undertake comparative studies of education research because we can use another culture's 'lens' to better understand the limitations and strengths of our own practice. Making comparisons is 'in the very nature of intellectual activity' and 'a fundamental part of the thought processes which enable us to make sense of the world and our experience of it… *only* by making comparisons can we properly defend our position on most questions of importance which require the making of judgements' (Philips, 1999: 15, *italics* original). Indeed, comparing is by nature a human higher-order thinking process that leads to critical judgement of questions at hand or situations under study and helps to challenge our taken-for-granted viewpoints towards the familiar education practices at home. Therefore, comparisons provide us with new understandings through acquiring a new perspective on the familiar, though this should not lead to an unquestioning assumption that there can be a transfer of practices from one country to another. Given the aforementioned benefits of comparisons, we are also aware of concerns regarding if there can be any transfer of practices from one country to another without qualitative judgements that emphasise context and history (Pereyra *et al.*, 2011).

In their book *Comparative Education Research: Approaches and Methods* (2nd edn), Bray et al. (2014) provide useful reviews on comparative education research from historical perspectives before the millennium to emerging dynamics and emphases in the 21st century and identify several issues that emerged in the development of this field. These issues include 'uncertainties about the nature, scope and value of the field of comparative education' in the mid-1950s and 'no internally consistent body of knowledge, no set of principles or cannons of research that are generally agreed upon by people' in the field (Kazamias & Schwartz, 1977: 151). Moving into the 21st century, the development of comparative education research appears to be even more dynamic, thanks in particular to the advances in information technology and globalisation. For example, Crossley and Jarvis (2000) examine the changing phases of comparative education research and attribute them to a combination of factors including:

> the exponential growth and widening of interest in international comparative research, the impact of computerised communications and information technologies, increased recognition of the cultural dimension of education, and the influence of the intensification of globalisation upon all dimensions of society and social policy world-wide. (Crossley & Jarvis, 2000: 261)

Among these factors, the growing interest in international comparative research, the impact of globalisation and increased recognition of the cultural dimension of education are particularly relevant to the foci of this book – cross-cultural comparisons of two studies in Taiwan and England. To concentrate on our discussion of the benefits and potential problems of comparisons in the field of comparative education, I highlight various procedures, purposes and levels of comparisons before the delineation of carrying out comparisons between the two sociocultural studies in Taiwan and England.

Comparative education research has different procedures and purposes. Philips (1999: 16) highlighted several important benefits of the study of educational issues in a comparative context. He argues that the comparative study of education:

- provides a body of descriptive and explanatory data which allows us to see various practices and procedures in a very wide context that helps to throw light upon them;
- contributes to the development of an increasingly sophisticated theoretical framework in which to describe and analyse educational phenomena;

- plays an important supportive and instructional role in the development of any plans for educational reform, when there must be concern to examine experience elsewhere;
- helps to foster cooperation and mutual understanding among nations by discussing cultural differences and similarities and offering explanations for them;
- is of intrinsic intellectual interest as a scholarly activity, in much the same way as is the comparative study of religion or literature or government.

There are also different 'levels' of comparison including the comparison of policies, organisations, cultures, values and classrooms. Bray's (2014: 19–20) recent delineation of different categories of people, such as practitioners, policymakers and academics, helps us to understand who may benefit from undertaking comparative studies of education at which levels. For practitioners (e.g. school principals and teachers), they 'make comparisons in order to improve the operation of their institutions'. For policymakers, they 'examine education systems elsewhere in order to identify ways to achieve social, political and other objectives in their own settings'. For academics, they 'undertake comparisons in order to improve understanding in many domains, including the forces which shape education systems and the roles of education systems in social and economic development'.

Despite the different emphasis of why certain categories of people undertake comparative education studies, Philips (1999) and Bray (2014) share views in common that comparative education research can provide us with an alternative 'frame' of thinking from a wider cultural context and thus facilitate the development of education systems and processes. However, a closer look at the research literature of comparative education studies in the past few decades indicates a greater interest at the level of macro-national educational systems than micro-school and classroom processes (Alexander, 1999). The overt emphasis on international comparisons of policies or organisations as macro-national educational systems has not been without controversy.

In the last three decades, the level of comparing 'policies' has been particularly welcomed by policymakers thanks to the advances in information technology. For example, Wilson (2003: 30) points out that in the field of comparative education, 'the advent of web pages at international organisations and national statistical services has revolutionised how basic research is undertaken.... The development of Internet search engines ... has also transformed our research capabilities'. Bray *et al.* (2014) also point out that technology has spread the impact of comparative education research and made findings and insights from comparative educators accessible to a much larger audience. Therefore, the use of international data banks to compare educational systems is more convenient than before and considered by many as an effective way to identify and promote evidence of 'what works' (Auld & Morris, 2014). At the level of educational policy, cross-national comparisons of student performance are now essential to educational policy debates, and a growing number of studies have explored the ways in which comparative evidence has been used to initiate, or legitimise, patterns of 'borrowing' and 'lending' around the world (Auld & Morris, 2014).

One such example that has garnered more political and media attention and interest has been the Organisation for Economic Cooperation and Development's (OECD) PISA[4] study, representing the most widely reported of such comparative surveys in recent years. However, while PISA has become an influential tool, it also has limitations. For example, Meyer and Benavot (2013) argue that PISA's over-reliance on numbers and statistics is itself problematic. Bray (2014: 37) also points out that 'the comparisons in PISA have sometimes lacked the methodological insights that could have been brought by the tools and traditions of the field of comparative education. These include qualitative judgements that emphasise context and history'. In fact, it could be argued that PISA has always been a deeply contentious enterprise and the major issue is how do we validly lift pedagogic or institutional practice from one social and cultural context to another without having a whole ensemble of interlocking features to hold them in place.

In a much-quoted lecture delivered more than a century ago, Michael Sadler (1900/1964) reminded us that:

> In studying foreign systems of Education we should not forget that the things outside the schools matter even more than the things inside the schools, and govern and interpret the things inside. We cannot wander at pleasure among the educational systems of the world, like a child strolling through a garden, and pick off a flower from one bush and some leaves from another, and then expect that if we stick what we have gathered into the soil at home, we shall have a living plant. A national system of Education is a living thing, the outcome of forgotten struggles and 'of battles of long ago'. It has in it some of the secret workings of national life. (Sadler, 1900/1964: 310)

Indeed, we must be constantly aware of the warnings which began with Sadler's (1900/1964: 310) statement that education reformers should not 'wander at pleasure among the educational systems of the world, like a child strolling through a garden, and pick off a flower' expecting that sticking it in our own soil will produce 'a living plant'. In other words, while following the patterns of 'borrowing' and 'lending' around the world, we need to take into account the broader social and cultural context while undertaking comparative studies in order to avoid doing a naïve or superficial comparison. Therefore, the applications and developments in the form of comparative education must 'be understood with regard to their broader intellectual backdrop, and the social and political conditions within which they emerge, and to which they respond' (Auld & Morris, 2014: 131).

Furthermore, contemporary critiques of comparative education research argue that there is a need to move away from the comparison of a macro-national system to micro-school and classroom processes. For example, Alexander (1999) cautions against the traditional neglect of classroom processes such as pedagogy by comparative researchers. He argues that:

> comparativists have tended to concentrate on national systems and policies rather than school and classroom processes and that this imbalance of attention needed to be rectified... the growing prominence being given to 'process' variables... what happens in classrooms is actually rather important; and the equally belated development of pedagogy as a central focus for educational research. (Alexander, 1999: 109)

The cross-national and cross-cultural comparison of micro-school and classroom foreign language learning processes follows this call and is the central focus of this book. It is with this in mind that I turn to delineating the methods used to carry out comparisons through the approach of sociocultural theory to learning.

Carrying out comparisons: Sociocultural approaches to learning

This book derives from sociocultural fieldwork carried out in Taiwan and England between 2004 and 2015. The Vygotsky-inspired sociocultural approach to learning has been very useful in exploring the social processes and the development of students in learning foreign languages. Recent advocates of sociocultural theories of second or foreign language learning and development have suggested that conventional second language acquisition (SLA) models require new, theoretical perspectives with different planes of analysis that take into account the socio-historical, sociocultural and sociopolitical contexts that shape language learning. To examine the foregoing sociological issues that shape language learning, we require a methodology that enables us to understand students' choices, views and experiences of foreign languages that motivate learning. Rogoff's (1995) model of three planes of analysis – community, interpersonal and personal – facilitates the development of an approach that seeks to understand such processes of thinking and learning as inseparable from the settings in which they are located. The intention therefore is to explore foreign language learning issues through a methodological lens derived from sociocultural theory that recognises learning as embedded in multiple settings. Students' personal decisions and views will be considered in a framework that takes account of the personal conditions, interpersonal processes in school and experiences in the wider communities as well as the homes in which they live. In Chapter 2, I delineate the theoretical and methodological underpinnings of sociocultural approaches to learning in more depth.

Two Nations, Nine Schools with Diversified Social/Institutional Groups

In the investigation of EFL and CFL learning and teaching in Taiwan and England from sociocultural and comparative perspectives, I was interested in understanding young people's choices and experiences of these two foreign languages. In line with sociocultural approaches to learning, foreign language learning is viewed as a situated practice whereby the socio-historical, sociocultural and sociopolitical contexts which shape language learning are taken into account. Towards this end, I identified school settings across various regions in Taiwan and England separately. For example, as shown in Figure 1.4, the four Taiwanese schools were chosen to represent the four major ethnic groups – Holo, Chinese Mainlander, Hakka and indigenous – located in urban and rural areas. The four schools in England were chosen to represent the state and independent schools where Chinese is a recent addition to the school curriculum. An additional school – St Mary's – was a state school in England not observed, but where I taught interested students about Chinese language and culture as taster lessons in the summer of 2013 and 2014.

In the following section, I introduce the nine schools in turn and provide a flavour of some of the students' ethnic and cultural backgrounds in these schools. Since learning does not take place in a social vacuum but is always embedded within particular contextual levels, these students' cultural origins, in particular in Taiwan, and the specific features of the schools are viewed as pivotal to the analysis of classroom learning and teaching processes. To protect the schools' identities, all names are pseudonyms.

The four participant schools in Taiwan

Urbany School: Urbany School was located in the urban area of Kaohsiung, the largest city in southern Taiwan. It was founded in 2000 as a new, municipal, junior high school, five storeys high with modern facilities, such as lifts for the benefit of people with disabilities and inbuilt visual aids for teaching, particularly TVs, in each classroom. In 2005, it

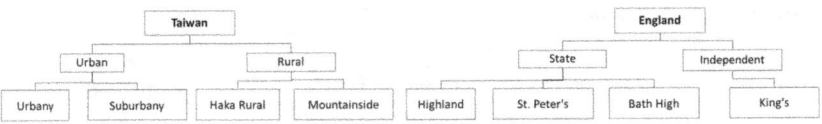

Figure 1.4 Comparisons between schools in Taiwan and England

comprised 62 classes with some 2521 students, mainly ethnic Holo (70%), Mainlanders (19%) and a small number of urban Hakka (10%) from the school catchment area, as shown in Table 1.3. In addition to the visually elegant appearance of its schoolrooms, the school campus had been carefully designed and maintained for bilingual purposes (Chinese and English). Following the primary aims of a bilingual school, the school intended to provide a subtly designed bilingual environment, including ubiquitous bilingual noticeboards and classroom signs, and this received solid support from parents and was welcomed by the local educational authority. This bilingual school vision enabled Urbany to continue to take in its full allowance of students while the falling birth rate in Taiwan led to lower enrolment in most secondary schools.

Suburbany School: Suburbany School, located in a suburban region approximately eight miles from downtown Kaohsiung, was established in 1970 and at the time of the research was composed of 105 classes, with a massive number of 3329 students, largely ethnic Holo (74%) and Mainlanders (26%). The relatively 'giant' size of Suburbany's population existed for good reason; it had been famous for its unique experimental gifted classes (*zī-yōu-bān*) for high-ability students, selectively recruited. Popular belief in the slogan that 'enrolling children in elite schools is a prerequisite for future success' within Taiwanese society, as well as individual parental ambition, guaranteed Suburbany's flow of applicants with superior ability, not only from within its catchment area but beyond, making it one of the largest junior high schools in Kaohsiung. In contrast to its large student population, Suburbany's school campus seemed rather small. Its schoolrooms were of three types: traditional, modern and unfinished. It was intriguing to see that its high-ability classes, including the one observed, were allocated modern classrooms situated centrally on the

Table 1.3 Demographic features of the four schools in Taiwan

Locales	Classes	Population	Ethnicity
Urbany	62	2521	Holo: 70%
			Mainlander: 19%
			Hakka: 10%
Suburbany	105	3329	Holo: 74%
			Mainlander: 26%
Hakka Rural	15	486	Hakka: 88%
			Non-Hakka: 12%
Mountainside	Senior: 11	Indigenous: 269	Indigenous: 97%
		Non-indigenous: 20	
	Junior: 13	Indigenous: 403	Non-indigenous: 3%
		Non-indigenous: 8	

Note: Figures were estimated in 2005.

campus adjacent to staff offices so that, according to the school principal, noise from outside traffic and potential interruption from other normal classes might be avoided. In contrast, the other normal class observed was situated in the row of traditional, three-storey classroom buildings.

Hakka Rural School: Hakka Rural School was situated in a rural township, near craggy foothill terrain, surrounded by a rice farm landscape, about 20 miles from downtown Kaohsiung. A new highway system, built some five years before the research was conducted, allowed the local town people to travel to downtown Kaohsiung within an hour. Hakka Rural School was an old junior high school founded in 1946, composed of 15 classes, with some 486 students who were predominantly ethnic Hakka (88%) coming from a cluster of Hakka villages. At over 70 years of age, Hakka Rural School looked old and traditional. However, it had a number of newly built schoolrooms mixed with traditional ones. Grades 7 and 8 students were allocated the new settings, while Grade 9 students were still taught in the old settings adjacent to the main staff offices. Like most secondary schools in Taiwan, the student population in Hakka Rural School had been in decline, the effects of a falling birth rate accentuated by the growing popularity of newly built, competing schools in urban areas which attracted applicants with higher potential.

Mountainside School: Mountainside School was located in an indigenous Paiwan village, 45 miles from downtown Kaohsiung. The Paiwan tribe (*pái-wān zú*) is the third largest indigenous tribe among the 16 officially recognised indigenous groups in Taiwan. Mountainside School was a junior high school founded in 1968 and extended to become a comprehensive junior-senior school in 2002 as part of the Taiwanese government's focus on the educational rights of minority groups. At the time of the research, the junior department was composed of 13 classes and the senior department 11 classes with a total student population of about 700 students. Mountainside School was a unique, indigenous boarding school (58% boarded) with 97% of its indigenous students coming from the local Paiwan village and other, remote, inner-mountain tribal communities. The same governmental focus on the educational rights of indigenous people enabled Mountainside to be financed for the construction of a modern school campus, including brand new schoolrooms and, in particular, a distinctive, multipurpose gymnasium and a standard 400 metre track and field for the development of athletic sports. Recent government funding had also made possible the introduction of subsidies for part of the student tuition and boarding fees for indigenous students at the secondary education level. Enchanting sculptures and paintings representing Paiwan's tribal customs were ubiquitous both on the school campus and in the community, ranging from the three Paiwan warriors in the central village square to the distinctive twin Paiwan warriors atop the school gate and the paintings of Paiwan cultural customs and historical legacies on the school walls, celebrating ethnic and culture identities that play a vital role in Mountainside School's hidden curriculum.

The five participant schools in England

Highland School: Highland School was a girls' state school with 1200 students at the time of the research in 2015 in an urban city in southwestern England. Students were located across two campuses just opposite each other on a narrow street surrounded by residential houses. As claimed in the Highland School prospectus, it provided a single-sex learning environment engendering high academic aspirations and aimed to encourage girls to fulfil their academic and career potential. It also aimed to enable students to develop well-rounded abilities, including taking leadership roles across the school and participating in extracurricular activities. Working in partnership with nearby partner secondary schools, Highland School took part in the local Education Network. The aim of this social network is to improve the educational experience of young people in member schools and colleges, and more importantly to share local educational resources such as learning CFL. For example, Highland School had opportunities to share teaching and learning activities and resources, such as workshops, with partner schools. An annual Chinese Day was usually held in Highland School where students from all partner schools in the network (e.g. St Peter's School) demonstrated their Chinese learning outcomes through performances.

St Peter's School: St Peter's School was an 11–18, state, co-educational Catholic school located in the suburban area close to Highland School. It was rated 'Outstanding' by Ofsted[5] and had also been rated as an 'Outstanding Catholic' school. St Peter's School was a member of the local Education Network and had opportunities to share teaching and

Table 1.4 Demographic features of the five schools in England

Feature	School Names	Categories	Students Learning Chinese
State	Highland	Girls'	n = 6 Year 13 (5 years)
	St Peter's	Co-ed (Catholic)	n = 10 Year 7 (beginners)
	Bath High	Boys'	n = 15 Year 10 (1 year)
	St Mary's*	Co-ed	n = 60 Year 9 (beginners)
Independent	King's School	Co-ed	n = 18 Year 9 (2 years)
			n = 11 Year 11 (4 years)

*St Mary's was the only participant school not observed but directly taught by me.

learning activities and resources, including the annual Chinese Day event, with other local partner schools. St Peter's School also established an international education partnership, linking schools in Jiangsu province in China (mainly in the Shanghai and Suzhou areas – 'Suzhou Link') with a number of nearby partner schools including Highland School and Bath High School. Each summer, St Peter's School hosted a group of 20 Year 7 Chinese students at the college for two terms. They came to improve their English skills and joined in a full St Peter's School programme of study and activities. These young Chinese visitors, hosted by St Peter's families, brought a host of experiences to share with St Peter's students in lessons and performances, and ran a regular Chinese club with activities including Chinese language lessons and culture learning such as calligraphy, Kung Fu and Chinese kites.

Bath High School: Bath High School was an 11–18, boys' state school located on the hillside near the same urban city as Highland School. Like St Peter's School, Bath High School was judged by Ofsted as 'Outstanding'. In its school vision, Bath High School aimed to develop boys' learning potential and academic performance at GCSE, which is usually outperformed by girls nationally in England. As claimed in the school prospectus, Bath High School aimed to do better than boys of similar ability across the country in areas such as reading and writing abilities. Apart from this school vision aiming to develop boys' potential as active individuals, in contrast to Highland School (the all-girl sector), Bath High School had ample athletic facilities such as a rugby field and football pitch. Like Highland School and St Peter's School, it was also a member of the local Education Network and had opportunities to share teaching and learning activities and resources in education, including the annual Chinese Day event held in Highland School where students from all partner schools performed their Chinese learning outcomes.

St Mary's School: St Mary's School was a co-educational state school with 1353 students (in 2015), located in a village about 20 minutes from the same city centre where Highland School was located. It had a mixture of buildings ranging from original 1960s classroom blocks to a new building opened in 2013 and a brand new sixth form centre opened in 2015. Before 2013, St Mary's School did not have Chinese on the school curriculum, but was excited to try it after my suggestion of two weeks of taster lessons in Chinese language and culture in the summer of 2013 and 2014. I instructed two Chinese classes (30 students in each) and students were invited to provide written accounts about their perceptions of their Chinese learning experiences and future perspectives before and after the two weeks of lessons. After the students revealed their enormous interest in learning Chinese and in responding to parents' expectations, the school language head (a French language teacher) enrolled in a local

Chinese teacher training programme in 2014 and eventually started teaching Chinese to a class of students at St Mary's School in 2015.

King's School: King's School was an independent co-educational school, located in a city adjacent to a tourist seashore area in southern England. A sixth form college with a long history, it was founded in the mid-19th century and was the first 'public school' (i.e. private fee-paying school) to be founded in the area. It had gothic revival buildings with the main entrance building looking very much like the 'Trinity College at Cambridge University' to me. The school appearance seemed to send an embodied image to students that they were bound to enter Oxford or Cambridge some day in the future. In fact, nearly 30 students from King's School were accepted to Oxford or Cambridge universities (among some 1800 applicants) in 2015. Although the school buildings looked historical, a mixture of new modern campuses was under construction, and it had a junior sector (elementary school) just a few blocks away on the same street. As an elite 'public school', front gate security checks and reception procedures appeared to be stricter and more formalised than the other state schools observed. Unlike the other state schools observed, King's School had a historical chapel located at the centre of the school campus, which had a dual function as an educational (e.g. morning assembly) and religious (e.g. choir) facility. The school ethos also appeared to be somewhat different from the state schools observed. As a fee-paying, elite school, school teaching and extra administrative work loads for teachers were demanding, somewhat similar to the elite schools in Taiwan such as Suburbany School.

Implications of this Book

This book has implications both within the academic community and beyond in policy arenas and professional institutions.

Academic implications

Sociocultural research has historical roots inspired by Vygotsky's (1896–1934) – a Soviet developmental psychologist – challenge to individualistic approaches to the human mind and requires multiple methods, within multidisciplinary approaches, involving areas of psychological, sociological, anthropological and linguistic investigation, for the understanding of human learning. Within the academic community, the sociocultural investigation into English and Chinese language learning in Taiwan and England has the potential to make a major contribution to international research on the pedagogy of English and Chinese language learning. It informs theories of learning by highlighting how classroom activities are embedded within multiple settings involving ethnic or other social group cultures, family and community resources and school visions or goals. It also underlines the need for cross-disciplinary integration in attempts to understand human learning in general and foreign language education in particular.

In addition, inspired by Mills' call for comparative and historical study, this book demonstrates a comparative education research that has expanded the temporal reach of analysis to a cross-cultural comparative modality, thereby enhancing our analytical thinking and understanding of limitations and strengths in foreign language education in our own culture such as in Taiwan or England. In particular, the study has investigated classroom learning and teaching processes as situated in broader cultural contexts such as school, home and the community. Lastly, inspired by recent calls from comparative educationists to move from a traditional focus on the 'macro' system level to more nuanced classroom teaching or learning processes, as many comparative studies have emphasised in the past few decades, this sociocultural and comparative inquiry has explored the 'micro' and 'meso' planes of analysis. Both the micro individual learning process and the meso interactional process between students and teachers were explored. In fact, this comparative sociocultural study contributes to pushing academic research boundaries to a new and innovative niche that significantly informs our understanding of human learning and education.

Political and practical implications

Given the emphasis that the Taiwanese government has seen English language learning as contributing to economic development within global markets and the increasing popularity of Chinese language learning in England, this book has the potential to make a major contribution to the politics of educational and economic inclusion. It is the first sociocultural investigation of learning EFL in Taiwan, illuminating how different ethnic groups recognise, access and value the English language and pointing out why some achieve less well than others in doing so. It suggests that teachers' capacity to share students' ethnic culture and mother tongue in pedagogical practice facilitates their intersubjective meanings (Rogoff, 1990). Its findings illuminate why some ethnic groups are relatively highly motivated to learn English and are able to gain privileged economic positions in the job market. In a similar vein, the sociocultural investigation of learning CFL in England reveals how different social groups (state and independent schools) recognise, access and value Chinese. It suggests that learning Chinese, like English in Taiwan, is gradually being viewed from learners and state aspirations as one of the keys to success in England's economic globalisation. Learning Chinese becomes a value-laden practice whose difficulties are exacerbated by heightened political pressure to ensure the UK's place in the global economy. Through this sociocultural lens, we may speculate that learning Chinese in England may create a bigger gulf between social classes than before if incipiently unequal access to Chinese were to become entrenched. Towards this end, English society may be at risk of augmenting an 'educational apartheid' that already exists in language teaching in secondary schools in the process of learning Chinese, exacerbating forms of social inequality within classroom settings and beyond. These insights can form the basis for recommendations to education practitioners, parents and policymakers in Taiwan, England and many other countries who are concerned to improve young people's English or Chinese language capabilities in an era of rapid globalisation.

Structure of the Book

In this chapter, some current issues of foreign language learning have been briefly introduced, and the theoretical and methodological approaches of the studies which inform the studies reported in this book have been outlined. In Chapter 2, sociocultural theoretical perspectives on foreign language learning, appropriate and useful in exploring social processes and student experience and development across different cultural contexts in learning a foreign language, are explored. Chapter 3 sets the scene for a cross-national examination and comparison of learning English and Chinese as foreign languages in Taiwan and England, respectively, by describing appropriate features of their historical and cultural contexts. Chapters 4 through 6 draw theoretical analyses together with fieldwork based on empirical research in Taiwan and England that follow Rogoff's (1995) model of three planes of analysis as an analytical framework. For example, in Chapter 4, I examine how secondary students in the two regions gain access to English and Chinese in their everyday practice of the two foreign languages. In Chapter 5, I describe students' classroom life, with the foci on teacher–student interactional processes, in order to depict how teachers apply certain pedagogical strategies such as 'scaffolding' (Woods *et al.*, 1976) to help students reach higher levels of knowledge acquisition and gradually shift more responsibility for the learning process to students. In Chapter 6, I explore the identity issues emerging in the process of learning English/Chinese with an attempt to understand individual students' learning trajectories in the 'communities of practice' (Lave & Wenger, 1991; Wenger, 1998). The last two chapters offer thematic discussion and a synthesis of key findings from the fieldwork through a cross-cultural comparative lens. Chapter 7 delineates the global and neo-political framing of foreign language learning and further discusses emerging issues of linguistic and cultural globalisation, presenting two themes regarding potential social inequality due to language competition and social gender identities in learning the two target foreign languages. In the final chapter, I offer suggestions to educationalists, scholars and policymakers who are concerned with young people's foreign language learning in countries such as Taiwan, England and many others facing economic competition in an era of globalisation.

Notes

(1) A key stage is a stage of the state education system in the UK setting the educational knowledge expected of students at various ages. Key Stage 4 is the legal term for the two years of school education which incorporate General Certificates of Secondary Education (GCSEs) and other examinations. In England, KS4 is normally known as Year 10 and Year 11 (ages 14–16).
(2) 'Public' here refers to a traditional term with historic origins. While this term is still in common use, the more accurate term is 'independent school'; one where students are academically selected and with more or less costly tuition.
(3) Care needs to be taken in interpreting the quantitative results (percentage) presented in the national data as the number of pupils learning Chinese, as a lesser-taught language, is usually very small. Unfortunately, exact figures of pupils involved in learning Chinese were not available in these national data.
(4) The OECD Programme for International Student Assessment (PISA) examines student knowledge in science, reading and mathematics. The OECD claims that PISA results provide educators and policymakers with the quality and equity of learning outcomes achieved elsewhere, and allow them to learn from the policies and practices applied in other countries.
(5) Ofsted is the Office for Standards in Education, Children's Services and Skills. Ofsted inspects and regulates services which care for children and young people, and services providing education and skills for learners of all ages in the UK.

2 A Theoretical Insight: Sociocultural Views on Language Learning

In Chapter 1, I noted that several 'levels' of comparison are often made in comparative education research, including comparisons of policies, organisations, cultures, values and classrooms. Unfortunately, the comparison of micro-school and classroom processes historically has tended to be neglected. In arguing for a new way forward in comparative education, Broadfoot (1999) contends that in the late 20th century the focus of educational debate is moving gradually towards 'learning and how it can be best facilitated, rather on teaching' and in this context:

> socio-cultural studies have gained an increased prominence in their capacity to provide a conceptual link between individual perspectives and the broader social context; to link culture with both individuals and institutions in an intellectual coherent way that provides guidance for the facilitation of learning. (Broadfoot, 1999: 27)

Indeed, sociocultural approaches, which regard culture as a core concern, have been increasingly used to explain students' learning and development (e.g. Cole, 1996; Lin, 2007; Rogoff, 1990; Wertsch, 1998). Vygostky-inspired sociocultural theory challenges contemporary theories of learning in psychology by questioning deeply held, yet controversial, views about 'individual cognition' (e.g. Chomsky, 1968, 2000) and identifies that thinking and learning take place between people and between people and tools in situated settings (Lin, 2007; Lin & Invison, 2012).

Sociocultural approaches to learning employ a methodological lens that recognises learning as embedded in multiple settings and involves different planes of analysis that take into account the broader sociocultural contexts that shape language learning. Inspired by Vygotsky, Rogoff's (1995, 2003) model of three planes of analysis – community, interpersonal and personal – is taken to be appropriate and useful in assisting the exploration of both sociocultural processes and student development across different cultural contexts in learning foreign languages. It informed the methodological backdrop to the research design of the fieldwork in Taiwan and in England drawn upon in the following analysis.

In this sociocultural inquiry, I investigated students' foreign language learning processes by starting with school and family resources, including school visions and parental encouragement, and went on to explore broader national, societal, ethnic and cultural forces which shape curricula at the community plane. Then, I focused on observation of the classroom processes of student–teacher interactions on the interpersonal plane, followed by mapping individual students' learning trajectories, including motivation and identity on the personal plane. Individual learners were the central focus of inquiry, within wider social and cultural background forces seen as shaping learning. Individual pathways of foreign language learning were seen as situated within a broader sociocultural context (see Figure 2.1).

Employing such a sociocultural approach makes possible a movement from a comparison of macro-national systems to micro-school and classroom processes, as Alexander (1999) suggested. Remembering Sadler's classic 'garden' metaphor concerning the importance of taking into account broader social and cultural contexts when undertaking comparative studies, such an approach leaves open the extent to which 'forces and factors outside the school matter even more than what goes on inside it' (Kandel, 1933: xix). Fieldwork in Taiwan and England seeking to investigate differential processes and achievements in English/Chinese as foreign languages and relationships between culture and language learning in particular classroom cultures thus entailed the adoption of cross-disciplinary approaches involving areas of psychological, sociological, anthropological and linguistic investigation, using multiple methods, including questionnaires, classroom observations and semi-structured interviews, yielding both quantitative and qualitative analysis (Lin, 2007).

To contribute in meaningful ways to our understanding of why sociocultural theoretical and methodological approaches are deemed appropriate and useful in mapping foreign language teaching and learning processes, it is worth delineating at some length contemporary debates

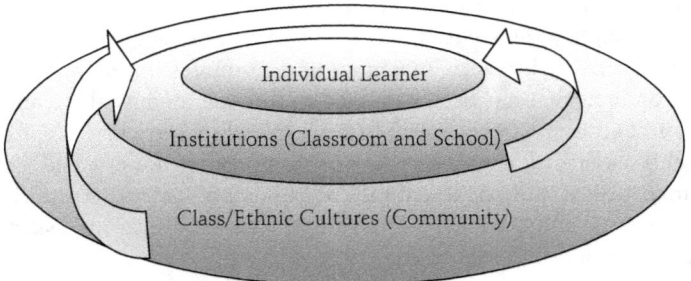

Figure 2.1 Sociocultural approaches to learning

over intertwining relationships between 'mind' and 'society' in relation to learning, and the development of sociocultural approaches. I start with a brief description of dominant cognitive theories before Vygotsky's work began to influence theories of learning. This will be followed by a depiction of Vygotsky's move in challenging the individualistic mind and more recent neo-Vygotskian studies which have underpinned assumptions about the social formation of the mind that inform this study. These provide the context for my choice of sociocultural methodologies in foreign language learning inquiry.

Challenge to the Individualistic Mind in Learning

The tendency for cognitive psychologists to focus their efforts on understanding a fixed and isolated human information processing system – 'cognitive machinery' (e.g. Chomsky, 1968) – has had an immense impact on the contemporary study of human cognition (mind) and on theories of language acquisition. Chomsky was interested foremost in the study of problems of language and mind. He viewed language as depending upon the existence of inner mechanisms individual to the human mind. Viewing language from an 'internalist' perspective, he argued that human beings come into the world with a 'language capacity' that 'constitutes the innate organization that determines what counts as linguistic experience' (Chomsky, 1968: 27). By reducing language to a closed system, Chomsky created new problems. Sociocultural theorists, among others, have challenged Chomsky's view of the mind as an internal mechanism.

Challenge of the individualistic mind

Criticism of this individualistic interpretation of the mind mounted during the 1980s from developmental and cross-cultural studies. The challenge, among others, was captured by Shweder's (1990) insightful remarks distinguishing cultural psychology from cognitive psychology:

> Cultural psychology is premised on human existential uncertainty (the search for meaning) and... intentional concept of 'constituted' worlds. The principle of existential uncertainty asserts that human beings... are highly motivated to seize meanings and resources out of a sociocultural environment that has been arranged to provide them with meanings and resources to seize and to use. The principle of intentional (or constituted) worlds asserts that subjects and objects, practitioners and practices, human beings and sociocultural environments interpenetrate each other's identity and cannot be analytically disjoined into independent and dependent variables. (Shweder, 1990: 1)

In Shweder's words, cognitive psychologists such as Chomsky appeared to invoke an inherent central processing mechanism that tends to deny any relations with sociocultural environments and specifically neglects the irreducible, fluid and intentional nature of the human mind by suggesting a discrete, individualistic model of mind/brain. The word–world relation which entails the intimate mutuality of subject matter (e.g. mind, self or emotion) and its sociocultural environment was missing from Chomsky's internalist interpretation of the human mind and language faculty.

In the field of language acquisition, Tomasello (2003: 328) called into question individualistic approaches to the study of the mind in suggesting that a language acquisition theory needed to invoke 'a variety of cognitive and social-cognitive processes that originate from outside the domain of language per se'. Furthermore, Hymes (1972) proposed the notion of 'communicative competence', challenging the reliance on a cognitive mechanism and arguing that this linguistic theory tended to ignore sociocultural dimensions of language use. He noted:

> It takes the absence of a place for sociocultural factors, and the linking of performance to imperfection, to disclose an ideological aspect to the theoretical standpoint.... The controlling image is of an abstract, isolated individual, almost an unmotivated cognitive mechanism, not, except incidentally, a person in a social world. (Hymes, 1972: 271)

Other, particularly neo- and post-Vygotskian studies also presented major challenges to individualistic approaches to the study of the mind, following Vygotsky's seminal work in challenging the notion of an internal cognitive mechanism in his attempt at a better understanding of the relations between language, mind and culture.

The Social Dimension of Human Minds

Vygotsky's move from the individualistic to the social

Vygotsky's tenets can be summarised in terms of the following basic themes: a reliance on developmental analysis; the assertion that higher mental functioning in the individual derives from social life; and the claim that human activity (on both social and individual planes) is mediated by tools and signs. These interlocking themes encapsulate his underlying approach to a theory of the mind that shifted from an individualistic to a sociocultural perspective. The shift towards the social origin of the human mind is best captured by Vygotsky's 'general genetic law of cultural development':

> Any function in the child's cultural development appears twice, or on two planes. First, it appears on the social plane, and then on the psychological plane. First, it appears between people as an interpsychological category, and then within the child as an intrapsychological category....

> It goes without saying that internalisation transforms the process itself and changes its structure and functions. Social relations or relations among people genetically underlie all higher functions and their relationships. (Vygotsky, 1981: 163)

Children's cultural development, in Vygotsky's terms, is a process that takes place between people as an interpsychological category. This social dimension of the human mind is not only radical but also positive because it points out that psychology should focus its attention on uniquely human higher mental processes (Kozulin, 1990). This positive psychological programme has brought back what cognitive psychologists viewed as 'noise' (i.e. culture) into the picture.

According to Vygotsky, higher mental functioning processes rely on mediation or psychological tools. Language, in Vygotsky's approach, was considered to be the most important psychological tool. He suggested that the primary function of speech is the function of communication, social contact, influencing people in the speech community. Language as a psychological tool or as mediational means was understood by Vygotsky as speech. As Daniels (1993) argues:

> For Vygotsky, speech was an important psychological tool, which was at one time a social and cultural element but also served to mediate social processes in the process of internalisation. Such psychological tools not only function externally/socially, they mediate or regulate internally the action of mental processes. (Daniels, 1993: 53)

If we accept Vygotsky's notion that language provides psychological tools that internally regulate the action of mental processes, their essential property is that they are culturally, historically and institutionally situated (Wertsch, 1998). Indeed, Vygotsky was one of the first psychologists to start with the social forces when addressing human mental development and helped to bring educational pedagogy into the realm of psychological development.

From this necessarily limited discussion of Vygotsky's main ideas, I intend to develop an account of human beings seen as 'making themselves from outside' (Daniels, 2001: 56), whereby the 'mind is in society' (Rogoff, 1990: 36). Vygotsky's ideas constitute a radical shift away from the world view of isolated individual minds. His ideas set the stage for a broader understanding of the importance and the connection between social, cultural and historical forces involved in the development of the human mind. However, a problem solved in social science almost inevitably means a new problem raised. Drawing on Vygotsky, we need a situated practice approach to language learning to supplement contemporary accounts of second or foreign language acquisition if we wish to pay more attention to actual experiences, practices and uses involved in the processes of language teaching and learning. In some measure, these may be found in neo-Vygotskian studies.

Neo-Vygotskian Studies

Building on Vygotsky's heritage, there has been a rapid growth in the number of approaches attempting to investigate the development of cognition in actual contexts which challenge early, cognitivist approaches to the mind. Relevant research has examined issues, such as how cognition is situated in everyday social contexts (Rogoff & Lave, 1984), how cognitive processes may be socially distributed (Salomon, 1993) and how certain forms of social interaction (e.g. mother–child dyads) may be appropriated to organise individual mental processes (Rogoff, 1990). Among these efforts, a few strands can be broadly characterised as, for example, cultural-historical activity theory (Cole *et al.*, 1997), sociocultural approaches (Wertsch, 1998) and situated learning models (Lave & Wenger, 1991). These neo-Vygotskian studies all share a common view in seeking to investigate or in attempting to understand processes involved in the social formation of the mind. Within neo-Vygotskian approaches, sociocultural accounts of learning or development are viewed as sociocultural processes that recognise historical, political, economic and institutional forces that influence learning.

As a way of concretising arguments over language learning inspired by Vygotsky's formulation, I will turn to a brief review of Scribner and Cole's (1981) empirical cross-cultural study of Vai literacy and provide a theoretical examination of contemporary 'situated learning theory' (Lave & Wenger, 1991), including Wenger's (1998) work on 'communities of practice'. This conceptualisation of neo-Vygotskian endeavours in investigating the relationship among mind (cognition), culture (society) and language significantly influenced the fieldwork on English language learning in Taiwan and Chinese language learning in England.

Practice approach to literacy: The Vai study

Scribner and Cole (1981: 8), standing on Vygotsky's shoulders, recognised that in order to support the assumption that literacy makes a difference in mental processes, 'psychological analysis has to be joined with cultural analysis'. With the notion of 'language as cultural mediator' in mind, their choice of literacy as a domain for testing a sociocultural approach to cognition proved to be useful. A brief depiction of the background and process of the Vai study is helpful for conceptualising the significance of its contribution to the contemporary understanding of the social origin of literacy.

The Vai study comprised a research design of within-culture comparison where different languages used by literate and non-literate people provided an ideal research project. The study was carried out in Liberia and investigated the speculation that literacy learning (reading and writing) fosters the development of higher intellectual skills. The Vai are one of the few peoples in the world with an original writing system, invented some 180 years ago. The system is a syllabary with approximately 200 characters representing the structure of the Vai language. The reading and writing of Vai are diffused from one villager to another through individual tutoring rather than through schooling. Possible school effects are, for this reason, irrelevant to the Vai study, allowing investigators to examine the cognitive implications of literacy which would be impossible in most modern societies where it is intimately related to schooling. Three literacies are commonly used in Vai society: English, Arabic and Vai script. English, used as the official language, is primarily learned in government-run schools for the purpose of reading English information or knowledge from newspapers or government announcements. Qur'anic literacy (Arabic writing) is learned predominately for religious functions, where reading is for remembering. Vai script is different in that it is used exclusively in secular, pragmatic and personal domains where the purpose of reading is related to actions in practical activities such as letter writing.

Scribner and Cole's intention to test out a Vygotskian sociocultural approach to cognition led them to carry out their research strategy by taking into account the cultural circumstances relating to the specific learning activities of literacies. They found activities that seemed to invoke links between 'literacy practice' and specific, cognitive skills, and observed that Vai literacy remained close to everyday give-and-take activities. Scribner and Cole (1981) declared that:

> we approach literacy as a set of socially organized practices which make use of a symbol system and a technology for producing and disseminating it. Literacy is not simply knowing how to read and write a particular script but applying this knowledge for specific purpose in specific contexts of use. (Scribner & Cole, 1981: 236)

The Vai study had several implications for both the contemporary understanding of linkages between literacy and cognitive skills and the specific nature of our study of English language learning in Taiwan and Chinese language learning in England. It provides a broader framework for understanding interrelationships between sociocultural activities and psychological processes involved in literacy which were described as a 'practice account of literacy'. The notion of a 'practice account of literacy' is significant because it not only deepens the scope of existing theories about literacy and cognitive skills but also helps to inform investigation of foreign language learning, particularly in taking research design 'outside of the classroom' in order to examine foreign language learning within historical, cultural and institutional settings (Lin, 2007).

Situated learning theory

Vygotsky-inspired studies compatible with Scribner and Cole's Vai study have been carried out elsewhere. The cognitive anthropologist Jean Lave (1988, 1996), among others, has been at the forefront of contributing to the formation of 'situated learning theory' that has furthered our understanding of learning as a situated practice. Everyday situated theory has its roots in practice theory and psychological accounts in the Vygotskian tradition. Situated learning theory challenges conventional assumptions of cognition, implying a social construction of the mind and its implications for learning which takes place in ubiquitous, everyday practices. As Lave (1988) points out:

> Practice theory has eclectic roots in the work of Marx, Bourdieu.... This work emphasises the dialectical character of relations fundamental to the socially constituted world – dialectics provides an obvious relational model for synthesis. And it is focused in part on experience in the lived-in world. (Lave, 1988: 15)

Situated learning refers to the idea that learning does not take place in a vacuum but in ubiquitous contexts with cultural specificity, emphasising 'persons-acting-in-setting' as its unit of analysis. In fact, 'there is no activity that is not situated'. The whole person is actively involved in learning, such that 'agent, activity, and the world mutually constitute each other' (Lave & Wenger, 1991: 33).

In school settings, students' learning activity is seen as constituted in relation to the sociocultural structuring resources (e.g. school, family and ethnic groups) that regulate learning processes. This argument has reshaped contemporary models for understanding knowledge acquisition or learning from that of individualistic and de-contextualised learning in classrooms to activity in the everyday, lived-in world. We can argue that learning activities, such as foreign language learning, do not take place in a social and cultural vacuum. The learning process 'is integral to the cultural fashioning of everyday life.... Such processes are generated in the complex structure of lived situations, rather than in the underdevelopment of the human mind' (Lave, 1988: 141).

Drawing on a model of situated learning, Lave and Wenger (1991) propose that learning is not a discrete and isolated activity but an integral aspect of active participation in a broader community of practice. 'Communities of practice' look into the way in which groups of people use their abilities to share past experiences and create joint understandings of new knowledge. This concept is significant, echoing various notions such as 'the practice account of literacy' (Scribner & Cole, 1981) and shedding light on English/Chinese language learning issues involving meaning negotiation and identity formation in language learning communities of practice.

Given the notion of a practice approach to literacy, situated learning models and an extended concept of communities of practice, we move away from individualistic approaches to human cognition towards understanding learning, or foreign language learning, as sociocultural processes situated in everyday, lived-in worlds. Foreign language learning is viewed as an open-structure-in-practice, such that investigation of foreign language learning has to be studied in actual contexts of persons-in-acting.

Chapter Summary

A sociocultural theoretical perspective allows more attention to be paid to individual levels of learning identity, to pedagogic issues on a micro-interactional plane within classroom settings and political issues at broader community levels. It allows researchers to incorporate and relate various planes of analysis in capturing holistic pictures of foreign language learning, such as those presented here in English and Chinese. From sociocultural perspectives, empirical exploration and observation of why and how young people learn English and Chinese may help us to broaden the focus to view foreign language learning as everyday practice influenced by sociocultural forces including political, economic, family, institutional and personal settings, circumstances and values.

In this chapter, I have attempted to delineate the appropriateness and usefulness of applying sociocultural theoretical perspectives to language learning in order to set the stage to challenge the problematic assumptions that English or Chinese as a foreign language benefits all students equally, as a neutral language tool with no connection to the unequal distribution of power along lines of race, class, religion and ethnicity. I hope to highlight that English or Chinese language practices that take account of the sociocultural backgrounds of students both reflect and affect the learning milieu in educational settings, a matter of concern in the following chapters.

3 Learning English/ Chinese as Foreign Languages: The Contexts

Chapter 2 sought to explain why sociocultural theories of learning are appropriate and useful in exploring both social processes and student development across different cultural contexts in learning foreign languages. In this chapter, as a way of contextualising the broader sociocultural forces that shape foreign language learning, we need to look at the historical, political and cultural contexts of learning English and Chinese as foreign languages (EFL/CFL) in Taiwan and England, respectively, in order to set the scene for our cross-national or cross-cultural examinations and comparisons. It is worth noting that, in comparing educational practices across nations, few would deny that cultural forces inevitably accompany and influence many facets of education (Mason, 2007). Comparative educationist Robin Alexander (2000) argues that

> Life in schools and classrooms is an aspect of our wider society, not separate from it: a culture does not stop at the school gates. The character and dynamics of school life are shaped by the values that shape other aspects of ... national life.... Culture, in comparative analysis and understanding, and certainly in national systems of education, is all. (Alexander, 2000: 29–30)

Other comparative educationists caution against the danger of overgeneralising or stereotyping. For example, Mason (2007: 166) warns against 'treating culture as monolithic, and of overstating its influence in a hybrid world characterised by complex interactions and influences' while comparing one culture with another. In particular, in an era of rapid globalisation, the usual political entity of nation-state boundaries is now loosely constituted due to the process of ever increasing travel, mass migration and intermarriage. For example, the meaning of being British refers today to more than a group of people who share a common monolithic national cultural identity. Being British today may mean driving a German car to an Irish pub for a glass of Belgian beer; then travelling home, grabbing an Indian curry or a Turkish kebab on the way; to sit on Swedish furniture and watch American shows on a

Japanese TV. Another example is the changing concept of the 'national English dish'. The dish may be named from the list of a traditional 'roast beef and Yorkshire pudding' or 'fish-n-chips' to become 'curry and rice' nowadays. In fact, 'modern nations are all cultural hybrids' according to the anthropologist Edward T. Hall's (1994) observation. Indeed, the process of globalisation appears to have heightened this cultural hybridity. As Mason (2007: 177) contends, 'the cultural hybridity of the modern nation-state, masked as a homogenous unity by the myths of national culture, is exacerbated almost to the point of displacement of the national culture by the processes of globalisation', that the answer to whether national identities truly are as unified, coherent, consistent and homogeneous as they appear in the representations of national culture, is negative. Most modern nations were born out of violent conquest of one or more groups by another. While this commodity-centred exemplification may seem rather superficial, there is no doubt that nations are historically divided from within by regional, economic, political, class, ethnic, gender and linguistic realities in relation to which global influences have very differentially penetrated. In this study, both Taiwan and England are 'nations' that were born out of more or less remote or recent processes of violent conquest of one or more groups and complex patterns of internal and external migration. As delineated in Chapter 1, the history of Taiwan contains linguistic oppression and ethnic conflict among four major social groups (Holo, Chinese Mainlanders, Hakka and indigenous). In Britain (or, more properly, the United Kingdom) there are four nations – England, Wales, Scotland and Northern Ireland, each having its own cultural-historical and linguistic roots and complex migration patterns, with England as the centre of political and economic power. Any attempt to attribute certain aspects of educational consequences to the homogeneous 'national culture' of Taiwan or Britain would be both difficult and problematic.

Bearing this caution in mind, I will acknowledge that in comparing English and Chinese language practices in Taiwan and England, certainly cultural influences are important and have real consequences; but inferentially locating the source of the significance of these consequences in culture has to be treated with care. Towards this end, I will go beyond the only partially useful notion of macro national cultures of Taiwan/England and further locate micro sources of cultural forces in their subnational ethnic, class and other cultural formations which may shape EFL and CFL learning.

The Political Framing of Foreign Language Learning

EFL context in Taiwan

Globally, the history of teaching and learning English as a foreign language has deep economic and political roots. According to Crystal

(2010), the English-speaking population whose mother tongue is not English now outnumbers native speakers of English by three to one. The global spread and use of English appears to have become the key force contributing to rapid globalisation in the 21st century. The importance of English as a common means of communication across the world and its strength as the first foreign language of choice for most non-Anglophone Asian countries such as China, Japan, Korea and Taiwan has grown alongside this rapid globalisation.

Historically, although several foreign languages are learned and used in Taiwanese society including English, Japanese and other European languages (e.g. Spanish, French and German), English has been the dominant foreign language, notwithstanding Japanese occupation ended in 1945. EFL teaching in China stretches back 150 years to the opening of the first English language school (*tóng-wén guǎn* 同文館) in 1861 during the Qing dynasty because of concern over a shortage of diplomatic specialists. English has since played a pivotal role in the education history of Taiwan. In 1912, following its overthrow of the Qing dynasty in 1911, the Republic of China government, led by Dr Sun Yat-Sen, announced that English was the compulsory foreign language in secondary education. Following the Japanese invasion in 1937, the English language was made non-compulsory in the secondary curriculum. However, when the Chinese Nationalist government (KMT) retreated to Taiwan in 1949, English was still its major foreign language. Since the 1980s, learning English as an international language has become crucial to Taiwan's economy in terms of providing access to the world's community and has been regarded as one of the keys to the success of Taiwan's economic globalisation. Being able to speak English carries considerable prestige and it is generally believed that speaking better English fuels upward occupational and social mobility. Knowledge of and skill in English is seen as affording a 'survival kit' for economic success, and learning it has become so popular as to trigger a 'national movement' for its acquisition (Lin, 2007; Lin & Byram, 2016).

Accelerated by the need to communicate with the outside world of business, diplomacy, and scholarship, English has become a dominant foreign language in the public sector, job markets and schools in Taiwan. For example, in the public sector, official action was taken in 2002 to create an English-friendly environment in Taiwan as part of an effort to align with global trends and attract more foreign visitors. A plan to establish a bilingual environment was incorporated into the Challenge 2008 National Development Plan (*tiǎo-zhàn* 挑戰 2008). The Research, Development and Evaluation Commission (RDEC) of the Executive Yuan compiled an English translation glossary containing the names of government agencies and signs posted in public places in 2003. A Chinese–English signage system was placed on roadways and in public places and tourist sites in order to boost a bilingual environment helpful to foreign visitors. Bilingual websites were created, English news programmes produced and laws and regulations translated into English. Incentives were provided for academic institutions and the private sector to establish a more extensive 'bilingual environment' (*shuāng-yǔ huán-jìng* 雙語環境) – Chinese and English – in Taiwan.

In recent years, the rise of China with its economic influence worldwide and the growing trend of learning Chinese makes some young people in Taiwan, especially those who do not enjoy EFL learning, question 'Will Chinese replace English as the common means of communication across the world?'. This is not the place to predict the answer; however, the importance of English as a common medium of communication across the globe and its momentum as the first foreign language of choice for most non-English-speaking countries, such as Taiwan, is likely to remain unchanged.

Foreign language learning context in England

In England, the picture of foreign language learning is very different. Questions like 'Why learn a foreign language?' or 'Which foreign language to learn?' appear to be the centre of debate in academia and among the general public in Britain. Since the 1960s, it has been the case that 'the big three' (French, German and Spanish) have been the dominant foreign languages for young British people. For example, a national survey in the 1960s revealed that students presenting themselves for the General Certificate Education (GCE) 'O' level in languages were French (169,435), German (31,902) and Spanish (9,171) (Statistics of Education [1964], quoted in the Incorporated Association of Assistant Masters in Secondary Schools, 1967: 8). French appears to be the most dominant foreign language, with more than five times the number of learners than other foreign languages. In 2014, this ranking order of the 'the big three' remained unchanged, according to the survey from the British Council (2014).

However, as noted in Chapter 1, the context of foreign language learning in England reveals a historically limited success and a 'reluctance' towards learning foreign languages, albeit there has been a 'slow but steady' growth of interest in Chinese learning in recent years. The essence of such 'reluctance' can be captured, as early as the 1960s, in *The Teaching of Modern Languages* (authored by the Incorporated Association of Assistant Masters in Secondary Schools). When reflecting on the fundamental question – 'Why learn a foreign language?', we can see the frustration as follows:

> Only too often the English student, already struggling with our national bashfulness and self-consciousness, is made to feel that his efforts earn ridicule rather than admiration. Worst still, we are all familiar with the

sight of the modern foreign language teacher using hammer and chisel methods on passive or sullen students. Worst of all, and particularly in old-established industrial areas, there are parents who 'cannot see any earthly use' in the subject and actively discourage their children. (The Incorporated Association of Assistant Masters in Secondary Schools, 1967: 5)

This frustration in the 1960s prevails through the decades of the 1970s and the 1980s when the teaching of English monopolised the school curriculum in England. For example, in arguing for a balanced school curriculum for teaching and learning both English and a foreign language, the British language educationist Eric Hawkins (1987) challenges the 'parochialism of teachers of English'. He argues that the report *A Language for Life*, by Alan Bullock (1975), exemplified such 'parochialism' of the English language:

> What astonished modern linguists about the Bullock Report was the complete absence from its 600 pages of any reference to foreign languages in the curriculum or to the fact that we live in a polyglot world and that the pupils whose 'language for life' the report describes will, as adults, be brought (in their jobs, their politics, their leisure activities) into ever closer interaction with neighbours whose mother tongue is not English. (Hawkins, 1987: 33–34)

In fact, we can argue that such 'parochialism' in teaching and learning English somehow helps us to conceptualise the ignorance and reluctance to learn a foreign language in England, albeit there are certainly other forces that contribute to this social phenomenon of 'reluctance'. One of the driving forces is no doubt the importance of English as a common means of communication across the world and its strength as the first foreign language of choice for most non-Anglophone countries.

There is limited space in this book for a full study of the cause of the 'reluctance' towards foreign language learning in England. However, it is worth noting that there is an ongoing debate among linguists and educationists over the issue of language education in school. In particular, the debate relating to common questions such as 'why learn a foreign language?' and 'at what point does knowledge of a foreign language acquire solid worth?'. For example, in the late 20th century, Hawkins (1987) was at the forefront of challenging the 'parochialism of teachers of English', as noted earlier, and striving to promote a balanced school curriculum in England for teaching and learning both English and foreign languages. He notes that the educational value of foreign language learning is that 'it can offer the pupil an experience different from that of the mother tongue and so contribute to an understanding of the polyglot world, and emancipate the learner from parochialism' (Hawkins, 1987: 32). Foreign language education therefore should be embedded in the school curriculum to help young people avoid a narrow-minded emphasis on mother tongue education – English. In fact, the historical 'reluctance' towards foreign language teaching and learning in England has impacted on how modern languages have been taught. They were generally regarded as 'difficult', unsuited to less able pupils, the pedagogy was formal – grammar and grammar bound (predominantly taught in grammar schools) and low on oral content with an abortive language lab interlude – and due to the limitations of traditional pedagogy, English language instruction lacked the prestige of other subjects taught at that time.

Moving onto the 21st century, geopolitical changes in the world economy and politics seem to have shed some new light on the dismal picture of the 'reluctance' towards foreign language education in England. For instance, Graddol's (2006) analysis of global language trends suggests that the competitive advantage of English will retreat and that monolingual English speakers, unable to tap into the multilingual environments enjoyed by others, will encounter a bleak economic future. Graddol's analysis serves as a timely warning against contentment over the predominance of English worldwide in Anglophone countries in general, and in Britain in particular. In addition, John Wore, the director of strategy at the British Council, highlights the value of culture and the importance of languages and international skills for young people in Britain. In the report *Languages for the Future: Which Languages the UK Needs Most and Why* (commissioned by the British Council, 2013), he addresses the need for more people in Britain to embrace multilingualism and learn a broader range of foreign languages in the future:

> … in the UK we must accept that speaking English alone is not enough in a world where multilingualism is becoming the norm… we need far more people learning a much wider range of languages in the future. French, Spanish and German will continue to be important but we will also need significantly more Arabic, Mandarin Chinese and Portuguese speakers as well as speakers of Italian, Japanese, Russian and Turkish. (British Council, 2013: 2)

The report from the British Council shows that the top five foreign languages are Spanish, Arabic, French, Chinese and German. Interestingly, the list has altered the 'big three' foreign language learning tradition in Britain and has Chinese ranked as high as number four. This changed ranking order represents the growing importance of the cultural, economic and educational priorities of the Chinese language in future Britain.

Despite the aforementioned rather overburdened official/expert 'reports' which say little about individual motivations to learn foreign languages, this broader historical analysis of foreign language teaching and learning in Taiwan and in England gives us at least some tenuous grasp of trends in foreign language learning in the two locations. Now, we have two different pictures: zealous EFL learning as a 'national movement' of sorts in Taiwanese society and a somewhat gloomy picture in England painted by the historical 'reluctance' to learn foreign tones, with little light ahead. With these two distinctive pictures in mind, I turn to a delineation of the school systems before exploring the formal school curriculum and hidden curriculum that may regulate foreign language education at schools in both Taiwan and England.

Understanding School Cultures

In keeping with sociocultural approaches to learning, foreign language learning and teaching in classrooms must be situated in a broader cultural context. Comparing classroom lives and pedagogies should not be limited to what happens within classrooms but should be understood as situated practices within school, local and national contexts. Alexander's (2000) 'Five Cultures' study, conducted between 1994 and 1998 in England, France, India, Russia and the USA, provided a sound approach to the investigation and cross-referencing of analysis at different system, school and classroom levels. At the school level, for example, Alexander identified categorisations along five dimensions:

- School buildings and how space was organised.
- The organisation of school time (concentrated or dispersed, elastic or rigid, lesson length regular or irregular, lesson short or long).
- The organisation of people (including both adults, i.e. staffing structure and power relationships, and children, i.e. class sizes and the way students were organised and grouped).
- The idea of a school as held by the teachers (i.e. what they held to be the primary values and functions of schools).
- External relationships (i.e. the way schools were viewed by and related to parents, families and communities and how they handled demands and expectations).

These broader sociocultural contextual levels of analysis must significantly inform our understanding and comparisons of school cultures if we are to further examine and compare processes of English and Chinese learning and teaching, including on the intrapersonal and interpersonal plane of analysis (Rogoff, 1995). Bearing this in mind, I will briefly describe the two school systems in terms of their curricula for foreign language education, embedded as they are in hidden curricula involving the primary values of the school, the existence of supplementary cram schooling, and tutoring and educational visits to foreign countries which may shape students' English and Chinese practices.

The school systems in Taiwan and England

Apple (1988: 195) argued that 'we cannot fully understand the curriculum unless we first investigate the way our educational institutions are situated within a larger configuration of economic, cultural, and political power'. To fully understand education systems and their curricula, we have to first investigate the way educational institutions are situated within a broader sociocultural context. This has certainly been the case with respect to the recent curriculum reform in Taiwan, namely the Grades 1–9 curriculum (*jiŭ-nián yī-guàn kè-chéng* 九年一貫課綱) and the 12-Year Basic Education Curricula[1] (*shí'èr-nián guó-jiào xīn-kè-gāng* 十二年國教新課綱) as well as historical changes to the education system in England.

In Taiwan, the primary and junior high school education curriculum, normally termed the 'Grades 1–9 curriculum', was introduced by the Ministry of Education, Taiwan (MOE) in 2001, legitimising English learning as early as Grade 5 in primary level. A description of the national curriculum is set against a brief portrait of the school system in Taiwan. There are four phases of schooling in Taiwan: three years of 'pre-school education' (*xué-qián jiào-yù* 學前教育); nine years of 'compulsory education' (*yì-wù jiào-yù* 義務教育) (six years primary and three years junior high school); three years of senior secondary education; and four years of higher education. Pre-school education is normally termed 'kindergarten'. Most kindergartens are private while public kindergartens are mostly affiliated to elementary schools. Students aged 4–6 are admitted for one to three years of schooling.

As a way of focusing the discussion, I will foreground the levels of compulsory education and senior secondary education and only briefly overview higher education. Mandatory or compulsory education was limited to six years of primary schooling when the Chinese Nationalist government (KMT) first moved from China to Taiwan. Subsequently, the fiercely competitive Taiwanese National Examination for Junior High School might be taken which deterred many from continuing with secondary education before 1968. To remove such pressure on students aspiring to junior high school and in recognition of the importance of education to the national development, a policy of nine years of mandatory education was introduced in 1968, known as Compulsory Education for Elementary and Junior High School Students (MOE Taiwan, 2006). Students aged at least 6 enter elementary school without a test, graduating with a diploma after age 6 and moving, aged at least 12, to junior high schools under the jurisdiction of county or city municipal governments.

Senior secondary education remains divided into six types of public or private schools: senior high, senior vocational, comprehensive, single-discipline, experimental and combined high schools. In applying for entry to this level, students are required to take the Comprehensive

Assessment Program for Junior High School Students (*guó-zhōng jiào-yù huì-kǎo* 國中教育會考) as well as meeting other requirements, including those of specific subjects required by individual schools. The most demanding subject standard requested is for English and this is usually formulated in terms of the General English Proficiency Test (GEPT), usually with elementary or intermediate level as the entry requirement for some elite senior high schools. More recently, the implementation of the 12-Year Basic Education Curricula in 2019 indicates that compulsory education in Taiwan will be extended from 9 to 12 years, i.e. to senior high school years.

In responding to the rapid changes in communication technologies that have dramatically accelerated intercultural interaction around the world, the 12-Year Basic Education Curricula cover three core changes. Lin and Godwin-Jones (2018) argue that

> The new curricula have three core changes; discourse-based (not decontextualized), usage-based (not grammar-focused) and the addition of listening practice to different English accents.... The third change to include understanding of 'Global Englishes' reflects the recognition of a growing importance of intercultural training in the global context. In the new EFL curricula for senior high schools... the core literacy involves cultivation of multicultural understanding and appreciation, understanding of global issues, and capability of international mobility. This also leads to a rising demand for intercultural communication pedagogy not only in senior high school level but also in higher education in globalized Taiwan. (Lin & Godwin-Jones, 2018: 3)

Various types of schools and institutions make up higher education, including five-year and two-year junior colleges, four-year or two-year institutes of technology/universities, universities and independent colleges and graduate schools. Universities and independent colleges are run by either government or private bodies. Until recently, high school graduates were selected through a variety of means, including passing entrance examinations, submitting personal applications and high school recommendations. The recent 'open-door policy' for higher education has meant that at least 95% of senior high school graduates each year attend universities. Those who complete the course requirements within the designated time are granted bachelor's degrees (see also Lin & Byram, 2016). Unlike the centralised education curriculum guiding the school systems in Taiwan, the education system in Britain does not seem to have a general curriculum for all students.

As mentioned in Chapter 1, since the schools under study are in England, we need only focus, from this point, on the English education system, which has enough internal variations. In a general sense, the English state school system contains primary, secondary and higher education institutions: nursery schooling, beginning at age 3, is limited, with compulsory primary school education beginning at age 4 in Reception class, followed by Years 1–6 and secondary school systems from Year 7 to Year 12. The final two years of the latter are traditionally referred to as sixth form and some exist as separate colleges, alongside or now increasingly merged with tertiary colleges, mainly for 16–19 year olds, offering a mix of academic and vocational programmes. Over the last 70 years, the English system has seen transfers between primary, middle (now virtually disappeared) and secondary schools at every age between 7 and 14. The English higher education system is split into two levels – undergraduate programmes that include bachelor's degrees, foundation degrees, higher national certificates (HNCs), higher national diplomas (HNDs) and postgraduate programmes that include master's degrees and doctorates. Higher education is provided both at universities and colleges in addition to specialist centres such as art institutions.

In addition to the traditional routes described, the English higher education landscape is currently undergoing further, limited reform with the introduction of higher and degree apprenticeships, aimed at providing a degree level of education for students who are trained in the workplace. These apprenticeships are offered in vocational and professional areas, which are expected to become a more popular choice for students wanting to avoid the high cost of tuition associated with the traditional university route. To further complicate the English education system, there are regional variations due to the choice that local educational authorities have in establishing the local school system. For example, in Gloucester (mid-England), there are secondary schools (age 11–16) as well as grammar schools (age 11–18) and tertiary colleges (e.g. Gloucestershire College) that offer courses for ages 16+ including A levels – traditionally provided by secondary or grammar schools. Moreover, central government policy has persuaded more than half of English secondary schools and a growing number of primary schools to leave their long-established local authority (LEA) control for individual or group autonomous status with continued state funding. Finally, it should be borne in mind that many schools are provided and governed by religious bodies, while also being essentially wholly state funded, while private schools (confusingly historically referred to as 'public' but who now prefer to be known as 'independent') provide for about 16% of students at 16+ and about half that number before that age.

Historically speaking, the English education system has gone through several reforms. For example, a particular change from grammar to comprehensive school form in the second half of the last century; the removal of schools from local governmental control into free and academy format control; effective forms of 'neoliberal' privatisation as a determination of the curriculum details (e.g. Exley & Ball, 2014); and staff employment conditions and student entry loosened or removed from centralised control. And perhaps even more importantly, to better understand the English education system and its curriculum patterns, we need to examine how it is situated within the larger structure of economic, cultural and political power. For example, Lawton's (1975) historical analysis of the way English education is intertwined with broader cultural and social class divisions is still apposite. In his book *Class, Culture and the Curriculum*, Lawton (1975) defines curriculum as a selection from the culture of a society. He argues that:

> Throughout the nineteenth century there were two quite distinct traditions of schooling which developed along very different lines and established two distinct kinds of curricula which were not only different but contain aims and assumptions which hardly ever overlapped or even came close to each other. On the one hand there was the public school/grammar school tradition of education for leadership, which give rise to a curriculum for 'Christian gentleman' who would become the leaders of the society.... On the other hand, the elementary school tradition was especially intended to train the 'lower orders'. Elementary schools were designed to produce a labour force.... It was also important that the pupils should be trained to be obedient and to have respect for the property of their betters. (Lawton, 1975: 1)

These two distinct kinds of curricula that shaped the two traditions of schooling in Britain in the 19th century went through several changes in the 20th century in what may now have become an attenuated quest for more equal opportunity in education, not least in pursuit of aspirations of greater 'classlessness' and 'egalitarianism'. These moves were exemplified in the 1944 Education Act, which marked a significant change in attitudes towards the two 19th-century traditions of selective secondary public school/grammar schooling and universal elementary provision.

However, the realisation of a more egalitarian provision was still difficult due to a complex site of struggle between different classes and, explicitly or implicitly, political rivalry between the two mainstream political parties, Conservative and Labour. In general, Conservative policies supported a fee-paying sector and student selection in state schools that privileged middle-class and aspirant working-class interests. Labour policies questioned but never sought to remove private school privilege, though it eventually prioritised comprehensive school formats where student intakes were not formally selected but might widely differ by locality and be less thoroughly internally differentiated in creating teaching groups. There was general consensus between the parties after 1945 that state schools should be controlled by LEAs, within national guidelines, which also protected the established privileges and degree of autonomy of religious – mainly Anglican and Roman Catholic – providers. In the decades that followed, there was real change in the direction of greater child-centredness or progressivism in primary schools freed from the shadow of secondary school selection. School and teacher autonomy with respect to pedagogic and curricular practice increased significantly, though in a system that still showed huge variation in quality and output and remained under constant scrutiny and criticism concerning its performance in supporting economic and labour force demands. Such discontent was underlaid by mixed enthusiasm, particularly among an increasingly heterogeneous middle class, for more 'comprehensive' schools and less traditional pedagogic modalities.

The Conservative Party's 1987 general election manifesto put forward radical proposals for change in education, which led to the 1988 Education Reform Act and a centrally determined national curriculum and pupil assessment system, accompanied by changes in school inspection systems and new metrics for determining school performance and ranking. A succession of changes, also embraced by successive Labour governments, encouraged schools to leave LEAs for self-management and greater curricular specialisation (though still under direct central government financing), and sought to increase parental choice at school entry and transfer.

Examining the historical changes in English education through the impact of neo-liberal educational reforms may also help to better our understanding of the English education system and its curriculum patterns. For example, Ball (2012) argues that:

> ... English education policy has come full-circle – from the first constitution of a state system of education in 1870 (or 1833) to the beginning of the end of state education in 2010 – and that this circularity can be understood in relation to what we might call the reluctant state. That is, I want to draw a link or a parallel between the period of the early to mid-nineteenth century, and what we might call the first liberalism, and the late twentieth–early twenty-first century, and what we might call the second liberalism, or what is often called neoliberalism. (Ball, 2012: 89)

Ball and colleagues (Exley & Ball, 2014) continue to point out that 'neo-liberalism is everywhere'; schools and universities are neo-liberal and it seems that neo-liberalism is an 'economisation of everything', presented and increasingly accepted as rational and normal that affects English education policy.

This is not the place to dig deep into the political battle between the political parties and the myriad of change wrought in English schools, but it could be argued that, as with income and wealth distribution and social mobility in society where neoliberalism prevails as the 'economisation of everything', there are wider gaps, less equal distribution and even more variations in patterns of institutional governance and provision than ever before.

The curricula for foreign language education

Grades 1–9 curriculum in Taiwan

In Taiwan the implementation of the Grades 1–9 curriculum for elementary and junior high schools restructured the development of foreign language learning and teaching. Responding to a dramatic sense of sociopolitical and economic change and conscious of global trends in educational reform, the Taiwanese government introduced unified guidelines regulating curriculum goals, pedagogic methods, timetables, content and evaluations. These had important implications for EFL teaching and learning within a curriculum comprising 10 core competences and 7 major learning areas (MOE Taiwan, 2015). As shown in Table 3.1, among these learning areas, 'Language Arts' is composed of Mandarin Chinese and English, focusing on the skills of listening, speaking, reading and writing in order to develop basic communicatory competences, as well as knowledge of culture and social customs.

Table 3.1 The structure of learning areas in the Grades 1–9 curriculum

Learning areas	Grades 1–2	Grades 3–4	Grade 5	Grade 6	Grade 7	Grade 8	Grade 9
Language arts	Chinese	Chinese English	Chinese English	Chinese English	Chinese English	Chinese English	Chinese English

The two languages, Chinese and English, share weekly classroom hours. At the elementary level, more time is devoted to Chinese as it is the medium used for teaching other subjects, and less (approximately 1–2 hours weekly) is provided for learning English. In junior high school, on the other hand, at least 6–8 hours per week are typically equally divided between Chinese and English (see Table 3.2).

The average time (3–4 hours weekly) spent learning English includes one supplementary slot (*fǔ-dǎo kè*), an official after-school revision class. Given the strongly increasing trend of EFL learning, most junior high schools are desperate to further increase its dedicated classroom hours, which somewhat compromises sessions deemed 'not so important'. For instance, as noted in Chapter 1, some teachers tended to replace mother tongue education class with an English session in a Hakka rural school. Some English and Chinese bilingual schools have created new class formats to achieve their visions, while some others have replaced extracurricular activities with English sessions, or even added Saturday classes for high-ability students (e.g. in elite urban schools). By such means, 4–5 hours per week tend to be devoted to English education in junior high schools in Taiwan. The actual EFL classroom content and pedagogies will be further explored in Chapter 5.

Foreign language curriculum in England

In contrast to foreign language curriculum guidelines in Taiwanese society, no consistent foreign language curriculum is specified for English schools as a general guide for the development of students' competence. Inconsistent foreign language official policies, to some extent, are to blame for the limited success of foreign language learning in England. For example, Hawkins (1987) observed a downturn of sixth-form entries (i.e. upper secondary) in modern languages from 1965 to 1985 as a 'spiral of decline'. Tracing the factors causing this downturn, he argued that initially the insistence of the old selective grammar school (largely replaced in most LEAs by comprehensive forms over this period) on a broad curriculum, including a foreign language up to 16+, was strongly supported by the policy of the universities. Until the mid-1960s, they tended to require a spread of five subjects for entry on degree studies, including the prerequisite that a language other than English was included. While it would be true to say that there is both the concept and reality of a core curriculum in English education comprising Maths, English, Science and Computer Literacy, the remainder is increasingly varied and many subjects, particularly creative arts, are in retreat, including modern languages.

Regarding the phenomenon of an 'inconsistent' foreign language policy in England, it would be interesting here to use a relevant personal foreign language learning anecdote from Roger Smith (pseudonym), a university professor of language education in England, who used to learn French, Spanish and Chinese as foreign languages. In an interview in June 2013, he stated that the inconsistent foreign language policy in England was a consequence of the linguistic reality – the dominance of the English language in Europe – that led to ignorance of other foreign languages. He argued that, in contrast to those Asian-Pacific Anglophone countries, like Australia, the British government seems to be 'messing around'. He continued to reveal the reality about Britain's inconsistent language policy and said:

> In contrast, in Britain, we are still messing around, and government policy has been very inconsistent on modern languages in general.... I remember seeing a poster on the wall, with Tony Blair, the former Prime Minister, saying, 'how important it was to use foreign languages, you know, for the future of Britain, and all the rest of it'. But then, I think almost that same year, they took modern languages out of the compulsory list, they made modern languages just an optional subject. It wasn't a necessary part of the curriculum anymore. (Roger Smith)

In fact, all modern languages were indeed 'out of the compulsory list' in 2007, an unfortunate language policy that may, directly or indirectly,

Table 3.2 Subjects and weekly teaching hours

Subject	School Grade	Primary School III, IV	Primary School V, VI	Junior High School I, II	Junior High School III
	I, II				
Language	4–6	5–8	5–8	6–8	6–9
Mathematics	2–3	3–4	3–4	3–4	3–5
Health and Physical Education	2–3	3–4	3–4	3–4	3–5
Life Curriculum	6–9	0	0	0	0
Social Studies	0	3–4	3–4	3–4	3–5
Arts and Humanities	0	3–4	3–4	3–4	3–5
Science and Technology	0	3–4	3–4	3–4	3–5
Integrative Actives	2–3	3–4	3–4	3–4	3–5
Flexible Learning	2–4	3–6	3–6	4–6	3–5
Total Number of Classes	22–24	28–31	30–33	32–34	33–35

Source: MOE Taiwan (2015: 30).

exacerbate the already limited success of foreign language learning in England. However, despite the fact that people from Australia are trying to catch up on Asian foreign languages such as Japanese and Chinese because of economic and geopolitical concerns as argued by Smith, it is not without problems for Australians to learn Asian foreign languages. For example, the high dropout rate in learning Chinese in Australia (Orton, 2008) and problems of low intake of local Australian students learning Chinese whereby 'Chinese risks becoming perceived as a "ghetto" language to be taken only by students of Chinese background' (Asian Studies Association of Australia –ASAA, 2009: 6), which we will refer to later in Chapter 7.

To concentrate on our discussion of the newly emergent foreign language learning and teaching – Chinese in England, I focus on the inquiry into how Chinese is situated in the secondary school curriculum, including state and independent schools. According to the report 'The Language Trend 2014', commissioned by the British Council, Chinese is classified as one of the less taught languages in England, and is mostly taught in after-school clubs as enrichment classes in most state schools (see Table 3.3). In some independent schools, however, Chinese is set in the standard curriculum and has regular weekly class sessions. In rare situations, Chinese is compulsory in the school curriculum, such as the case in the participant school, King's School, with three weekly class sessions to ensure that students are provided with enough academic scaffolding to learn this new foreign language and as a way to match its school vision – a Forward Thinking School, which will be described in more detail later in this chapter.

The survey report demonstrates, as previously mentioned, that Chinese is categorised as a less taught language as opposed to the 'big three'

Table 3.3 Schools where all or almost all students study a language throughout Key Stage 3

Schools	2009	2010	2011	2012	2013
State (%)	97	96	97	95	93
Independent (%)	99	99	98	97	99

Source: British Council (2014: 105).

foreign languages and is mostly taught in after-school clubs as enrichment classes in most state schools (11%). Independent secondary schools have a greater percentage (38%) of after-school clubs with Chinese language programmes. Furthermore, they also have a higher percentage of students studying Chinese than those in the state schools.

It is worth noting that the study of Latin stands out as an important language subject in independent schools, rather than in the state sector. In Britain, as in other European countries such as France, Latin is considered an elite language and is associated with the traditions of education which go back to the first grammar schools in Britain in the 17th century. As Hawkins (1987: 101) puts it, '… Latin remained the lingua franca of Europe it was an essential vocational tool for any youth aspiring to further education or to work in the public service. It was taught in the grammar schools by a mixture of "grammar/translation" and learning by use…'. Learning Latin is also said to be a good intellectual exercise and useful for learning Romance languages such as French and Spanish. It is linked to the Roman Empire which shaped Europe and which is still present in many ruins and other signs of the empire in today's Europe. Learning Latin therefore gives a better understanding of the history and development of European languages. However, apart from the so-called 'benefits' of a classical education and a better understanding of other European languages, Latin is used by many independent schools to mark their elite status and there may be a similar approach to Chinese which is seen as not only useful but also a distinguishing factor (Tables 3.4 and 3.5).

In comparing language resources or capital, the stark differences in foreign language provision between the state and independent sectors have an impact on students' access to foreign language learning. Issues

Table 3.4 Languages taught in state secondary schools, 2013

Stages	French (%)	German (%)	Spanish (%)	Chinese (%)
Key Stage 3 (Year 7–9)	95	50	69	6
Key Stage 4 (Year 10–11)	95	53	74	5
Post-16	81	49	61	6
Outside curriculum	8	8	10	11

Source: British Council (2014: 105).

Table 3.5 Languages taught in independent secondary schools, 2013

Stages	French (%)	German (%)	Spanish (%)	Chinese (%)	Latin (%)
Key Stage 3 (Year 7–9)	96	71	83	10	48
Key Stage 4 (Year 10–11)	98	78	87	8	48
Post-16	97	79	84	8	48
Outside curriculum	6	8	7	38	10

Source: British Council (2014: 105).

relating to unequal resources at school and at home for young people in England will be discussed in the following chapters.

Understanding the hidden curricula

In Taiwan, school visions, cram school attendance and access to foreign teachers or tutorials are considered to be sociocultural forces that influence students' learning. In a similar situation in England, school visions and foreign culture experiences are also regarded as significant factors that impact on those students who are given access to foreign language learning, which is almost non-existent at the primary school level and is severely restricted by ability even by mid-secondary school. A further major difference between the two systems is that 'cram school attendance' as a cultural scaffolding mechanism is unavailable in England but is highly prevalent in Taiwan.

The school visions in four schools in Taiwan

School visions are regarded by principals, teachers and parents as playing crucial roles in shaping school cultures. An investigation of such putative, shared beliefs may lead us towards a broad understanding of what is commonly valued in most schools, including what aspects of English teaching and learning may be regarded as of most worth. As mentioned in Chapter 1, a school vision or ethos is recognised in Taiwan and England as integral to establishing purposes and goals for teaching and learning in schools. In the context of Taiwanese schools, principals are normally expected to develop their 'school vision', which is more specifically an issue of their choice of aims, values and objectives for the school. In Taiwan, the school vision is also intended to be shared by all members of the school community, providing guidelines and directions throughout all stages of a school's educational development, planning, implementation and evaluation. Each Taiwanese school in the present study claimed to have its unique 'vision' whose central aims were to ensure that its members pulled in the same direction, all having common features found in traditional educational values. For example, the underlying five elements – 'morality' (*dé* 德), 'intellectuality' (*zhì* 智), 'health' (*tǐ* 體), 'cooperation' (*qún* 群) and 'art' (*měi* 美) – are similar values commonly found in all Taiwanese secondary school visions, representing the emphases on holistic education.

Take Urbany School as an example, emphasis on English teaching and learning as part of a bilingual education was the distinguishing characteristic of this school. Certain everyday English activities, such as lunchtime English broadcasts with an English DJ and regularly issued bilingual publications were aimed at reinforcing students' English competence. A young school, Urbany had engendered remarkable cohesion, involvement and support for bilingualism. In contrast, Suburbany School had developed a general school vision of 'holistic education' (*quán-rén jiào-yù* 全人教育) that sought to incorporate a spirit of humanism, an international perspective, an emphasis on integrated competencies, democratic thinking and concepts, and lifelong learning. Being a popular, elite school with a group of students labelled 'talented' (*zī-yōu-shēng* 資優生), Suburbany aimed to build a unique working vision committed to fostering students' cognitive competence within a school ethos where all members and parents felt involved and engaged. Academic excellence, regarded as high-quality education, was claimed to be Suburbany's distinctive characteristic, mediating students' everyday actions. Equating 'high-quality' education with cognitive competence met both parental expectations and the imperatives of the competitive culture within Taiwanese society. The motto (*biao-yü* 標語) located right next to the school's main entrance, which read 'running high-quality education in the modern era; creating a high-tech innovative world' (*jīng-yíng dà-shì-jì yōu-zhì jiào-yù; kāi-chuàng gāo-kē-jì chuàng-xīn tiān-dì* 經營大世紀優質教育、開創高科技創新天地) appeared to be intended to serve as a cultural tool or artefact mediating students' thoughts and actions. In this vein, academic eminence defined what counted as high-quality education and explicitly directed Suburbany School's endeavours and sense of direction.

Hakka Rural School was situated in a rural Hakka community. The school had developed visions that aimed to enhance students' core competence, moral values and, in particular, an understanding of Hakka culture. Hakka people in Meinung village are traditionally known for their unique attachment to agriculture and intimacy of kinship between family members. A pervasive working vision emphasising the enhancement of students' core competences in order to achieve school excellence seemed to echo the Hakka cultural legacy of valuing 'academic study'. Education, somewhat narrowly interpreted as cognitive competence, was generally viewed by local people as the ticket out of poverty and a laborious agricultural lifestyle. The booming 'cram schools' in the village appeared to best exemplify this impulse.

Lastly, Mountainside School was situated in a culturally distinctive Paiwan community. As the island's minority group, its celebration of its indigenous identity was implicitly embedded in everyday school life as its hidden curriculum. The core school vision in Mountainside School ranged from the goal of holistic education, incorporating intellectuality and humanity, to seeking to cultivate indigenous students' full potential by means of improving their skills in career planning and motivation for lifelong learning in a healthy learning environment. It might be said that these seemed to highlight the indigenous people's existing social and cultural deficiencies, if not stereotyped problems. Indigenous Paiwan parents experienced relatively little in terms of education and had disproportionately humble occupational backgrounds. Intentional career planning alongside the motivation for lifelong learning might have been cast as the solution to such problems. Alcoholism and associated domestic violence, high divorce rates and accidental death, all contributing to a 'single-parent syndrome', were salient in the Paiwan village. Such dysfunctional family features served as sociocultural constraints hampering students' academic attainments and future ambitions, as detailed in Chapter 6.

However, indigenous people in Taiwan are known to be gifted at singing and dancing and, in particular, for their athletic prowess. For these reasons, athletic sports and their shared values were regarded as crucial to the achievement of students' full potential. At Mountainside, modern school sports facilities, athletic high-ability classes and incentive bursaries had been created in the hope of inspiring students' athletic potential. Through sport, a number of students strove for futures as professional athletes or coaches, some being sent to departments of physical education in universities without an entrance examination and little by way of an academic qualification to match their athletic potential. For some students, athletic prowess was collectively considered to be their ticket out of poverty, towards dignity (Table 3.6).

Table 3.6 Characteristics of the four schools' visions in Taiwan

School visions	Urban		Rural	
	Urbany	Suburbany	Hakka Rural	Mountainside
Holistic education	✓	✓	✓	✓
Elite education		✓		
Bilingual education	✓			
Athletic education				✓
Ethnic culture education			✓	✓
Maintain ethnic dialect*			✓	✓

* Both Hakka Rural and Mountainside held a specific class for learning ethnic dialect that was not compulsory.

The school visions in the five schools in England

As a girls' state school, Highland School developed a school vision and values aiming to provide an inspirational environment in which girls flourished. The school claimed to strive to help all girls develop a strong sense of belonging and enjoy freedom from stereotyping and limited aspirations. It provided a wealth of opportunities both in and out of class aimed at engendering in students the self-confidence, resilience and moral courage requisite to achieving ambitions. As part of the school vision, for example, Chinese lessons had been provided and taught by Ms Wang (from Taiwan) since 2005 and had been running for 5 years before the fieldwork took place in 2014. Along with Bath High School and St Peter's School, Highland School was part of the 'Suzhou Link' (see Chapter 1) school and provided opportunities for Chinese cultural experiences through educational exchange visits each year.

St Peter's School, a Catholic state school, developed its school mission claiming to imitate Jesus Christ and his loving religious practice: '… our inspiration is Jesus Christ.… We will help our students to discover their vocation in life, to achieve their full potential and to use their gifts for the greater glory of God'. As with Highland School, St Peter's School was also part of the 'Suzhou Link' school and provided students with opportunities to experience Chinese culture through educational exchange visits each year. This unique activity fostered relationships between teachers and students by welcoming incoming Chinese groups to Year 7 in school for a 10-week 'language immersion' experience, in the summer term. The partnership also supported two-way teacher visits that were considered to be an important experience for both countries. Chinese lessons had been provided and taught by Ms Byrne (from England) since 2007, 7 years before the fieldwork took place in 2014.

Bath High School, a boys' state school, characterised itself as aiming to provide the best possible education for boys and to set the highest possible standards in all areas of school life: academic, sporting and beyond. As with Highland School, Bath High was also part of the 'Suzhou Link' school and provided students with opportunities for Chinese cultural experiences through educational exchange visits each year. Chinese lessons had been provided and taught by Ms Wang since 2005.

St Mary's School, as a co-educational state school, claimed that its mission was to develop young people with active and creative minds and that it aimed to be an outstanding school, offering a broad and challenging education to meet the needs of all its students. Its teachers were said to be committed to inspiring students to achieve the highest standards of intellectual and personal development through a stimulating and comprehensive curriculum. Its school vision pledged to develop students 'to be resilient and adaptable, equipped with the knowledge, skills and curiosity to continue their education and become fulfilled, confident, socially responsible adults'. As noted in Chapter 1, St Mary's School was the only school without formal Chinese lessons by the time of my first field visit in the summer of 2014. Following two-week taster lessons in Chinese in 2014 and 2015, a formal Chinese curriculum was set up.

Lastly, as an independent school, King's School carried with it the mission to develop students' academic and career potential. Given the fact that students were selected and mostly academically able, it had developed a school mission sending a powerful and effective image to students that they were bound for entry to Oxford and Cambridge in the future. In January 2016, it claimed to have 39 students gain acceptance at Oxford and Cambridge, a new college record. It was reputed as the 'Most forward thinking school in Britain' by the local press and perhaps one of the best examples of this reputation was its decision to make Chinese compulsory in 2006. In an interview in 2015, the deputy head claimed that 'we do it very successfully'. Chinese lessons are taught in the formal school curriculum by Ms Tan (from China), Mr Blake (from England) and other Chinese teachers and have been running smoothly (Table 3.7).

Comparing the school visions: Taiwan and England

Following Bernstein's (1990) fundamental claim that instructional discourse (school vision) – aimed at producing competence – was always grounded in and regulated by regulative discourse – the school's image of conduct, character and manner, we discovered that the school visions in the nine participating schools indeed played vital roles in shaping school cultures. As can be seen from Tables 3.1 to 3.7, the most distinctive similarity lies in the claim that all nine schools celebrated versions of 'holistic education' which encompassed intellectual competence and moral education – both embedded in the daily pedagogic practice of all school subjects. The salience of moral education appeared to be more overt within Taiwanese school contexts, less visible in English school life except for St Peter's and King's School, the former a Catholic faith school

Table 3.7 Characteristics of the five schools' visions in England

School visions	State				Independent
	Highland	St Peter	Bath High	St Mary's	King's School
Co-education		✓		✓	✓
Single-sex education	✓		✓		
Holistic education	✓	✓	✓	✓	✓
Elite education					✓
Foreign language education	✓	✓	✓	✓	✓
International link	✓	✓	✓	✓	✓

Note: Only King's School made Chinese learning compulsory.

where moral ethos was built into the school curricula and the latter, though not controlled by the Church of England, having its own chapel on campus, where religious practice and moral education were part of students' school life.

In the four Taiwanese schools, moral education was undertaken through activities both in their overt and hidden curricula, the former exemplified in school class timetables such as daily 'morning assembly', where official announcements were made; weekly 'school assembly', where school heads addressed students in highly moralistic terms; and 'class meetings' and 'civics' where democratic and civil practices were taught through activities. These 'hidden' curricular practices were exemplified in the deferential classroom demeanour of students through daily, afternoon, classroom cleaning chores where students were assigned by their homeroom teachers to share responsibility for cleaning and tidying places within and beyond their own classrooms.

Perhaps more interestingly were the differences in the school vision among the nine schools. In Taiwan, Urbany School was the only institution to highlight bilingual education, placing English learning and teaching at the centre of school life. Suburbany was the only school that stressed elite education by setting up a number of high-ability classes. The two rural schools, Hakka Rural and Mountainside School, both celebrated their ethnic culture in the hidden and overt curriculum, in line with recent government policy emphasising local ethnic cultural identities and encouraging the revival of ethnic language and specific cultural customs. However, Hakka Rural did not seem to be particularly enthusiastic about preserving the Hakka mother tongue, but privileged 'academic study' in compliance with traditional Hakka cultural values. Mountainside School, in contrast, listed the Paiwan tribal mother tongue on its 'menu', proficiency in the ethnic dialect having become one of the fundamental criteria for securing some indigenous bursaries for school education. In addition, Mountainside was the only school that placed athletic prowess, entailing daily training practice, at its core. One observed class taught by Ms Lin illustrated the case, where approximately one third of students were 'missing' on official absence because they undertook regular athletic training drills after 15:00. Such activities affected some students' normal lessons, including English, as we will see in the following chapters.

In England, both Highland School and Bath High School were single-sex establishments while all four Taiwanese schools were co-educational, like many other secondary schools in Taiwan. And since EFL is compulsory in all Taiwanese secondary schools, foreign language education or bilingual education (e.g. Urbany School) was an important school priority. Yet, all five English schools had international links either with European schools through schemes run by the European Union (i.e. Erasmus Programme) or with China with language and a cultural exchange programme while none of the Taiwanese counterparts had such international links below senior high school, when more contacts with international schools become available, in particular in some academic elite senior high schools.

Cram schools in Taiwan: A unique and lucrative business

In addition to formal English and Chinese learning, attendance of after-school revision classes in cram schools in Taiwan and tutorial lessons in England must be addressed. Cram school (*bŭ-xí bān* 補習班) attendance provides a distinctive academic learning culture within Taiwanese society. As a result, and in view of the importance of English proficiency for senior high school entry, engagement in after-school revision classes in cram schools has become widespread among junior high school students. Cram school attendance and, to a lesser extent, one-on-one tutorials are useful for many as a 'cultural tool' (Wertsch, 1998) for dealing with the growing complexities and difficulties of English as a junior high school subject in Taiwan. The availability of cram schools does not guarantee students' academic improvement because of the reluctance of some students to attend and the passivity of pedagogic practice within cram schools that tends to deter full participation.

In fact, when informant students were asked where they started learning English, a strikingly high percentage of them revealed engaging every day in after-school revision lessons either in cram schools or private language institutes. It is worth noting that private language institutes, commonly known as 'children's American English institutes' (*ér-tóng měi-yǔ bān* 兒童美語班), tend to focus on oral expression with the help of foreign English teachers and are popular with elementary school students. Cram schools, in contrast, focus more on cognitive competence in school subjects and are popular with junior high school students. Here, we use the term 'cram school' to cover both. Table 3.8 reveals that more than 60% of students on average gained access to English taught by cram schoolteachers. The popularity and availability of cram schools in urban areas, with Holo and Mainlanders (both 89%) and the Hakka rural township (61%) made cram schools important social settings outside homes and normal schools in regulating English learning activities. The far lower availability of cram schools in the nearby Paiwan indigenous community seemed to

Table 3.8 Learning English in cram schools

Practices	Urban			Rural		All students (n = 253)
	Holo (n = 98)	Mainlander (n = 28)	Hakka (n = 64)	Indigenous (n = 53)		
Cram schools (%)	20	18	14	8		15
Private language institutes (%)	69	71	47	19		52

constrain students' access to English (27%). Cram schools have become a lucrative business in urban Taiwan and Hakka communities, foreshadowing our later discussion of students' cram school learning identities as part of English learning communities of practice which will be addressed in relation to the personal plane of analysis in Chapter 6.

Foreign English teachers/tutorials in Taiwan

Foreign English teachers, generally called '*lǎo-wài*' – 老外 (literally, 'old outsiders'), worked in both cram and formal school settings, particularly in urban settings. The introduction of foreign nationals in English language teaching in elementary and junior high schools in Taiwan since 2004 has become an important milestone highlighting the growing awareness of the importance of English. These foreign English teachers were deployed primarily to elementary schools in remote areas, attempting to tackle an already well-marked 'urban–rural disparity' (*chéng-xiāng chā-jù* 城鄉差距) or 'English divide' (*yīng-yǔ luò-chā* 英語落差). The first cohort of five Canadian English language teachers was introduced to Taiwan on 24 October 2004, followed by another 14 (12 Canadian and 2 British) on 14 February 2005 (MOE Taiwan, 2004). In later years, the MOE signed cooperation memos with several governments in America and Australia to facilitate educational and cultural exchanges, especially the introduction of English teachers to elementary and junior high schools in Taiwan (see also Lin & Byram, 2016).

Given foreign English teachers' native accents and more interactive pedagogic orientation than local teachers in providing a window on a foreign culture, they were usually perceived as 'better English teachers' and were very popular with students and parents. Despite the fact that some of them lacked formal teaching qualifications, many parents still regarded them as much better than Taiwanese teachers of English, with their choices of language cram school influenced by their presence or absence. Most foreign English teachers choose to live and work in urban city areas for convenience and, among other things, more lucrative working conditions, so an urban–rural divide inevitably existed in students' experience of them. For example, our two urban groups were three times more likely to have been taught by foreign English teachers than the two rural groups, as can be seen in Table 3.9. An average of 70% of students who had been instructed by foreign teachers reported enjoying it. Regarding their first impression of their teaching, all four groups described them as 'funny and playful', as well as 'passionate', 'employing interactive pedagogy', able to 'share a foreign culture' and, of course, having 'native English pronunciation'.

Student informants revealed some of the reasons for foreign teachers' popularity. Foreign teachers were reported to be less tied to the chronic school culture of grammar-based and test-oriented English teaching and

Table 3.9 Learning English from foreign teachers

Experiences	Urban			Rural		All students (n = 253)
	Holo (n = 98)	Mainlanders (n = 28)	Hakka (n = 64)		Indigenous (n = 53)	
(Yes)	90	93	33		13	57
Enjoy the teaching	66	58	71		86	70

learning, experiencing less school board pressure regarding the enhancement of students' language skills and abilities than local teachers. One informant from Suburbany School claimed that she liked the foreign teacher's class 'because there is no test'. Some students still received corporal punishment for unsatisfactory test performance, although the practice was officially banned in 2007; another student indicating that he liked his foreign teacher's classroom simply 'because it is a safer place to learn English'. Such revelations of the advantages of being taught English by foreign teachers, including increased appreciation of foreign cultures, contrasted sharply with the mounting pressure students disclosed in learning English in traditional classroom settings.

There were no signs of cram schools on the streets and limited evidence of foreign language in my English observations, though in affluent areas like London and Bath, private Chinese tutors were employed to enhance students' learning to sit the General Certificate of Secondary Education (GCSE). For example, Ms Wang, the participant Chinese teacher from Taiwan who taught at Highland and Bath High School at the time of this research, shared her tutorial experience in England:

> Sometimes I have 1 or 2 students in their home or my home. We use lots of interactive method to make Mandarin learning fun… as far as I know, there isn't any Mandarin cram school around, people need tutoring mainly because there isn't Mandarin offered in their schools…. In my current school, Mandarin tutoring is to help the top flyer to achieve A* or the D grade student to go up to C or B.

According to Ms Wang, the main purpose of tutorial help was for GCSE and A level exam preparation. Students benefit a lot particularly in speaking and listening because in class they do not have much opportunity to interact with teachers. Also on writing, 'one-on-one support enables them to clarify lots of common errors so their writing is more native and fluent'. For other general non-GCSE/A level purposes, tutees tended to just want to be able to speak Chinese, so the focus was on listening and speaking. They were not bothered with reading and writing Chinese characters. It is worth mentioning that even though tutees benefitted across ability levels, the tuition fees were worryingly expensive and unaffordable for many.

Foreign culture experiences for the British: The educational visit

Educational visits to foreign countries have been welcomed in England and regarded as useful hands-on experiences for students during the course of foreign language learning. Hawkins (1987) argued for the significance of an educational journey to foreign countries for students where they might compare and then justify what they have learned in the foreign language classroom while undertaking an educational visit abroad.

The Suzhou Link of the Bath Educational Partnership well exemplified the value of educational partnership with China and was much welcomed by students, schools and parents in the four English schools who joined the educational link with partnership schools in Suzhou province, China. In my field trip to St Peter's School in the summer of 2014, I saw a group of Chinese students (about 20) visiting for a summer term, financed by their parents. Students from St Peter's School could go on a return visit as long as it was financially feasible. Unfortunately, relatively fewer students could afford to travel to China for two weeks during a period of economic recession in Britain. Perhaps this was a different story in King's School, an independent school, where Steven (a student at King's School) reported enjoying his educational trip to China and was greatly inspired by having a genuine experience of Chinese language and culture in Beijing, a story which I will describe in more detail in Chapter 6.

Understanding Social Group Cultures

The historico-cultural legacies of social groups in Taiwan and in England are viewed as important forces that shape young people's foreign language learning processes. For example, the Taiwanese students from the four ethnic groups tend to be positioned differently in terms of access to English in their everyday lives at very basic levels. In England, the school curriculum seems to be intertwined with broader English culture and to be divided somewhat along class lines, so that students in state and independent schools are positioned differently in terms of access to Chinese in their everyday school curriculum.

Ethnic group cultures in Taiwan

Ethnic cultural variations in Taiwan are particularly pivotal for an understanding of how value is attached to English language learning. The four ethnic groups have both specific cultural roots and linguistic variations, which have intimate relations with each other. The Holo people, as has been noted, settled in the plains and developed seaports and river ports which provided good living conditions and close trade networks with the 'mother' country, China. For many, being a Holo, as Greenhalgh (1984) suggested, has meant aiming to move from small- to large-scale entrepreneurship and climbing the commercial ladder. For 300 years, the 'business Holo', arguably, with their historico-cultural legacy of business trading and contributing to economic growth and success, has become one of our most distinctive ethnic characters. As the largest business trading and social group in Taiwan, the Holo have firmly connected with English as a key foreign language. Taiwan's entry into the World Trade Organisation (WTO) in 2002 symbolised the depth of its engagement in global business.

When the Chinese Nationalist government settled in Taiwan in 1949, it brought with it about 1.2 million people, the majority in the military, civil service and education. They lived mainly in cities in unique clusters called 'residential military communities' (juàn-cūn 眷村). Many second-generation Mainlanders were brought up in these communities and were labelled 'outsiders' (wài-xǐng-rén 外省人) in contrast to local Taiwanese 'insiders' (běn-xǐng-rén 本省人). They brought with them their own customs, traditions and political influences, their cultural influence evidenced in art, food, literature and what rapidly became the widespread use of Mandarin. Their lifestyles as predominantly urbanites working either in the military or the civil service gave them what was generally considered to be relatively high political and social status. 'White-collar Mainlanders' (Greenhalgh, 1984) became distinctive ethnic characters differentiated from other social groups, whose second generation characteristically sought social mobility by moving from low to higher responsibility salaried public sector jobs, affording them more access than others to English as a foreign language.

The Hakka history and culture in Taiwan was nicely captured by a Hakka historian some 80 years ago:

> They are a strong, hardy, energetic, fearless race... Self-reliant and active, their rapid expansion and fondness of property have often brought them into conflict with their neighbours.... Fundamentally the Hakka is a farmer, forced by poverty to struggle with the unproductive soil ... They usually occupy the hilly and less fertile districts, while the Punti (bendi) (earlier Han Chinese inhabitants) remain in possession of the fertile deltas and plains.... The women folk are strong and energetic, and have never adopted foot-binding as a custom. (Hsieh, 1929, cited in Constable, 1996: 10)

Hakka women's dual gender roles in Meinung village have been unique in Chinese history, active in both domestic and farming work in contrast to those in other Chinese social groups where the sexes were 'strictly separated in domestic life', women tending to work inside and men outside the home. Hakka people have remained 'proud of the literary accomplishments of their ancestors' and are known for their traditional emphasis on 'academic study' (dú-shū 讀書). Jingzi Pavilion (jìng-zì tíng

敬字亭), the historical architecture, built in 1769 to burn papers with written words on them in order to promote the custom of cherishing them, represents traditional Meinung people's respect for literature since ancient times.

The resounding reputation of the 'town of PhDs' in the Hakka Meinung community strongly exemplifies this cultural legacy of emphasis on 'academic study'. Inspired by the old Hakka saying 'we would sell ancestor's farm lands rather than forget their words' (*níng-méi zŭ-zōng tián, bù-wàng zŭ-zōng yán* – 寧沒祖宗田, 不忘祖宗言), hundreds of PhDs and thousands of master's and bachelor's degrees have been attained in Meinung over the past three decades. Many students have achieved doctorates in education and work in professional educational positions outside the community. Encouraged by this cultural legacy, the gradual expansion of its cram school provision is related not only to economic opportunities but also to the popularity of English and academic study in general.

Tension has existed between the Hakka and other dominant social groups in terms of ethnic identity and spoken language rooted in conflict over scarce land resources. The 'invisible Hakka identity' characterises many of their urban migrants, Mandarin Chinese as the existing 'high language' and the recent rising tide of both local Holo and foreign English languages having become threats to the Hakka mother tongue and leading them to abandon it both as a means of obscuring their humble ethnic origins and privileging highly sought after academic success. Official 'multiculturalism' has done little to sustain many other endangered, minority dialects in Taiwan and the Hakka language is rapidly dying out. Mr Zhao, a senior Hakka English teacher and administrator at Hakka Rural School expressed concern that the Hakka dialect had moved to the stage of 'ICU' (intensive care unit in hospital) in face of the enormous influence of 'Mandarin Chinese'. Hakka students' choice of songs in school singing contests well exemplified the influence of such language discrimination on the Hakka mother tongue, as Mr Zhao said:

> Students were enormously influenced by 'Mandarin Chinese' (*guó-yŭ*). When we held a singing contest at school... the first choice of students was Mandarin, followed by Holo songs, the choice of Hakka songs were 'relatively rare' (*hĕn-shăo*).

The unpopularity of Hakka songs might have symptomatised language value asymmetry, as will be explored further in Chapter 6.

The Paiwan tribe located in the most southern regions around Pintong and Tai-tong counties is the third largest with a population of some 78,000. Among its many distinctive cultural features are beliefs in the sun and snake totems and a social hierarchy consisting of nobility and commoners, under which the nobility leased land to commoners for farming, while some members of the community concentrated on the arts. In terms of religion, though some 30% of modern Paiwan people believe in Western religions, particularly what they refer to as Christian and Catholic (detailed in Chapter 4), they also believe that their ancestral spirits, dwelling on Da-wu Mountain, come down every five years to visit their descendants. The Five-Year Ceremony (*Maleveq*) in the Paiwan language, is their most important ritual, celebrating a reunion with returned gods and ancestors; celebrated in Hu's (1984) anthropological film 'The Return of Gods and Ancestors: The Five-Year Ceremony' (cited in Graves, 1987). As became apparent during classroom observation, some attempt was made to refer to the rite in English teaching. Though many indigenous cultural practices appear to be in decline in the wake of widespread social and economic change, the *Maleveq*, which normally lasts for 3–5 days, is still celebrated today. According to local legend, the gods and ancestors bring fortune as well as misfortune. In the key rite of the *Maleveq*, individual families have to compete for gods' gifts, represented symbolically by 10 small 'balls' woven of bamboo stripes, called *qapudrung* in the Paiwan language. Five of the balls are said to represent good fortune and the other five misfortune. According to Graves (1987), the key rite of the *Maleveq* takes place after the gods and ancestors have arrived. This rite clearly reveals the essentially competitive nature of the *Maleveq*. In 2003, the competition was held on flat ground on a hill adjacent to Mountainside School. Each family put forward a champion equipped with a long 'bamboo pole' (*djuljat*) who sat on elevated stands arranged in a circle with other competitors holding long poles in a vertical position. At their centre, key religious figures stood while balls were tossed skyward, one after another, while competitors swayed their poles in a rhythmic effort to catch one of them on their sharpened tips. The rite continued until all 10 balls had been spiked, ending in gains for some families and losses for others.

The Paiwan group are particularly distinguished in terms of their artistic prowess, for example, the manufacturing of earthenware pots, glass beads and woodcarvings, participated in by men only and weaving, participated in by women only. Singing and dancing are favourite everyday activities, leisure activities transmitted between generations: 'Paiwan young people are able to sing and dance because they have seen and imitated these practices since childhood' (Chiang, 2004: 336). A junior high school team from the Bunun tribe who won the national English drama competition in 2004, the first ever indigenous competitors and champions in the four years since the competition began, amply exemplify indigenous people's talent for performance.

Indigenous Paiwan, as well as other tribes, share a powerful cultural legacy of athletic prowess that cannot be overemphasised. Physical fitness and athletic agility are traditionally celebrated and highly valued in the Paiwan annual athletic contest held each year. Successful models of international athletic performance inspire young Paiwan people, most notably Mr Chuan-Guang Yang (1933–2007) of the indigenous Ami tribe, known as the 'Iron Man of Asia' (*yàz-hōu tiĕ-rén* 亞洲鐵人), winning gold for Taiwan in the decathlon at the 1954 and 1958 Asian Games and setting a new world record in 1963. His most memorable competition was the duel with his fellow University of California, Los Angeles (UCLA) schoolmate, Rafer Johnson, at the 1960 Summer Olympics in Rome, where Yang was awarded silver. Yang's athletic prowess and achievement inspired thousands of his fellow indigenous youngsters to develop their athletic potential, as at Mountainside School as will be seen in Chapter 5.

Social group culture in England

As Coombs (1985: 256) suggested in Chapter 1, 'Any nation that encompasses various ethnic linguistic groups… inevitably faces the serious difficulties in achieving a binding sense of nationhood among its different peoples. These internal language difficulties are compounded by each country's need for linguistic bridges to the rest of the world'. British society has its counterparts in Taiwan's 'internal language difficulties' involving historical conflict of linguistic divisions and suppression of languages in the process of seeking linguistic bridges to the world community. Historically, the four nations – England, Wales, Scotland and Northern Ireland – constitute the commonly known United Kingdom, often referred to in everyday life as (Great) Britain. Each nation has its own unique linguistic and cultural roots that engender the complexities of multilingual reality in Britain. Despite the fact that mother tongues such as Welsh (Wales) and, to a lesser extent, Gaelic (Scotland) are well embedded in the relevant national curriculum of each region in order to pursue cultural and national identities, English is unquestionably the dominant high language across the four nations in Britain. But some degree of tension exists between the requirements of reaching out for modernisation or globalisation and those of internal cultural identification. As it is, English schools, while free of overt, historic internal language conflict, may be sites of contrasting class and regional cultural variants conflict, where students' mother tongues are often those of other ethnic immigrant groups.

English linguistic dilemmas, like those in Taiwan, remind us of the potentially conflicting themes of language and localisation (purer) or globalisation (newer), suggesting the inevitability of emerging competition between languages within British society. Moreover, as we have noted, Britain has long been seen to be 'constantly straining toward newer… more efficient solutions to the problems of today and tomorrow' (Fishman, 1989: 126) while possibly slipping backwards in the task of learning other foreign languages (e.g. French, Spanish, German and Chinese) as part of its perceived need to connect to the outside world. At the same time in Britain, and disproportionately in England, there are immigrant groups from south Asia (Indian, Bangladeshi and Pakistani), China and a recently much larger group from a variety of European Union countries, which make up a multilingual Britain. Despite the fact that English is always the dominant language, heritage languages are spoken at home for these immigrant groups (and the Welsh case, as we have already noted, is even more complex). In certain cases, with support from some local authorities to promote local group identities, heritage languages are provided as part of school education, though often with lessons restricted to after-school clubs or weekend schools. Chinese, for example, as the language of a minority has long been taught on a Saturday schools basis in order to maintain it as cultural heritage. In addition, for other European languages such as Polish, French, German and Spanish, they are now present in Britain as 'temporal' heritage languages.

In this context of Britain's multilingual reality, I will focus on an exploration of CFL learned at school as an additional subject in recent years. Its most obvious feature across different schools is what is referred to as the 'state–independent divide' in England, evident in the national survey conducted by the British Council in 2014. This divide engenders issues relating to resource disparity and various cultural capital and social class divisions that have impacts on students' learning not only in Chinese but other languages, particularly the classical ones (Latin and Greek), performing and other arts and physical education and games. The particular social class divisions in British society have historically impacted hugely on its education system and is perhaps key to the question of why more independent, fee-paying schools than state schools are offering Chinese to students.

The dominant characteristics of 19th-century education in Britain were two very distinct traditions of schooling – the public school/grammar school tradition of education for children of the upper and growing middle classes and the elementary school tradition intended to train the 'lower orders'. The 20th-century distinction modified the principle of equality of opportunity in education (e.g. the new institutional requirements of the 1944 Education Act, the rise of more child-centred primary school modalities and the growth of the comprehensive) to provide somewhat more ready access to improved and extended educational experiences for working-class children. But even in the 21st century, the 'state–independent divide' in England in the provision of CFL seems to mark the continued existence of very distinct traditions of schooling where fee-paying independent school students, backed by affluent parental and appropriate family cultural capital, are given more choices of foreign language learning (and other curricular) options than those in the vast majority of state schools. Giddens' (2006) declaration of the importance of class may be helpful here and applies to English society even though he formulates a more general statement:

> Although the traditional hold of class is most certainly weakening in some ways, particularly in terms of people's identities, class divisions

remain at the heart of core economic inequalities in modern societies. Class continues to exert a great influence on our lives, and class membership is co-related with a variety of inequalities from life expectancy and overall physical health to access to education and well-paid jobs. (Giddens, 2006: 333)

The 'state–independent divide' in England in the provision of Chinese inevitably lures us into thinking that the social class division with 'vestigial remains of feudalism' and 'economic inequalities' still exists today and has an impact on English education in general and on foreign language education in particular, a matter of concern which I will discuss in Chapter 4.

Chapter Summary

In this chapter, we have examined broader sociocultural forces that shape foreign language learning. These social forces include the historical, political and cultural contexts of learning English and Chinese as foreign languages in Taiwan and England, respectively. We have first examined the political framing of these two foreign languages, making us aware that learning English or Chinese should not be considered as an isolated school subject, but rather a practice embedded in wider political and globalised cultural contexts. We have also examined and compared school cultures within Taiwanese society and between Taiwan and England, involving school visions, curricula for foreign languages and the hidden curricula, including cram schooling in Taiwan and access to foreign cultural experiences. These school or out-of-school practices are important forces that shape students' English and Chinese learning. Lastly, the social group cultures in both countries have been examined and compared within and across cultures. In Taiwan, for example, the historico-cultural legacies of certain ethnic groups were found to have directed students towards specific orientations and thus influenced their English learning. In England, however, our focus has been drawn to differences between state and independent schools as social groups. In particular, the 'state–independent divide' in England in the provision of the Chinese language appears to relate to the traditional social class division in English society. With these cultural contexts in mind, we will further examine students' access to English or Chinese in their everyday lives in the next chapter.

Note

(1) More recently, in responding to the revolutionary changes in communication and transportation technologies that have dramatically accelerated intercultural interaction around the world, the 12-Year Basic Education Curricula was announced by the MOE in 2014 and was implemented in 2018 (MOE Taiwan, 2019).

4 Getting Access to English and Chinese: Everyday Practice

A sociocultural approach entails that what students do in learning English/Chinese cannot be divided from their experiences of foreign language practices in other settings, such as their local communities, schools and homes, and the historico-cultural legacies of their social groups. Students' participation in everyday English/Chinese learning practices should be seen in terms of a broader concept of 'apprenticeship' (Rogoff, 1995) characterised by dynamic relations between their activities in the communities and the institutions in which they occur.

This chapter presents empirical findings involving students' everyday participation in culturally organised activities within and beyond school settings. It reports students' access to English in Taiwan and Chinese in England in their everyday community, home, after-school learning (referred to as cram school in Taiwan) and school settings, mainly drawing upon their questionnaire responses and some interviews and informal conversational responses. The student questionnaires contained three sections: learning English/Chinese; use of English/Chinese in everyday life; and demographic characteristics. Mapping similarities between English/Chinese practices in everyday life in Taiwan and England permits the presentation of a broader picture of students' access to the target foreign languages in community, family and ordinary school settings. Regional and cultural differences in students' everyday use of English/Chinese reveal the existence of an 'urban–rural divide' in Taiwan and a 'state–independent divide' in England. In Taiwan, family resources and incomes are seen to be characterised by ethnic cultural varieties of disparate and unequal kinds and getting access to English in everyday settings seems to encourage language familiarity and academic achievement that helps to explain why some students from certain social groups learn English better than others. In England, the unequal provision of very limited amounts of teaching and learning Chinese between state and independent schools largely determines why some students from certain schools or family backgrounds gain access to Chinese more easily than others.

Variations in the cultural and economic resources of students' families lie at the heart of Bourdieu's (1986) notion of 'cultural capital', as a key to our understanding of why some students can do better in learning English/Chinese than others in the context of existing social class inequalities. In Bourdieu's (1986) words, it was:

> The notion of cultural capital... as a theoretical hypothesis which made it possible to explain the unequal scholastic achievement of children originating from the different social classes by relating academic successes, i.e., the specific profits which children from the different classes and class fractions can obtain in the academic market, to the distribution of cultural capital between the classes and class fractions. (Bourdieu, 1986: 243)

Bourdieu describes cultural capital in three forms or 'states': embodied, objectified and institutionalised. Academic qualifications exemplified the institutionalised state of cultural capital from which children could profit as members of their family, school or social class groups. 'With the academic qualification, a certificate of cultural competence which confers on its holder a conventional, constant, legally guaranteed value with respect to culture social alchemy produces a form of cultural capital' (Bourdieu, 1986: 248). We can expect cultural differences, variations in 'cultural capital' among Taiwanese social groups and between students in English independent and state schools to make an impact on students' English/Chinese learning.

Getting Access to English in Taiwan

The following data concerning students' experiences of English in everyday life in terms of listening, speaking, reading and writing were mainly drawn from a questionnaire, comprising 43 categories modified from Scribner and Cole's (1981) questions in their seminal study in Liberia, and were administered during fieldwork in Taiwan.

Everyday English practices

As shown in Table 4.1, when students were asked in what circumstances they would hear or listen to English, 87% reported listening to 'schoolteachers' and more than 50% across all categories listened to English from 'CD/audio music' (mean: 62%). On average, 52% also heard it from 'cram schoolteachers', masking large differences between groups, with only 17% of indigenous respondents doing so, in contrast to 75% of Mainlanders. Almost without exception, Holo and Mainlander respondents reported higher incidences across all categories. In Table 4.1, there were relatively smaller differences between social groups concerning access to a number of modern technologies or learning facilities, such as 'desktop' (48%). In terms of speaking English, most reported 'in class' (mean: 70%, indigenous students 80%) or 'in cram school' (mean: 48%, indigenous students

Table 4.1 Everyday English practices

Categories of practice	Urban			Rural		All students (n = 253)
	Holo (n = 98)	Mainlander (n = 28)	Hakka (n = 64)	Indigenous (n = 53)		

Categories of practice	Holo (n = 98)	Mainlander (n = 28)	Hakka (n = 64)	Indigenous (n = 53)	All students (n = 253)
Listening					
1. Schoolteacher (%)	86	90	88	83	87
2. CD/audio music (%)	61	71	58	57	62
3. TV (%)	56	70	48	62	59
4. Cram schoolteacher (%)	68	75	47	17	52
5. Desktop (%)	54	57	45	36	48
6. Movie theatres (%)	54	57	25	25	40
Speaking					
1. In class (%)	66	77	58	80	70
2. In cram school (%)	64	64	44	21	48
3. At home (%)	33	50	33	36	38
4. On desktop (%)	43	42	36	22	36
5. On the street (%)	9	18	13	15	14
Reading					
1. School lessons (%)	74	83	67	87	78
2. TV programmes (%)	42	64	47	40	48
3. Websites (%)	60	46	47	34	47
4. Email (%)	49	46	41	21	39
5. Shopping (%)	39	50	36	28	38
6. Household objects (%)	31	57	25	28	35
Writing					
1. Schoolwork (%)	85	97	77	84	86
2. Taking school notes (%)	72	96	80	82	83
3. Birthday cards (%)	65	75	53	51	61
4. Email (%)	36	39	30	28	33
5. Chat room (%)	35	29	36	21	30
Categories of services					
1. Help from others (%)	47	71	37	45	50
2. To teach others (%)	64	82	15	10	43

21%), as with their listening practice. Mainlanders spoke markedly more English at home, while indigenous students did markedly less so 'on desktop' (22%), explaining a well-documented 'digital divide' between urban and rural regions within Taiwanese society. Indigenous students tended to be less well provided with internet-mediated English practice facilities, including those at Mountainside boarding school, though they might pay to access it from a nearby cybercafé in the village.

In terms of reading English, most reported that it occurred through 'school lessons' (78%) in the highly textbook-oriented school culture in Taiwan. Nearly 50% of the respondents read English from 'TV programmes' (48%) or 'websites' (47%); however, once again, the main general feature of these distributions reveals a relative lack of access among indigenous and, to a lesser degree, Hakka respondents, than their urban, particularly Mainlander, counterparts. In terms of writing English, most reported 'schoolwork' (86%) and 'taking school notes' (83%). While Mainlanders again scored most highly across all but one category (chat room), group differences were generally much smaller and of less surface significance than for other practices. Lastly, when students were asked if they had ever asked anyone who could speak, read or write English to help them, a mean of 50% reported that they did so with friends/classmates, schoolteachers or family members. A mean of 43% also reported having taught someone how to speak, read or write English, urban groups again outnumbering their rural counterparts in both respects. For example, very few Hakka (15%) or indigenous (10%) students taught others as opposed to their urban peers, i.e. Holo (64%) and Mainlanders (82%).

Given this broader picture of students' access to English in everyday life, two particularly salient points emerged. Overwhelmingly, 'institutional' (school-based) practice appeared to count as students' major form of access to English in everyday life (i.e. 87%, 70%, 78%, 86% in the four language skills on average, respectively). However, differences between social groups demonstrated that Mainlander students consistently had the highest range and incidence of everyday English practices, in certain respects related to the availability of facilities in their towns and homes, as well as learning within school and cram school settings. For example, in terms of speaking English, both urban groups (64%) reported that they did so in cram schools. However, less than half (44%) of Hakka and only 21% of indigenous students reported speaking English in cram schools.

Family resources: Aiding access to English

Students' parental encouragement, engagement and arrangements appeared to play pivotal roles in contributing to the nature and extent of everyday English practices in their homes. It is crucial to understand whether anyone encouraged respondents to learn English and whether their family members' knowledge of English had influenced their English learning. In Taiwan, travelling or study abroad for English immersion is widely considered by parents to be effective strategies for improving English and parental encouragement and engagement or arrangements in respect of them are pivotal. In addition, certain ethnic cultural formations, for example, indigenous peoples' attachment to Western religions (classified, somewhat confusingly, as 'Christian' and 'Catholic'), or

Hakka cultural legacy emphasising academic study, appeared to help explain the behaviours, the 'whys', that differentiated students' access to everyday English.

In terms of parental encouragement, more than 70% of students on average reported being encouraged to learn English, as indicated in Table 4.2, slightly more by parents than undisclosed others, with mothers on average almost four times more likely to encourage their children's English learning than fathers (30% vs. 8%). This familial resource of maternal encouragement seems to suggest mothers' overriding responsibility for children's schoolwork at home within Taiwanese society. A further question asked if specific family members with knowledge of English had influenced English learning, to which respondents from urban groups were nearly twice as likely to report having been influenced to learn English in this way than those of rural groups (44%, 46% vs. 25%, 21%). Holo fathers were unusual in being twice as likely to be the source of influence as mothers (37% vs. 19%) and four times less likely in indigenous families (9% vs. 36%). Overall, whereas more than two in five urban families provided some influence, barely one in five rural families did so. Undoubtedly, parental education and career background play a part in valuing English at home and encouraging and helping their children.

Foreign travel has long been valued by Taiwanese parents as key to learning English well. Travelling abroad for cultural immersion, whether for sightseeing or study tours, is a strategy supported and endorsed by students and parents alike but with very different access by different social groups. More than half of Mainlander students (52%) reported foreign travel and cultural experience but only 4% of indigenous students did so (Table 4.2). Moreover, 11% of Mainlander students, in complete

Table 4.2 Familial influence on English learning

	Urban			Rural	All students
	Holo	Mainlander	Hakka	Indigenous	
Encouragement from others					
(Yes) (%)	72	75	72	67	72
Mother (%)	31	32	33	25	30
Father (%)	11	4	11	6	8
Familial influences (parents with knowledge of English)					
(Yes) (%)	44	46	25	21	34
Mother (%)	19	46	31	36	33
Father (%)	37	46	13	9	26
Travel abroad					
Been abroad (%)	34	52	22	4	28
Lived abroad (%)	1	11	0	0	3

contrast to other groups, reported they had lived abroad at some time in the past. Mainlander students had more opportunities to travel for sightseeing than other social groups while almost no indigenous students did so.

Parental education and occupation

Students' family backgrounds, including parental education, occupation and involvement, have been persistently recognised as contributory influences on students' educational achievement. In his ethnographic observation of a fishing village in rural Taiwan, Stafford (1995) pointed out that the pressure driving the educational system came from parents, rather than school or state. Indeed, this tendency also applies to urban Taiwan where, mediated by an urban, competitive culture, anxious parents 'swarm' to engage their children in learning English as early as possible. While being cautious of oversimplifying the causation between parents' education and occupation and children's English as a foreign language (EFL) performance, given the other complex social and cultural forces that also shape English learning, a closer look at the differences in parents' education and occupation across various social groups certainly points to ways in which family cultural capital and family access to social and economic resources play a part in children's access to English learning.

As shown in Table 4.3, urbanite Holo and Mainlander parents had higher overall educational levels than others. More parents with college education levels or above were found in Mainlander groups, while the lowest parental educational levels were found in the indigenous group, most being educated only at or below junior high school level. Mothers were generally as well educated as fathers across all ethnic groups, except at postgraduate level, though less than a third of all indigenous mothers and a quarter of fathers had education beyond junior high, in contrast with over 80% of Holo, nearly all Mainlander and over three quarters of Hakka mothers and even higher percentages of fathers. In addition, parental occupation appeared to bear close correlation with parental education level. Table 4.3 indicates that while mothers' occupations were dominated by domestic and unskilled employment, they were remarkably similar across ethnic groups, with the exception of government employment and business, appearing to echo a common-sense belief that 'men work outside and women work at home' within Taiwanese society that gives rise to the sort of social gender identity which will be addressed in Chapter 6. Indigenous (65%) and Hakka (49%) males disproportionately occupied unskilled labour positions and were severely underrepresented in business, government and police/military categories. In his study of Taiwanese rural society in the 1980s, Thompson (1984) found large numbers of the rural population had gone to work in cities, impelled by

Table 4.3 Parents' education and occupation

	Urban			Rural	All students
	Holo	Mainlander	Hakka	Indigenous	
Mother's education					
Elementary school (%)	6	0	2	42	12
Secondary school (%)	51	40	57	49	49
College (%)	29	43	33	6	28
University (%)	14	18	8	4	11
Postgraduate or above (%)	1	0	0	0	0.3
Father's education					
Elementary school (%)	1	0	3	40	11
Secondary school (%)	46	19	50	49	40
College (%)	25	41	39	12	29
University (%)	26	26	8	0	15
Postgraduate or above (%)	3	15	0	0	5
Mother's occupation					
Domestic (%)	23	27	23	24	24
Labour (unskilled) (%)	9	4	19	28	15
Business (%)	35	35	35	8	28
Government official (%)	19	23	4	2	12
Temporary work (%)	8	0	9	20	9
Military/police[a] (%)	0	8	0	2	3
Father's occupation					
Labour (unskilled) (%)	24	11	49	65	37
Business (%)	48	37	22	6	28
Government official (%)	14	30	11	6	15
Military/police (%)	1	15	2	6	6
Temporary work (%)	1	0	2	6	2
Domestic[b] (%)	0	0	0	0	0

Note: 'Government official' includes teachers.
[a]'Military/police' means military personnel and police officers.
[b]'Domestic' means unemployed or working at home.

the relative unprofitability of agriculture. This remains true in modern Taiwan and applies particularly to rural Meinung and Paiwan parents. Many of them, mostly fathers, tended to migrate to urban cities to engage in comparatively lucrative off-farm or full-time employment. In contrast, as can be seen in Table 4.3, almost half of Holo fathers worked in 'business' (48%) while Mainlander fathers were at least twice as likely as those of any other group to work as 'government officials' (30%).

Looking at the distribution of male parental occupations from a historical perspective, the phenomena of 'business Holo' and 'white-collar

Mainlanders' seems to be alive. The distributions tend to confirm Greenhalgh's (1984) ethnographic account of two generically different routes followed by these groups in climbing to the top of the commercial and social ladders. 'Being a Holo' has meant going through small- to large-scale entrepreneurship and 'being a Mainlander' moving from low to higher responsibility, salaried jobs. The data suggest that better educated Mainlanders tend to secure civil servant or teaching jobs, in what are widely known as 'iron rice bowls' (*tiĕ-fàn-wăn* 鐵飯碗), which not only contribute to their higher social status and politico-economic power but also provide cultural capital for their children's English learning.

On the contrary, rural parents' educational and occupational styles seemed to impede involvement in their children's education and, in turn, access to English in everyday life. Following the economic boom in the 1970s, indigenous people started to flow into urban cities in search of employment, primarily in poorly paid manual positions, such as construction and heavy industry. National statistics demonstrated that 16% of indigenous people were engaged in construction work and that the proportions of indigenous people also working in agriculture, factory, fishing and animal husbandry were higher than those of the general population in Taiwan. Some indigenous parents, therefore, waited or 'hunted' on urban street corners for temporary jobs with new building projects, travelling back to their rural homes on a weekly basis or only for festive occasions. As a result, a grandparental child-rearing style prevailed in both Hakka Meinung township and the indigenous Paiwan village, leading to a lack of immediate daily parental involvement in children's education. For instance, in talking about the scarce parental engagement of some low achieving classmates, one Mountainside student in Ms Lin's class (Vanessa) reported that

> Those who live with grandparents cannot get any help from there.... Some of my classmates are from single-parent families, some of them are living with their grandparents. I even have a classmate who lives alone which is 'really scary' (*hăo-kĕ-pà*)! ... It is quite common for parents working outside of the community.

This grandparental child-rearing style posed another challenge to speaking English 'at home' for students from the same two groups. The fact that most Meinung grandparents could only speak the Hakka dialect, while Paiwan grandparents spoke either their tribal language or some Japanese, made any English-speaking practice at home difficult or impossible for their student grandchildren. For example, one Paiwan student complained:

> When I am trying to speak English with my grandparents, it ends in recrimination...for one thing, they do not understand this language at

all, and for another, they tend to question me why I choose to speak a foreign language rather than our mother tongue. (Informal conversation, 3 August 2004)

The emerging consequence of the grandparental child-rearing style upon these intergenerational relations within these two rural groups seemed to intensify the influences of ethnic identity and the value asymmetry of various languages (ethnic mother tongues, official/national language and foreign languages) in use within Taiwanese society, which will be addressed in Chapter 7.

Getting Access to Chinese in England

The previous section described some features of the contexts and situations in which Taiwanese secondary students gain access to English in their everyday lives at home, in school and at the broader community level. In delineating English students' reports on their experiences of everyday Chinese practices, family resources which aid access to Chinese, parental education backgrounds and reasons for learning Chinese as parallel as possible, data drawn from a questionnaire survey in King's School and observational and conversational encounters in St Mary's are given below. The questionnaire was also informed by Scribner and Cole's (1981) study in Liberia, fashioned according to students' contexts in England. The data are limited and reflect the facts that independent schools are four times more likely than state schools to provide the limited amount of Chinese on offer and that the relatively smaller number of state school students enrolling in Chinese do so mostly in after-school club sessions as an enrichment curriculum. With this limitation in mind, it was practical and appropriate to undertake the questionnaire survey only in the cooperating independent school (i.e. King's School) where Chinese had been compulsory since 2006 and there was a reasonably large cohort of respondents ($n = 92$) available in October, 2015. However, in order to indicate some incipient features of a more general picture of Chinese practices in secondary schools in England, observational and interviewing data regarding students at St Mary's School as to their attitude and reasons why they want to learn Chinese will be added.

Everyday Chinese practices

The demographic features of the English students from King's School are shown in Table 1.4. As Chinese had been compulsory since 2006, students learned Chinese for a duration of two to four years with Chinese lessons taught on a weekly basis. Table 4.4 reveals students' everyday practices when they reported the circumstances in which they would listen, speak, read and write Chinese, summed up as total percentages across four categories (i.e. at least once a day/once a week/once a month/

once a year). In terms of listening to Chinese, as high as 95% reported access through listening to 'schoolteachers' and 70% through listening to 'friends speaking'. More than half of the respondents reported access through listening to 'internet/social media' (57%) and 'CD-stories/lessons' (55%). For example, one student said:

> I hear Mandarin when I am revising my vocabulary for a test or just for a revision on online websites with audio of the vocabulary. I also hear it in Mandarin class when my Chinese teacher or other pupils are speaking, or when an audio file is played on the computer for an exercise we are doing.

Unlike in Taiwan, there was no cram school teaching. In terms of speaking Chinese, almost all reported 'in class' (97%) and half of them 'at home' (53%), with markedly less 'on desktop' (35%), 'on the street' (34%) or 'in after-school club' (30%). For example, one student said:

> Often in conversations with friends, we will say certain things in Chinese, simply for fun, and to test our abilities to make sentences. This begins in class where we will be asked to do this by the teacher; however outside the classroom we have occasionally done the same thing, trying to integrate Mandarin into our daily lives as I know speaking it as much as possible can only improve my Mandarin.

In terms of reading Chinese, most reported through 'school lessons' (85%) in the textbook-oriented school lessons and more than half read Chinese from 'websites' (57%), a practice which might also link to school lessons as homework. To a lesser degree, less than half reported out-of-school Chinese practices with respect to activities, such as 'shopping', 'street-aids' or 'email' (46%, 42% and 41%). For instance, one student reported that 'I read Mandarin throughout Mandarin lessons, on the whiteboard and in my textbook and exercise book. I also read Mandarin at home on the computer for revision and practice of the language'. In terms of writing Chinese, markedly similarly to EFL practices in Taiwan, most reported 'schoolwork' (92%) and 'taking school notes' (83%). For example, one student said 'I write Mandarin when I'm practicing for tests or for controlled assessments at home. I also write it in class when practicing the characters of words, or doing other exercises'. Another student reported that 'I occasionally use Mandarin to abbreviate my notes in other subjects (e.g. using 国 or 国家 in history notes instead of "countries")'.

Lastly, when students were asked if they had ever asked anyone who could speak, read or write Chinese to help them, 32% reported that they did so with friends/classmates, schoolteachers or family members and 40% had helped to teach someone how to speak, read or write Chinese (see Table 4.4). The categories of language assistance would include, for example, 'confirming grammar and vocabulary choices when writing an assignment from friends' or 'asked friends who can speak Mandarin to help me with homework or knowing how to say something'. This might also happen outside of school, in particular during their education trip abroad in China. A student reported that 'when we were in China our teacher translated things for us'. At home, one student said: 'I taught my dad how to speak a bit of Mandarin at a Chinese restaurant'.

As in Taiwan, overwhelmingly, 'institutional' (school-based) practice appeared to count as students' major form of access to Chinese in everyday life, which stood out to be the key source for students to access Chinese. Incipiently, several practices outside school in the community

Table 4.4 Everyday Chinese practices

Listening	
1. Schoolteacher (%)	95
2. Friends speaking (%)	70
3. Internet/social media (%)	57
4. CD-stories/lessons (%)	55
5. Cram schoolteacher (%)	0
Speaking	
1. In class (%)	97
2. At home (%)	53
3. On desktop (%)	35
4. On the street (%)	34
5. In after-school club (%)	30
Reading	
1. School lessons (%)	85
2. Websites (%)	57
3. Shopping (%)	46
4. Street ads (%)	42
5. Email (%)	41
Writing	
1. Schoolwork (%)	92
2. Taking school notes (%)	83
3. Birthday cards (%)	35
4. Shopping memos (%)	30
5. Chat room (%)	28
Categories of services	
1. Help from others (%)	32
2. To teach others (%)	40

seemed worth noting, such as using Chinese on the street or in Chinese restaurants. For example, according to one student, 'I occasionally use Mandarin words or phrases with fellow learners of Mandarin outside the classroom, and have sometimes spoken a little to Chinese people outside school after being encouraged'. Another student would speak Chinese 'sometimes in Chinese restaurants when ordering food' and another would intentionally try to read Chinese for practice. She/he said 'sometimes if I see a sign somewhere in English, that has a Mandarin translation below, I will look at some of the characters to see if I can understand what is being said'.

Family resources: Aiding access to Chinese?

Given that parental encouragement, engagement and arrangements appeared to play pivotal roles in contributing to the nature and extent of everyday English practices in Taiwan, it is interesting to explore whether anyone encouraged the English respondents to learn Chinese. Both in Taiwan and England, travelling or study abroad for foreign language immersion is widely considered by parents as effective in improving English/Chinese. In terms of encouragement from others to learn Chinese, 22% of students reported being encouraged by 'school and teachers' (see Table 4.5), slightly more than by parents and siblings (13%). In contrast to Taiwanese parents' encouragement of 72% on average (see Table 4.2), this relatively less familial resource of parental encouragement in King's School seems to suggest schoolteachers' overriding responsibility for students' Chinese learning as schoolwork. A further question asked if specific family members with knowledge of Chinese had influenced their Chinese learning. Only 2% of students reported that their 'parents' knew Chinese. As opposed to Taiwanese parents' knowledge of English (34%), students in England have much less opportunity to practice Chinese with their parents, albeit they could do that with siblings (12%) at home or friends in school.

Foreign travel for cultural immersion, whether via sightseeing or study tours, has long been valued by some parents as key to learning foreign languages well, more so in Taiwan than England. In the latter, travelling abroad is supported and endorsed by parents and the nation alike, by individual and local school arrangements and by regional networks, such as the 'Erasmus+ Programme' (e.g. youth exchange) under the European Commission framework. Education exchange visits to China were restricted by differing family economic situations at both ends during our period of study in the urban city in south-western England. For example, in the summer of 2013, fewer British students from St Peter's School were able to visit China (i.e. for the Suzhou Link with China) than those Chinese students visiting England at a time of

Table 4.5 Familial influence on learning Chinese

Encouragement from others	
(Yes)	36
School and teachers (%)	22
Parents (%)	13
Siblings/relatives/friends (%)	1
Familial influences (family with knowledge of Chinese)	
(Yes) (%)	14
Siblings (%)	12
Parents (%)	2
Travel abroad	
Been abroad (outside of UK) (%)	96
Lived abroad (%)	35

economic downturn in Britain as a whole, as well as for other individual family reasons. In independent King's School, where parents were generally more affluent, an overwhelmingly high percentage of students reported foreign travel and cultural experience (96%). Among them, 35% reported they had lived abroad (see Table 4.5). When asked what was the farthest place they had travelled to outside England, students reported the USA (21%), Australia and China (both 13%). Of the students who had been abroad, 22% of them had done so 1–10 times and 27% for 11–20 times. The high percentage of travelling experience for the English students is in sharp contrast with the Taiwanese students (28% on average) and 52% for Mainlanders students (see Table 4.2). It could be argued that this high 'modernity and mobility' could be associated with parental education backgrounds and involvement, a matter turned to in the following section.

Parental education backgrounds

Following Stafford's (1995) ethnographic account of Taiwanese parental forces driving the educational system, it would be interesting to explore a potential correlation between parents' education backgrounds and children's access to Chinese in England. However, we only have data relevant to it from the questionnaire administered in one independent school. As shown in Table 4.6, English independent school parents have an overall high educational level. Over 80% of mothers and fathers have a university and above educational level. While acknowledging its unrepresentativeness, it offers a clear affirmation of the link between parental education background as 'cultural capital' and students' presence in high achieving school contexts and access to Chinese.

Table 4.6 Parents' education backgrounds

Father's education	
Elementary school (%)	1
Secondary school (%)	7
College (%)	7
University (%)	60
Postgraduate or above (%)	26
Mother's education	
Elementary school (%)	0
Secondary school (%)	5
College (%)	14
University (%)	48
Postgraduate or above (%)	33

Impact of historico-cultural legacies on foreign language learning

Looking closely at students' familial resources and affordances in getting access to English or Chinese, we discover that the historico-cultural legacies of certain social groups in Taiwan seem to have some influence on students' English learning, which is not available to their British counterparts in learning Chinese. For example, in Taiwan, the historico-cultural legacies of both the Hakka and indigenous social groups must loom large in any attempt to map students' family resources and affordances in getting access to English. One historico-cultural legacy in the Hakka Meinung community was its resounding reputation as the 'Town of PhDs' arising from its historic emphasis on academic study, as delineated in Chapter 3. Religious belief, primarily of family origin, seemed to provide another example of the regulation of students' access to English, especially among indigenous students. According to Greenhalgh (1984: 537), the majority of Taiwanese historically 'identified themselves as Buddhists or folk religionists (e.g. Taoism)'. Having ancestral altars in their homes, they tended to 'worship' (*bài-bài*) their ancestors through burning incense or paper money and contributing to local religious festivals on an occasional basis. This anthropological account reported three decades ago still matches the scene in contemporary Taiwan.

As can be seen in Table 4.7, more than half of Holo (60%) and Mainlanders (50%) reported that they held either Buddhist or Taoist religious beliefs. Indigenous students, in contrast, claimed to hold Western religious beliefs, nearly 70% Christian (67%), including Catholic (28%). Western religions are important historico-cultural legacies for indigenous people within Taiwanese society. Following the Han immigration, the footprints of foreign missionaries (mainly Christian) brought Western customs to the mountains, alongside religious doctrine,

Table 4.7 Students' religious belief

Religion	Urban		Rural		All students
	Holo	Mainlander	Hakka	Indigenous	
(Yes) (%)	60	50	36	67	53
Buddhism (%)	35	18	29	0	21
Taoism (%)	21	25	7	0	13
Christian (%)	4	7	0	67	20

Note: (a) Percentages do not always add up to 100 due to missing values. (b) Taoism usually refers to local folk religion in Taiwan.

which interweaved with tribal culture. It might be expected that such a historico-cultural legacy of Western religion had implicitly inclined indigenous students to value foreign culture. Ms Yang (the indigenous teacher in Mountainside School) certainly described herself as an 'xenophile', saying that 'most Paiwan students, including myself, are churchgoers.... We tend to recognise Western culture rather than Han Chinese culture'.

Urban–rural divide and cultural differences

Drawn from students' experiences of English or Chinese in various settings in everyday life, this section provides further discussion of the 'whys' of regional and cultural differences, particularly urban–rural and ethnic cultural variations in Taiwan, including family resources and income power as a form of 'cultural capital' and how such differences may lead to resource disparity, hence social inequality in learning English across various social groups within Taiwanese society. In England, as argued in Chapter 1, the major difference in access to Chinese lies in the fact that there is a 'state–independent school divide' rather than urban–rural or ethnic cultural variations as in Taiwan.

In Taiwan, regional differences which prevail across students' experiences of English in various settings in everyday life are reflected in the long-standing 'urban–rural divide' in attaining, for instance, the annual National Basic Competence Test (see Chapter 1). If we conceptualise the English language as a 'cultural carrier', regional discrepancy can be understood by perceiving cities as modern cultural 'beachheads' (Coombs, 1985) whereby urbanites naturally have easier access to it than their rural counterparts. As Coombs (1985) puts it, interbreeding of cultural infusions in developing countries since the Second World War has been vast and penetrating. The infusion of American culture and its English language into Taiwan has been among its best examples. The English language, alongside its cultural importations and influences, has had enormous effects, especially in urban contexts. These heavily Westernised, modern, cultural 'beachheads' have made it possible for English, as a powerful foreign language, to be available to urbanites in various settings, including family, school, cram school and town, exemplified in students' differential access to it through engagement in modern leisure activities (e.g. via movie theatres), perceiving signs of English 'at home' (e.g. through use of household objects such as electronic products) and 'in town' (e.g. through road/traffic signs while shopping), as can be seen in Table 4.1.

Apart from these broad regional differences in students' everyday English practices, a careful look at those existing between ethnic groups reveals complex socio-historical roots. Within the ethnic hybridity of Taiwan, the historico-cultural legacies of each ethnic group account for many differences in students' experience of English in everyday life. For example, Mainlander students have the greatest accessibility to English in various settings, including speaking English 'at home', perceiving 'household objects' written in English or things 'in town' and 'getting help from others' or 'teaching others' English. The historical roots of Chinese Mainlanders seem to play a pivotal part in this regard. Immigrating from Mainland China in 1949, first-generation Mainlanders were predominantly urban dwellers who have, in large measure, produced succeeding generations (our students counting as the third) more adapted to greater modernisation and exposure to English material culture in urban arenas than those of other social groups. Their higher social and political status as soldiers, military officials and civil servants have made possible forms of cultural capital which bestow superior social positions on Mainlander students, including getting access to English. On the contrary, indigenous students, as members of one of our rural groups, are positioned in an inferior social status with respect to access to English. Their lower percentage usage of information technology, including listening, speaking, reading and writing on 'desktop' exemplifies an existing urban–rural digital divide within Taiwanese society, though the overall percentage using computers in English learning was low.

In England, the variations in 'cultural capital' in the independent schools had a significant impact on students' access to Chinese. According to Bourdieu (1986), cultural capital can be transmitted from one generation to the next, depending on the effectiveness of the social capital of a group. Bourdieu describes social capital as follows:

> …the aggregation of the actual or potential resources which are linked to possession of a durable network of more or less institutionalized relationships of mutual acquaintance and recognition… to membership of a group – which provides each of its members with the backing of the collectivity-owned capital, a 'credential' which entitles them to credit. (Bourdieu, 1986: 248–249)

Indeed, students from the independent sectors in England are provided with a social network which helps their access to Chinese and makes possible Chinese learning practices such as cultural trips in China. If we consider the 'school vision' of independent schools and the 'family resources' of the students as cultural capital that supports learning, these two forms of cultural capital indeed shape independent school students' academic learning in general, and Chinese learning in particular.

With 'forward thinking' as the unique school vision, King's School made Chinese compulsory in 2006 and provided all students' access to this new and very different language from other European languages. An interesting comparison can be made between the Taiwanese 'white-collar' Mainlander students as urbanites and independent school peers in England. We discover that they both share something in common, namely the relatively ample family resources of parents' higher educational levels and thus children enjoy relatively high 'modernity and mobility' and English/Chinese foreign language immersion. However, such abundant family resources as parents' educational backgrounds and associated foreign cultural experiences, a close relevance to economic power, may contribute to the unequal access to English/Chinese. A new form of social inequality in the access to English/Chinese is therefore at issue and worth our further attention.

State–independent divide: Resource discrepancy in England

Now we have discovered the urban–rural and ethnic cultural variations and the potential impact on English learning among four Taiwanese ethnic groups, it would be interesting to explore if similar cultural variations and impacts on Chinese learning also exist in state and independent schools in England. Unfortunately, due to the limited duration of the fieldwork in England, it was not possible for us to explore as many cultural forces affecting pupils' everyday Chinese practice as we did in the Taiwanese fieldwork. Besides, the limitation of getting access to their overall internal school exams on Chinese at all participating schools made it impossible for us to carry out a cross-institutional comparison between state and independent schools in England.

However, King's School had more student respondents ($n = 92$) and thus it would be possible to look at their Chinese performance at school and if family resources have any impact on their performance. For example, when students were asked if they had ever taken any Chinese proficiency test, about 9% ($n = 8$) had a GCSE in Chinese at A level (one got a GCSE higher A level), albeit some said they had not yet done it but would do so in the future. Most of them had done school internal exams such as 'controlled assessments', the Chinese proficiency test carried out by the classroom instructor but different from regular internal exams at school.

An example of Chinese ability from the results of an internal school exam in two Chinese classes taught by Mr Blake at King's School served as a general indicator for our understanding of how students perform during the course of learning Chinese. As shown in Table 4.8, it is

Table 4.8 Exemplified Chinese performance at internal school exam

Chinese Ability (total out of 100)	(n = 41)
High (80–100)	37%
Intermediate (60–79)	34%
Low (0–59)	29%

Note: Internal exam results from the Fourth Form (Year 10) group in the fall term of 2015.

Table 4.9 Family affordances in King's School

School	Student	Year	Gender	Parents	Education	Engagement
King's School	Steven	Year 11	Male	Father	Post G.	✓
				Mother	University	✓
	Angela	Year 11	Female	Father	University	✓
				Mother	University	✓
	Holly	Year 10	Female	Father	College	
				Mother	University	✓

interesting to discover that about one third (37%) of the students were high achievers in learning Chinese, one third (34%) intermediate and the last one third (29%) low achieving students. Among the high achieving, one third or 20% scored in the range from 90 to 100.

A close look at three high achieving students from King's School revealed (see Table 4.9), to some extent, how family affordances or 'cultural capital', in Bourdieu's sense, may have contributed to their Chinese ability performance, although more examinations such as their interactions with classroom teachers (see Chapter 5) and their individual motivations and experiences (see Chapter 6) are still needed. These three high achieving students were interviewed and revealed that they were provided with ample cultural capital such as high parental education and encouragement. Chapter 6 provides a more detailed description of these three and other high achieving students, as central participants in the Chinese learning communities of practice, in terms of their Chinese learning trajectories.

Chapter Summary

In this chapter, we have examined how sociocultural contexts, such as locale, region, economic and family background and religion influenced the values that each group attached to learning English in Taiwan and Chinese in England. The results demonstrated that these sociocultural contexts seemed to regulate access to English/Chinese as culturally organised activities. In ethnicity-mixed Taiwan, resources like family affordances are embedded within ethnic group cultures and family values. Family background including parental encouragement and an emphasis on education as cultural value appear to play crucial roles in student investment in learning English. Rural students appear to be impeded by lower parental involvement in their education with respect to academic achievement in English.

In England, though encouragement or actual help was not forthcoming from parents, high parental educational backgrounds and students' associated high level of foreign cultural experiences seemed to contribute to their knowledge of and attitude to learning Chinese, albeit a more in-depth students' account (see Chapter 6) will be needed to support this claim. Certain forms of 'guided participation' (Rogoff, 1995) seemed to have emerged as sociocultural values serving to direct mutual participation between students and parents in learning activities within family settings in Taiwan and England. The involvement of students' parents as crucial 'social partners' and resources as a form of 'cultural capital' seemed to provide ample family support and may shape the directions in which students are encouraged to go or are discouraged from going. In the next chapter, we will further examine if such a 'guided participation' takes place within classroom settings and impacts on students' English and Chinese learning, with particular focus on pedagogic interactions between teachers and students.

5 Classroom Life and Pedagogical Comparisons

The preceding chapters have broadly located the sociocultural settings of English as a foreign language (EFL) learning in Taiwan and Chinese as a foreign language (CFL) learning in England within their community contexts. In this chapter, how learning English and Chinese takes place within classroom settings is investigated, with a particular focus on pedagogic interactions between teachers and students. Rogoff's (1995: 146) notion of 'guided participation' 'stresses the mutual involvement of individuals and their social partners, communicating and coordinating their involvement as they participate in socioculturally structured collective activity' at the interpersonal level. In these terms, classroom teachers are students' key social partners in everyday activities in learning English and Chinese, which we saw in Chapter 4 to be dominantly school-based practices.

Law's (2007: 321) reminder that 'comparative studies of pedagogy should not be confined to what happens within classrooms, but should be comprehended as practices within the school, local and national contexts' is taken as axiomatic for comparing EFL and CFL pedagogies across cultures. Although micro-interactional processes of teacher–student reciprocal engagements are foregrounded here, broader, sociocultural contexts, including students' daily schedules in terms of class timetables, the material culture in their classrooms across the schools studied and portraits of their teachers are not neglected in attempting to chart the wholeness of their foreign language learning processes. In this chapter, I will begin with descriptions of the classroom material culture before getting to know what these classrooms sounded and felt like through comparisons of pedagogy across cultures in Taiwan and England.

English Language Classrooms in Taiwan

The school features described in Chapters 1 and 3 are pivotal to a consideration of analyses of classroom interactional detail. In this section, each school's daily schedules which structured students' everyday school activities are outlined and are followed by delineations of classroom contexts as material cultures, portraits of the eight EFL teachers in the four schools and analyses of textbooks, reference books and note-taking as mediational tools (Wertsch, 1998).

Class timetables as daily schedules

Class timetables regulate students' everyday recurring school activities. In Taiwanese junior high school, routinised schedules are structured by uniform guidelines for curriculum, instructional material and equipment prescribed by the Ministry of Education (MOE) which sets down national curriculum standards for elementary and junior high schools in the Grades 1–9 curriculum. It regulates and structures the time–space framework of the school day throughout the school year, from early September to the end of the following June, though slight changes in class timetables may occur in the second semester (from February to June), if necessary. In a generic sense, each class abides by the national curriculum guidelines and has a fixed timetable as its formal schedule.

A generic structure of daily school timetables across the four schools is illustrated in Table 5.1. Almost every Taiwanese junior high student has to arrive at school before 07:30 every school day. Some may arrive nearer to 07:00 to carry out cleaning chores inside and outside classrooms and in some public areas of the school campus and beyond, such as the sidewalks surrounding the school walls. These cleaning chores are assessed by weekly competition between classes and are valued as an important part of moral education. The following half-hour morning session (*zǎo-zì-xí* 早自習) is regarded as an important starter to the school day. Supervised by homeroom teachers, the first 20-minute slot is usually used as a student self-regulated reading session. It may sometimes be used by homeroom teachers to review certain lessons or it may be 'borrowed' by core subject teachers (i.e. of Mandarin Chinese, Maths, Science and English) if they find themselves behind the schedule and need to 'catch up' (*gǎn-kè* 趕課) prior to monthly exams. Sometimes, it is used to test, for example, English vocabulary, especially when monthly exams are drawing near. The latter part of the morning session is a 10-minute or so 'morning assembly' (*shēng-qí* 升旗), valued as another important means of moral education when students sing the national anthem and salute the national flag in the playground. This ritual is always followed by staff announcements related to student academic or disciplinary matters and, most importantly, the school headmaster's short address. A similar, 1-hour, morally oriented ritual termed 'school assembly' (*zhōu-huì* 週會) is carried out weekly when the results of the weekly cleaning chore competition may be revealed, with winners regaled with banners, followed by a longer speech either by the headmaster or guest speakers.

Following morning assembly, students start formal class sessions, four in the morning and three in the afternoon, with a supplementary

Table 5.1 Standardised structure of everyday school timetable

07:30–08:00	Morning session (reading time and morning assembly)
08:10–11:50	Morning class sessions (four class sessions)
12:00–13:00	Lunch time and siesta (30 minutes each)
13:10–16:00	Afternoon class sessions (three class sessions)
16:05–16:50	Supplementary slot (evening class session)

Note: Each class session is 45 minutes with a 10-minute break in between.

slot of one 'evening class session' (*fǔ-dǎo kè* 輔導課). It is worth noting that, as Taiwan is located in a subtropical region where the average daily temperature may run as high as 25°C–30°C, a 30-minute siesta (*wǔ-xiū* 午休) is required immediately after lunch time, when students lie with their face downwards on their desk for a nap; this is believed to benefit concentration during afternoon lessons. Morning sessions, like siesta periods, are supervised by homeroom teachers to maintain classroom order. A 'dizzy syndrome' (*dǎ-kē-shuì* 打瞌睡) is often at issue during the course of the first afternoon class session, particularly in summer, as students tend to feel sleepy following their short siesta. For this reason, most core subjects are usually not allocated to this time slot, tending to be confined to morning sessions.

A supplementary slot of one evening class session, predominantly for Years 8 and 9, indexes heightening academic pressure on junior high students. Core subjects are mainly taught in this time slot for supplementary purposes, though, on occasion, tests for reviewing lessons are given, especially before school monthly exams. Some students are still not entitled to call it a day even after supplementary classes. Approximately half of each class (except in Mountainside School) continues in private cram schools for core subjects such as English. Some may have only one subject with which they have to engage, so they only need to go to cram school two days a week. Others, however, may pursue more than one subject, attending on a daily basis. Given the general structure of school timetables, class timetables in schools may demonstrate certain similarities and discrepancies that may appear inconsistent with national curriculum standards and reflect aspects of specific school visions, as was the case in our four study schools.

Comparing class timetables in the four schools

Although each class in the four school settings had a fixed class timetable complying with Grades 1–9 curriculum guidelines, flexibility existed, mirroring individual 'school visions' and related commitments. While all four schools had the same number of English classes in a week in terms of formal and supplementary sessions (see Table 5.2), Suburbany School had unique, fortnightly, weekend English classes for high-ability students,

Table 5.2 Comparison of school class timetable

	Urbany	Suburbany	Hakka Rural	Mountainside
English classes per week	4	4+ *(2)	4	4
English supplementary class per week	1	1	1	1
Weekend English classes	0	*(2)	0	0
Extracurricular activities	1	0	1	2
Ethnic culture learning	0	0	0	1

*Suburbany's weekend English classes were taught fortnightly. The figures stand for numbers of class sessions.

highlighting its distinguishing characteristic. In contrast, Mountainside School was the only school emphasising ethnic culture as a subject matter but devoted only one optional hour weekly to it, including tribal language, performance (e.g. singing or dancing) and craftwork. It also devoted two more hours per week to extracurricular activities, as well as providing for athletic training practice every afternoon, underlining its commitment to a full school day of culturally organised activities. Hakka Rural School, in further contrast, did not provide lessons on ethnic cultural matters, despite the strength of the Hakka historico-cultural legacy involving, for example, singing 'Hakka mountain songs' (kè-jiā shān-gē 客家山歌) and crafting 'Hakka oil-paper umbrellas' (kè-jiā yóu-zhǐ sǎn 客家油紙傘).

In addition, as pointed out in Chapter 3, there were two important differences worth noting involving the availability of specialist teachers (i.e. native speakers of English) and cram schools reflecting the overt, 'urban–rural divide' in the availability of the former, from which Hakka Rural and Mountainside Schools suffered while the urban schools enjoyed such specialists as crucial, cultural resources. The availability of cram school learning as a cultural resource cut across urban–rural divisions, given the Hakka cultural emphasis on academic study, leaving students from Mountainside School as the only group without access to this after-school learning resource, with possible, consequent effects upon their very different English learning trajectories.

Material culture: The classroom contexts

The physical structures of classroom locales in the four schools were slightly different in terms of size and location (see Table 5.3). Whereas Class B in Urbany School was situated on a second floor, others were either first or ground floor. Class D in Suburbany School was the only one situated in a building that was more than 10 years old, the others in more modern classroom settings. Class D in Suburbany School was the largest at 40 students, Classes G and H in Mountainside School the smallest at 28 and 27.

Table 5.3 Physical structures of the classrooms

School	Urban				Rural			
	Urbany		Suburbany		Hakka Rural		Mountainside	
Class	A	B	C	D	E	F	G	H
Teachers	Mr Lin	Ms Wu	Ms Huang	Ms Sun	Mr Yuan	Ms Mei	Ms Lin	Ms Lu
Size	34	31	29	40	34	30	28	27

The interior physical structures of the classroom settings were quite similar, as shown in Figure 5.1, which is a generic diagram. Students' tables with drawers were arranged in rows in the centre of the classroom, a teacher's table, a podium upon which teachers stood and a wide piece

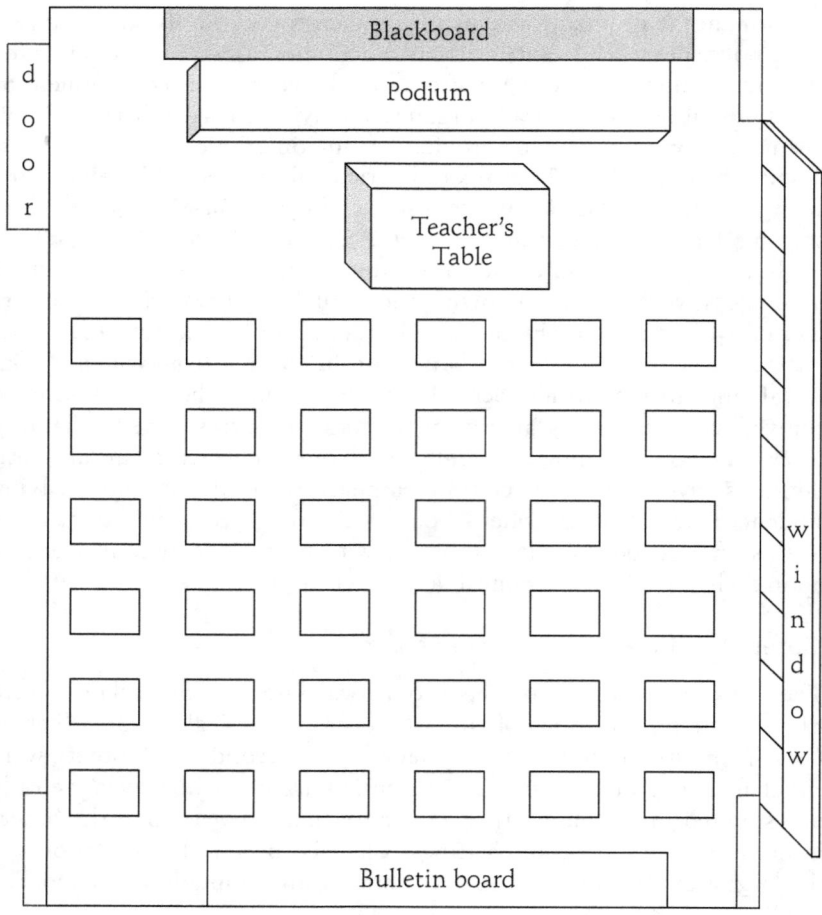

Figure 5.1 General physical classroom arrangement in Taiwan

of blackboard hanging on the front wall where they gave whole-class written instructions. The blackboard also functioned as the space where the numbers or names (two per day) of 'duty students' (*zhí-rì shēng* 值日生) were marked to identify who would be responsible for daily classroom routine, such as helping to fetch teaching aids, if any, or teacher's drinking water from the staff offices before each class session, erasing blackboard contents after class and locking the classroom after school. The rota of 'duty students' was also available in Ms Tan's class in England, allowing students to practice Chinese culture, a matter for further comparison later in this chapter. On the back wall, a wide noticeboard was used to place decorations, school notes and students' work. Most schools held a decoration competition each semester to encourage student creativity and active participation in school affairs. However, some differences also existed in each classroom.

In Urbany School, Mr Lin's class (Class A) had 34 tables arranged in rows in the centre of the classroom, a teacher's table, a podium and a wide piece of blackboard hanging on the front wall. Being a new, bilingual school, a TV set was positioned next to the blackboard for audio-visual and other teaching purposes. A loudspeaker sat atop the blackboard for daily staff announcements and the lunchtime English broadcast. Underneath the blackboard was a microphone plug, amplification being widely used by teachers. A unique space at the front right of the classroom was provided for teachers to mark school work. Urbany's new structure provided double corridors, allowing students more space for relaxation during the break. The smaller corridor faced outside and functioned as an ideal place for storing all sorts of tools for morning cleaning chores including mops, brooms and bins.

In Suburbany School, Ms Sun's class (Class D) had 40 tables arranged in rows in the centre of the classroom, a teacher's table, a podium and a wide piece of blackboard hanging on the front wall, with a microphone facility beneath it. Being a popular school with a large student population, tables were squeezed into a tiny space, with tools for morning chores leaning against the back wall, against which students sat. In Hakka Rural School, Mr Yuan's class (Class E) had 34 tables arranged in rows in the centre of the classroom, as well as other, familiar pedagogic accoutrements, including a loudspeaker set atop the blackboard. Like Urbany's new classroom design with double corridors, Class E also used an outside facing corridor as a space for storing tools. The classroom, though newly built, was smaller than that at Urbany, students sitting in the last row having even less space. In Mountainside School, Ms Lin's class (Class G), with 28 student tables was, again, not dissimilar. Two cupboards were put next to the blackboard in which some reference books and teaching aids were stored and at the back of the classroom there was another teacher's table and chair suitable for supervision and an ideal place for observation during my field research. Some back wall notices, in particular, caught my attention, particularly newspaper cuttings and guidelines and criteria for indigenous students' scholarships, clearly intended as incentives to encourage students' learning.

Portrait of the eight English teachers

Eight teachers took part in the observational phase of the study, bringing with them values informed by their previous English learning history. This may shed light on their current dialogical interaction with students within classroom settings, making it important to briefly depict teachers' biographical characteristics such as gender, ethnicity and years of teaching experience (see Table 5.4) before proceeding to the discussion of actual classroom interaction.

Urbany School: At Urbany School, Mr Lin (Class A) was both English and homeroom teacher. He was a young ethnic Holo with only two years' teaching experience. As a homeroom teacher, he dealt with issues ranging from students' classroom behaviour in all class sessions to academic attainments that might raise concern across subjects. Such 'housekeeping' chores were predominantly undertaken in morning sessions and class meetings, yet sometimes mingled with his regular teaching sessions, as was the case with many other junior high school homeroom teachers in Taiwan. Ms Wu, Class B's English teacher, was a Holo teacher with eight years' teaching experience who had also played an administrative role as the school 'English environment coordinator', taking most responsibility for Urbany's bilingual education scheme and its implementation, the school's core working vision. Like many other colleagues in Urbany School, these English teachers could be characterised as working with a dedicated school head teacher towards a cohesive, bilingual school vision.

Suburbany School: At Suburbany School, Ms Huang, an ethnic Hakka, was the English teacher of high-ability Class C. My prior acquaintance with Ms Huang had made it possible for me to 'slide in' through Suburbany's bureaucratic system and also, with her assistance, to access

Table 5.4 Characteristics of the eight English teachers

School	Urban				Rural			
	Urbany		Suburbany		Hakka Rural		Mountainside	
Class	A	B	C	D	E	F	G	H
Teacher	Mr Lin	Ms Wu	Ms Huang	Ms Sun	Mr Yuan	Ms Mei	Ms Lin	Ms Lu
Ethnicity	Holo	Holo	Hakka	Holo	Hakka	Holo	Holo	Paiwan
Sex	M	F	F	F	M	F	F	F
Age	mid 20	early 30	early 40	late 20	early 30	late 30	late 20	late 20
Year/teach	2	8	15	2	2	14	5	4

Ms Sun's class. She also arranged my one-month substitute teaching in Class C in the summer of 2004 which contributed greatly to my initial understanding of the underlying culture of this elite school. With her 15 years' experience and humorous interactional style, Ms Huang could be characterised as both senior and competent, regarded as one of the 'famous teachers' (*míng-shī* 名師) in Suburbany School. Her past English learning history was also important in accounting for her competence in teaching and humorous interactional style. A brief description of her past may help here. She graduated from a Taiwanese teacher's college where teachers were trained to teach primary school level. English was not particularly emphasised in teacher's colleges because English was not taught in primaries until the implementation of a new national curriculum in 2001. As she put it, 'I totally knew nothing about grammar whereby the only learning was to recite everything I learned from school'. Following many of her classmates' steps, she intended to register for a higher degree at a university, attempting to teach at junior high level, which was commonly regarded as 'upward job mobility'. She eventually enrolled in an English department becoming my classmate in 1987.

Due to Ms Huang's poor English ability, attending the English department in a top-tier Taiwanese university meant inevitable hard times and sometimes even humiliation. She recalled:

> I felt I was lagging behind when I attended the English department.... My problem was rather serious in English composition class... I remembered the teacher said something 'serious' and 'hurtful' (*zhòng-huà* 重話) addressing my low English ability. Seven students in class, including me, were 'humiliated' (*xiū-rù* 羞辱) in public by the teacher, saying 'you will feel easier if you attend another department'. I was also told by the teacher that 'I will fail you if you ever write English like this!'

This painful humiliation drove her to undertake intensive independent learning, including keeping an English diary every day and long hours of study in the library. As I recall Ms Huang, alongside six other more mature classmates with similar backgrounds, all worked diligently, unlike the rest of us, young and innocent students busy enjoying university life. Her English eventually improved so much that it surprised the same teacher who had previously humiliated her. Her successful struggle to learn English, prompted by her initial experience of being humiliated, seemed to have led her to develop a thoughtful and humorous interactional style. She described her approach to teaching as follows:

> Some of my former students have become English teachers at normal schools or cram schools.... I think I have a great deal of influence on students.... I teach them to keep a 'life-long interest in English' rather than just focus on getting high scores.... Many of my students are taking

advantage of having a good command of English, such as applying for senior high schools or top universities.

Ms Sun, a young Holo with only two years' teaching experience, was both the English and homeroom teacher to Class D. As a young colleague, Ms Sun was allowed to observe some English classes taught by 'famous teachers', including her own former English teacher. Such 'in-service training' or 'co-teaching' was unique to Suburbany School, whereby young colleagues like Ms Sun could benefit from such scaffolding or 'guided participation' (Rogoff, 1995) through the appropriation of more able colleagues' pedagogic skills.

Hakka Rural School: At Hakka Rural School, Mr Yuan (Class E) was a young Hakka teacher, also with only two years' teaching experience. Mr Yuan's additional administrative working schedule seemed to create implicit tension between himself and Class E, especially when he had to swap his teaching sessions for job-related school or out-of-school meetings. Mr Yuan seemed to suffer from his less than smooth relationship with Class E, complaining there were 'three big troublemakers' in this class who gave up learning English and required constant disciplinary attention. In the sense of having been brought up by his grandparents and his experience of cram school, he appeared to mirror the specific lifestyle and English learning activities of contemporary young Hakka people. He described his early schooling as follows:

> I lived in Meinung up to Year 4 because my grandfather was a local elementary school teacher. It was a 'grandparents' up-bringing' [He chuckles] because my parents were working in Kaohsiung. They took me 'out' (*chū-qù* 出去) in year 4. So I undertook my schooling in Kaohsiung city after that. But I would come back to Meinung on weekends or holidays.

For many Hakka students, being brought up by grandparents was not uncommon, many parents working in Kaohsiung city in lucrative jobs and passing responsibility for supervising children's schoolwork to grandparents. Such a shift in responsibility appeared to render English-speaking practice at home difficult as few Hakka grandparents understood Mandarin, let alone English. Cram school attendance had rendered Mr Yuan's competitive, urban school life after Year 4 'very busy'. As he recalled:

> I felt very 'busy' (*máng* 忙) because I had to go to cram school for 'composition' (*zuò-wén* 作文) and then rush to another cram school for English. Though I felt very busy, I was among the lowest achieving students in that English class.

Ms Mei (Class F) was a Holo with some 14 years' teaching experience. She had been teaching at a rural junior high school in Taipei for

10 years before moving to Hakka Rural. This experience seemed to have contributed to her understanding of Hakka students' English learning. Her marriage to a Hakka man was particularly significant because it had made possible her recognition of and determination to learn the Hakka language and culture. She spoke of 'getting entry' (*róng-rù* 融入) into a Hakka family and community through learning its language:

> I came here in 1999. I tried hard to listen to Hakka which was a totally new language for me.... I asked students to help me by speaking Hakka in class...they were willing to speak to me.... When I got married and lived with my mother-in-law I had to speak Hakka with her because she couldn't speak any Chinese or Taiwanese. I could comprehend some basic words in Hakka for the first three months... and gradually picked up through constant practice with her, my husband and students.

Ms Mei's intentional Hakka language learning had helped her to use the knowledge of Hakka traditions to achieve much shared understanding with her students. She made use of the Hakka mother tongue in her class as a mediational tool, alongside Mandarin Chinese, the predominant instructional language. As she put it, 'I can learn some Hakka from students while teaching English.... I can feel the way and the difficulty they may encounter in learning English from my experience of learning Hakka language'. Perhaps it was because of her personal experience of learning Hakka that she seemed to be able to build an intimate relationship with her students, even though she was reputed to be strict.

Mountainside School: At Mountainside School, Ms Lin (Class G) was a Holo with five years' teaching experience. She had taught in a non-indigenous junior high school in a nearby township, a somewhat different pedagogic experience that enabled her to take a contrastive but not overcritical view of indigenous students' learning. Our informal talk before the fieldwork survey in 2004 may serve as an example of her hesitation. She reminded me, in a slightly warning tone, that 'these indigenous students may not understand your questions well even though the questions are written in plain Chinese'. At interview, she identified her daunting experience of Paiwan students' learning styles:

> I taught English in Pintung county for three years...I am also teaching in a cram school.... I can make some comparisons between students from urban and rural regions...they prefer 'interactive' (*hù-dòng* 互動) learning style but they tend to be reluctant when it takes 'brain work' (*dòng-nǎo-jīn* 動腦筋). They tend to feel 'troublesome' (*má-fán* 麻煩) and 'boredom' (*pí-láo* 疲勞). Their learning attitude is not as proactive as their urban counterparts... there is an 'enormous gap' (*tiān-rǎng zhī-bié* 天壤之別).

Ms Lin tended to prioritise cognitive 'brain work' rather than interactive style with her students. Tension, therefore, existed between her and the class whenever students were verbally aggressive in responding to her pedagogic practice. The fact that Ms Lin transferred to another, non-indigenous junior high school in 2005 might have been related to this tension, though other reasons would also have contributed to her move.

Ms Lu (Class H), with four years' teaching experience, was herself an indigenous teacher born in this Paiwan village. She had lived with a relative in the suburban Kaohsiung area since elementary school year because of her parents' divorce. Like many other urban students, she commenced her initial English learning at a summer cram school called a 'summer pre-sessional class' (*shǔ-qí xiān-xiū-bān* 暑期先修班) right before attending junior high school. It was her 'good' English pronunciation that made her a popular candidate whenever teachers needed someone to read for the class. As she put it, '…at that time, I was encouraged by the way my teacher valued my English'. The account of why she liked learning English, even in the absence of parental encouragement, reported drawing on other motivations:

> I like it [English] out of my own interest and the 'fantasy' (*xiǎng-wǎng*) of visiting foreign countries…. I like to watch foreign TV programs, which makes me want to encounter with foreign things.

In terms of pedagogic practice, as with Ms Mei's use of the Hakka language in class, Ms Lu employed her Paiwan mother tongue with Class H and was able to refer to Paiwan cultural customs in relevant lessons. Perhaps it was her 'co-membership' (Cazden, 1988) with the indigenous community that allowed her to build intimate relationships with her class.

Textbooks, reference books and note-taking as mediational tools

The education system in Taiwan can be characterised as textbook oriented. A variety of texts involving textbooks, workbooks, reference books and notes were seen to be used in the course of classroom observations, serving as 'mediational tools' in Wertsch's (1998) terms, designed to assist learning from lower-level understanding to higher-level comprehension. While textbooks and affiliated workbooks were similar across schools, reference books and note-taking behaviour were more discrepant. Textbooks were and are used by Taiwanese teachers as their main pedagogic guides and learning sources. Based on the recently formulated Grades 1–9 curriculum, a number of private publishers have produced different versions of textbooks for commercial marketing. Decisions as to which to use are mainly left to teachers of the same grade year as a group, based on their judgement of pedagogic need. With respect to English as a subject, final decisions are normally made through committee meetings of English teachers at the same grade level, leading to the possibility that versions of text or reference books may be discrepant across the three grade levels. The workbooks which accompany textbooks are mainly used for homework assignments, given at the end of each lesson. They are checked, marked and returned to students within a few days of being handed in. Sometimes, workbooks are used as tests to monitor students' progress and scores are taken as a record of academic attainment.

Teachers' everyday pedagogical instruction progressed at an average speed of one textbook lesson per week, the first class session of each normally spent on vocabulary building, followed by an introduction to a section of reading or dialogue, alongside a test on vocabulary, for the second session. Tests were primarily used by teachers as tools to monitor students' progress and to keep attainment records. In the third session, an audio CD might be used for improving students' listening. Sentence patterns and grammatical structures, in particular, were tackled in this session, alongside drill practice from reference books, if time permitted. The last class session was often used for more practice, such as with exercises embedded at the end of each lesson in the textbook, followed by a homework assignment from workbooks or reference books. Within this tight schedule, 'interruptions', such as routine tests, extra drill practices or revision using workbooks or reference books, were common practices, engendering a feeling of haste among both students and teachers, such that the practice of 'catching up with the schedule' (*gǎn jìn-dù* 趕進度) became something of a nightmare for most English teachers and 'borrowing classes' (*jiè-kè* 借課) became a remedial mechanism pervasive in most junior high schools in Taiwan.

Reference books (*cān-kǎo shū* 參考書) are optional but particularly popular in urban schools. Most are edited by private publishers attempting to provide students with drill practice alongside textbook learning. They are expensive (between NT$100 and NT$200 per volume) and some students, especially in rural regions, do not use reference books for financial reasons. For teachers, reference books are regarded as pedagogically beneficial, though costly and grammar based. Their ready-made drills on sentence patterns or translation practices appear to save teachers' time and energy and fit students' need in preparation for school monthly exams. Reference books were used in the schools under study except Mountainside School due to students' financial concern.

Lastly, taking notes was another interactional tool observed in all classrooms. Students were encouraged, sometimes requested, by their teachers to jot down relevant grammatical rules and sentence patterns written on the blackboard. Like tests, some teachers considered note-taking to be a tool either for regulating students' classroom behaviour or for monitoring their progress by collecting notebooks for marking and reinforcement.

Chinese Language Classrooms in England

Class timetables as daily schedules

As in Taiwanese school class timetables, timetables in the English schools visited and observed, regulated and structured the time–space framework of the day, throughout the school year. However, whereas Taiwanese school years usually start and end on the same dates nationally (1 September and 30 June), in both public and private sectors in England, there are three terms with several 'half-term' breaks in the middle of each term. The two semesters, as in Taiwan, punctuate the whole school year though minor differences between state and independent schools in England exist in terms of term dates. Despite the fact that both state and independent schools start their year from early September, some schools finish the school year towards the end of the following July, with the independent sectors rather earlier, such as late June, as was the case in King's School. Certain extracurricular activities may be arranged in July (or other holiday periods), such as foreign travel for cultural exchange programmes.

Rather different from the Taiwanese school daily routine, students in England appear to have a more relaxed daily schedule. Although state schools in England are expected to timetable in such a way as to observe the requirements of a broadly defined national curriculum and especially its 'core' subjects, schools have autonomy as to specific timing, sequencing, amounts and even the inclusion of some subjects. This does not mean that timetables do not show considerable similarity across schools of each type, given the pressures on curricular patterns of transfers between stages, national testing requirements, public examinations and university entrance demands and the expectations of parents, increasingly courted and cultivated by schools with increasing autonomy over student recruitment. Independent schools have no obligation to follow national curricular requirements or metrics, but timetables are also dominated by traditional subject requirements, with better resourced creative arts, sport and extracurricular provision.

The daily schedule of King's School is illustrated in Table 5.5. In contrast to the 'early birds' in Taiwanese junior high schools, students in England enjoy a more relaxed morning attendance time, doing morning registration around 08:20 in their own 'houses', to which they were assigned at school enrolment. This 'house' system is a traditional feature of schools in the English-speaking world and at King's School, comprising single-sex students across different year groups. There are regular competitions, such as at school sports day, where houses compete with one another, thus providing a focus for group loyalty and social learning. Morning registration is carried out by house teachers, similar to homeroom teachers in Taiwan whose main role is more disciplinary than instructional. King's School students, like other British students, do not

Table 5.5 Daily schedule of King's School

08:20–	Morning registration at 'house'
08.30–09:00	Chapel as educational and religious practice
09:00–10:55	Periods 1–3 (09:00–09:40, 09:40–10:20, 10:20–10:55)
10:55–11:15	Morning break time
11:15–13:55	Periods 4–6 (depending on students' timetable and year group; lunch would be taken during one period between P4 and P6)
13:55–16:00	Periods 7–10 (afternoon registration in their houses at 13:55)
16:00–	No supplementary slot (the 'yellow carded' might need to stay for detention)

Note: In general, each class session was 40 minutes.

undertake cleaning chores, valued as an important part of moral education in Taiwanese schools. Instead, their school day may start by attendance at chapel (on campus), combining religious and moral practice. On Monday, the headmaster announced his weekly awards/certificates for extracurricular activities, such as dance or chemistry challenges, followed by a sports report concerning games played on the previous Saturday, and notices for the week including information about lectures/talks, writers' visits and the promotion of societies/clubs. He then normally gave a short speech based on a particular theme. There was junior chapel on Tuesday, after which a teacher volunteer conducted assembly and announced school activities, such as trips abroad. Lastly, there was hymn practice on Wednesday, when houses took turns to be in the chapel to practice hymns. The chapel time slot exhibited similarity to Taiwanese morning and school assemblies, where religious observation replaced singing the national anthem and saluting the national flag and had moral exhortation in common.

Following chapel, students start formal class sessions, five periods in the morning and five in the afternoon (depending on lunch as a moveable feast). The duration of each class period is more flexible than in Taiwan, depending on the students' timetable and year group. Some might have lunch during one period between Periods 4 and 6 with no siesta (*wǔ-xiū* 午休) immediately after lunch. Some house teachers may carry out registration after lunch break to make up for morning registration. All subjects are basically evenly allocated to any time slot of the day.

At the end of the afternoon, there was no supplementary slot for evening class, as in Taiwan. Since King's School had day and boarding students, day students then either went home or stayed for drama/music rehearsal, while boarding students went for dinner and homework supervised by a boarding tutor and then bed around 22:30, depending on the year group. Although there was no evening supplementary slot, as in Taiwan, King's School had a 'detention' system in place in order to monitor students' academic performance. There were three kinds of detention: if students received a 'yellow card' detention from a subject teacher, they needed to catch up on school work after 16:00 on that day; if a student received a departmental detention (weekdays from Monday to Thursday), a subject teacher arranged a time, normally in Period 10 if both were free, for a duration of one period of 40 minutes or longer. Teachers might also give a student some extra class work to do. For Friday detention, a school staff member would be waiting in a classroom and students were required to stay for an hour from 16:00 to 17:00 to undertake work, assigned by the teacher who placed them in detention, in areas where they needed to improve. Students might also take advantage of the time to catch up with homework.

Ms Tan tended to assign specific/extra work to students while placing them in detention because she considered 'they need to do something extra because it is meant to be a punishment'. For Saturday detention, there were options for teachers to require either one, two or even more hours of attendance, if necessary, supervised by duty teachers to ensure the work that was set was finished as required. Parents were notified in advance of Friday and Saturday detentions, considered by the school as 'big punishment' for students. According to Ms Tan:

> The detention system is one big punishment for King's School students, not just because their parents will know about this, but also it stops them doing certain activities with their friends (they normally have activities/rehearsals/games on Friday four pm/Saturday morning). Getting a detention will also affect their interim effort grade (so they cannot get the highest grade 1).

What was called a 'detention' in this independent school in England can be regarded as having something of a counterpart in Taiwanese elite schools, such as Suburbany School, functioning to ensure students' academic capability. Despite daily supplementary classes and individual out-of-school cramming practices, extra high-ability classes in Suburbany School were held fortnightly on a Saturday. For Year 9 Suburbany students, heightened academic pressure for entry to better senior high schools also entailed extra evening 'self-study' (*zì-xí* 自習), usually for 2 hours (19:00–21:00), supervised by their homeroom teachers or volunteer parents.

Material culture: The classroom contexts

The major difference in material culture between classrooms observed in England and Taiwan lay in class sizes and their impact on the physical structures of classrooms and the pedagogical processes within them. Whereas Taiwanese classes had between 30 and 40 students on average where English was a compulsory school subject, Chinese classes in England were relatively small in numbers (10–15 students), with even smaller class sizes of 5–10 in some observed state schools. The interior physical structures of classroom settings in England were quite different from those in Taiwan. As shown in Figure 5.2, students' desks were arranged in a U-shape, rather than in rows, in the centre of the classroom. There was no podium for teachers, just a teacher's table with a computer monitor on it. A whiteboard and an electronic whiteboard hung on the front wall where whole-class instructions and PowerPoint presentations could be displayed. In comparison to Taiwanese classrooms, electronic whiteboards are widely used by CFL teachers in England for audio-visual and other teaching purposes, but these were not commonly found in the EFL classrooms observed in Taiwan. Moreover, English teachers do not use microphones when teaching, which are deemed essential in Taiwanese class teaching due to the large class sizes.

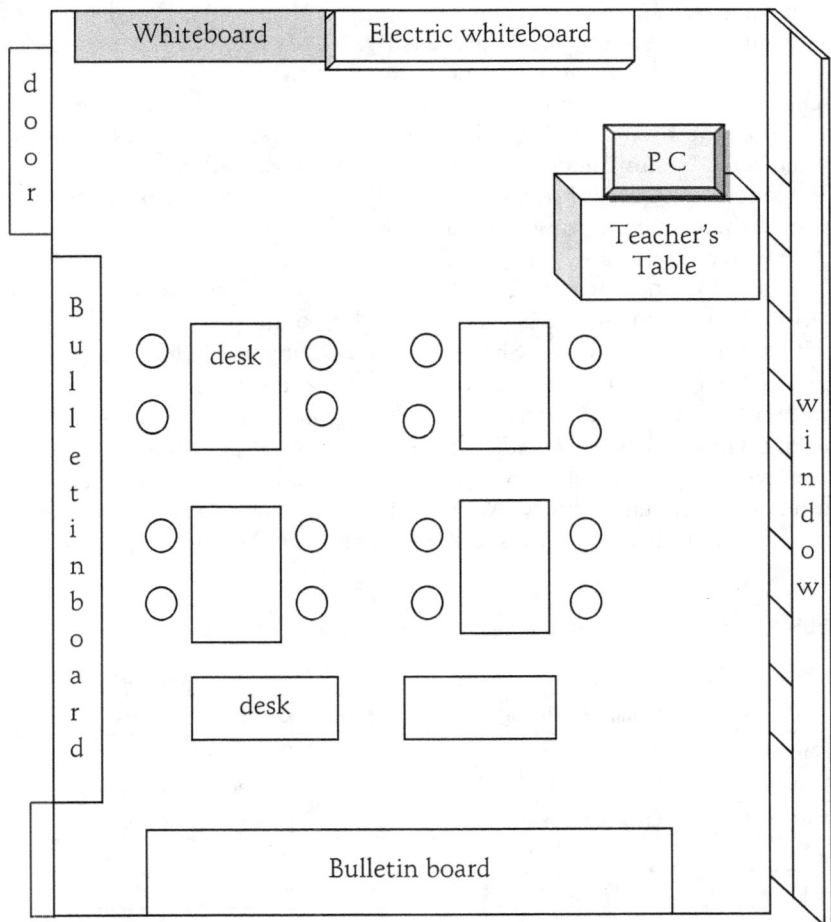

Figure 5.2 General physical classroom arrangement in England

In Taiwan, the blackboard functioned as the space where the numbers or names (two per day) of 'duty students' (*zhí-rì shēng* 值日生) were marked to identify who would be responsible for the daily classroom routine. In King's School, a duty student's name was also marked on the whiteboard in Ms Tan's Chinese class for the purpose of practicing Chinese culture. Although the duty students did not have to bring the teacher's drinking water from the staff offices, like their Taiwanese peers, they would erase whiteboard content after class and seemed to enjoy this honour. On the side and back walls, several noticeboards were used to display Chinese decorations and, more importantly, students' work about Chinese language and culture.

Portrait of the four Chinese language teachers

Four Chinese language teachers took part in the observational phase of the study in England – Ms Wang, Ms Byrne, Mr Blake and Ms Tan – of whom we highlight and offer most detail on Ms Byrne from St Peter's School (state school) and Ms Tan from King's School (independent sector). Like the Taiwanese English teachers, their previous Chinese learning and teacher training histories, particularly the Postgraduate Certificate in Education (PGCE), informed their pedagogic values and practices and shaped their interaction with students (Table 5.6).

Ms Wang: As a Chinese native speaker from Taiwan, Ms Wang started her Chinese teaching in 2001. She taught Chinese at various educational levels, including universities and secondary sectors, either as a private tutor or a lecturer. She had been teaching at Highland School (a girls' school) for three years since Chinese became part of its curriculum in 2011. The initial support from the headmaster and the language head at Highland School had made it possible for Ms Wang to teach Chinese to a relatively small class of six students despite the school's concern about its financial viability. With such support from Highland School, she eventually helped those six Year 12 girls sit the GCSE Chinese and

Table 5.6 Characteristics of the four Chinese teachers in England

School	State		Independent	
	Highland/Bath High	St. Peter's	King's	King's
Class	A	B	C	D
Teacher	Ms Wang	Ms Byrne	Mr Blake	Ms Tan
Nationality	Chinese (Taiwan)	British	British	Chinese (China)
Sex	F	F	M	F
Age	mid 30	mid 50	mid 30	mid 30
Year/teach	3	7	5	3

Note: All teachers' names are pseudonyms. Years of teaching were counted till 2015.

also engaged other younger learners at the beginners' level in Chinese. Ms Wang also taught Chinese in a nearby boys' school with a relatively larger class size of 15 boys.

Ms Wang was observed to be an enthusiastic teacher. She clearly loved teaching and had built an excellent rapport and good relationships with students:

> I love teaching, and it has been my greatest joy to see my students making progress and enjoying the subject. I believe that teachers play a very important role. They communicate their experiences of life and give children a new outlook. Teachers provide a positive image; they show youngsters what they can achieve. They are role models for their students. They know it is hard to learn Mandarin, but I always try my very best to make the lesson fun for them. I attend various learning needs and styles by applying kinaesthetic, multiple intelligence, audio, and visual method to maximise their learning and achieve the best learning outcome.

Unfortunately, in 2013, the new school headmaster at Highland School did not continue to support Chinese learning as much as his predecessor. Ms Wang submitted her proposal for making Chinese the second language option for the Year 7 curriculum, but was turned down, which eventually led to her leaving for another state school where Chinese was regarded as important as any other language. When she lost the support of the new headmaster, she was frustrated and complained that:

> So this is the issue of policy by the new Head. The previous Head could help me run the class even though I had only 6 students in my class. This new Head would not 'open the class' (*kāi-kè* 開課) without enough students... not even let students come and give it a try... just wouldn't open the Chinese class 'straightforward' (*zhí-jiē* 直接). The new Head had a 'very different' (*chà-hěn-duō* 差很多) attitude toward languages.

It seemed that having Chinese as part of the school curriculum required particular school visions towards this new foreign language and being able to cope with the financial problems while having relatively small class sizes. The new headmaster appeared to have a 'practical', if not passive, vision towards languages – a very small Chinese class would not be cost-effective. It was hardly surprising then that, following the completion of her PGCE teacher training programme in 2014, Ms Wang decided to leave for a school that supported her belief that Chinese needs to be learned from Year 7, providing learners with a solid foundation when reaching their GCSE year and the ability to pursue Chinese further to A level or pre-university.

Ms Byrne: As a senior teacher in her mid to late 50s, Ms Byrne had a very interesting Chinese learning background. She was an English native speaker from England and taught Chinese at St Peter's School. She completed a three-year degree in Chinese studies from a university in England in the late 1970s and spent four years at the Australian National University in Canberra, Australia, where she did a PhD in Chinese History. She worked as a business journalist in Hong Kong for four years on the China trade desk; however, after returning to the UK, she did little with her Chinese for about 15 years until she started teaching it as a foreign language. As a mature student, she trained to be a teacher achieving a PGCE secondary with religious education (RE). At that time in the 1990s, 'Mandarin Chinese was not a subject that many schools offered and certainly no PGCE courses would have accommodated'. She taught RE for several years and then, in 2006, while between jobs looking for another in RE, a language-teacher friend suggested that she might teach Chinese 'as schools were increasingly looking for teachers'. In the UK, having a PGCE secondary in any subject means teachers can switch subjects without needing further qualifications, meaning that she did not need to do any further training in order to teach Chinese. In fact, she said, 'I felt more comfortable teaching Mandarin as that was my degree subject'.

Ms Byrne was a diligent teacher and had been trying to keep herself updated with language pedagogy in general and Chinese specifically. She said:

> I have tried to keep up with language pedagogy, attending workshops... both general about language teaching and more specifically about teaching Chinese. I've also run workshops e.g. on teaching tones/pronunciation, running Mandarin clubs etc.

In addition, Ms Byrne was very resourceful in activities related to teacher development in Chinese. With an open attitude towards Chinese teaching resources and a more 'liberal' and relaxed teaching style, rather than being 'strict' over classroom management in a class of younger students, they seemed to enjoy her teaching style. At St Peter's School, Ms Byrne was welcomed by her students as a 'laid-back' teacher, nice and friendly, willing to offer individual help whenever students needed it. In a group interview with five girl students from a GCSE class, when asked if Ms Byrne could be classified as a 'strict' teacher, one girl said:

> for example... like our Maths teacher... you cannot talk to him... he is strict... you get afraid to talk to him... but to Miss is like... oh Miss, I need your help... we are not afraid of talking to her.

Mr Blake: As an English native speaker from England, Mr Blake had an administrative role related to Chinese teaching at King's School. Like

Ms Byrne, he also had a very interesting Chinese learning background, including having lived in Taiwan for three years and the ability to speak some Taiwanese/Holo dialect (*tái-yǔ* 台語). Mr Blake graduated from a Scottish university, majoring in Chinese because he liked 'challenges'. He then went on to another university in England for postgraduate study, majoring in translation. While in Taiwan, he worked for the information bureau of the Taiwanese government in early 2000 before working at King's School. Mr Blake was very creative in teaching Chinese, observed occasionally to sing and dance in class, and taught his students to greet him and me at the outset with Chinese hand gestures (*dǎ-gōng zuò-yī* 打恭作揖) by bowing and raising both arms with both fists held together, as a way of greeting elders in traditional Chinese culture.

Due to his early education in an experimental Steiner school, Mr Blake had a rather 'liberal' teaching style. He explained that students at King's School were themselves academic elite students, who already knew what to do in order to achieve success. There was no need for teachers to 'push' or add more pressure on them. In our informal conversation at one corner of the King's School campus, he described his teaching philosophy as captured in the following field note:

> Mr. Blake is a creative teacher who came from an experimental school where students are taught creatively. So he does not like to put 'too much pressure' on students, like many other teachers at King's School because exam is everything. In fact, students are hard-working and intelligent enough, so they will do the work themselves. He said some girls have already suffered from 'depression' due to academic pressure. I said to him that this situation is very similar to that in Taiwan. (Field note, 16 October 2015)

Given his caring personality and concern about students' mounting academic pressure, he was running an after-school 'transcendental meditation' club, hoping this extracurricular activity could release students' pressure.

Ms Tan: As a Chinese native speaker from China, Ms Tan was an English major graduated from a university in China. She gained her postgraduate degree and PGCE from universities in England. Though having greatly benefited from the PGCE teacher training programme, she then had a rather unpleasant Chinese teaching experience in London before working at King's School.

In 2012, Ms Tan went to Goldsmiths University for an academic year of PGCE training, during which she was assigned to a private girls' school in London where she stayed for about four months. She had enjoyed the mentorship with a local teacher who 'was very nice to me but also a very thorough teacher. It is the place where I learned most of my basic teaching style'. In 2013, she went to an East London state school where she did not learn much in terms of teaching techniques, 'but it expands my horizons in terms of how bad a classroom can be'. She felt that the teachers there had lower expectations of the students than she had encountered in the private girls' school and they had to focus a lot on students' behaviour for classroom management. As a female Asian teacher, on occasion she even encountered rather unpleasant situations in class involving students using racist and foul language towards her. Ms Tan recalled one time in class when, because she was very disappointed both with the class and herself for poor class management, she stormed out of the classroom when the bell went without saying 'class is over'. Her mentor saw this and gently told her off in front of other colleagues which made her feel guilty and more frustrated over why she had such unfair treatment and lack of support. She ended up crying embarrassingly in the staff office, though she still thought, 'it is not entirely my fault and I don't deserve this'. Although her mentor apologised later on, she felt she was not learning much from working at that school and eventually left. Perhaps it was also because of her Chinese cultural background which values hard work as a kind of virtue that she felt particularly frustrated to have seen students who were 'less intelligent but also lacking in effort' (*bèn-niǎo què-yòu bù-xiān-fēi* 笨鳥卻又不先飛). She noted:

> I don't accept 'being less intelligent but also lacking effort' because in Chinese education, if you come from poor background, you should make even more effort. These students and in fact their parents are relying on the UK benefit system, which made me even angrier and unconsciously turned my anger to the students. Why do I have to work so hard and suffer from people who basically used up the tax we contributed through our hard work?

Despite her unhappy Chinese teaching experience in London, Ms Tan revealed that she was very impressed and influenced by her mentor, who already had seven years teaching experience but still took teaching very seriously. 'I admire her strong work ethic and… make me complain less when I come to King's School. It's easier for me to adapt to the super-fast working pace. Funny though, I almost enjoy it every day'. In fact, during my observation at King's School, I was amazed by her 'super-fast working pace', to echo Ms Tan's words, and wondered how teachers here could cope with such a bustling routine in school life. In Ms Tan's case, her PGCE training history appeared to provide some answers. Besides, given such work experience at an independent school, she also developed an efficient way of working with absolute concentration because she had 'so much to do every day'. Lastly, it is worth noting that perhaps it was due to her teaching philosophy that she did not agree with 'being less intelligent but also lack of effort', Ms Tan was welcomed and considered by students as a 'good' and 'firm' teacher at King's School. One of her

Year 11 students (Jade), who was a hard-working and high achieving student, commented that:

> I'm very happy about learning with Ms. Tan. She's a really good teacher... she had taught me one and a half years of Chinese knowledge and vocabulary, just so that I could be in that very class today (GCSE class). I also think that Ms. Tan approaches lessons seriously but makes it interesting by adding variety so that we don't get bored, essentially.

These four CFL teachers revealed similar and different types of teaching styles, particularly in terms of the similarity between the two teachers with Chinese cultural identities – Ms Wang and Ms Tan, and that between the two teachers with British cultural identities – Ms Byrne and Mr Blake. Apart from their individual personalities, their different cultural value towards education between Eastern and Western cultures seemed to play a part in shaping their classroom pedagogy and this receives greater attention in the section titled 'Comparisons of Pedagogies across Cultures'.

Textbooks and note-taking as mediational tools

Like their Taiwanese peers, students in England had textbooks, exercise books, handouts and note-taking behaviour as mediational tools. There were no reference books, crucial tools in Taiwanese drill practice for learning English grammar and sentence structure. Textbooks were used at both independent and state schools. In both King's and St Peter's School, *Edexcel GCSE Chinese Student Book* by Pearson publishers was used and in the earlier stages, some teachers used *Jin Bu* by the same publishers (Pearson) and accompanying workbooks, as in Ms Byrne's class. However, though textbooks are usually the main pedagogic guides for GCSE students, handouts were important learning sources for most students in England because they were less 'scary' for early stage students. For example, as Ms Byrne put it:

> Because that particular group of early stage students were a bit scared of the textbook when they started on the GCSE Chinese course, I tended to use more handouts in the early stages.... Now they use it more and I've bought them the Go Chinese online support that goes with that textbook.

Teachers tended to use the accompanying workbooks as a teaching and learning set. However, students in Ms Tan's class tended to use notebooks with lined pages for writing Chinese characters as homework assignments or simply as note-taking tools. In her class, workbooks might sometimes be used to test listening and writing (e.g. dictation), serving to monitor students' progress with the scores taken as a record of academic attainment.

In Taiwan, teachers' everyday pedagogical instruction progresses at an average speed of one textbook lesson per week. However, the CFL lessons progress at various speeds depending largely on students' year group and their level of Chinese. In King's School, for example, there were 3-hour sessions of Chinese per week, compulsory for all students. In general, Chinese lessons progressed at a more relaxed pace as opposed to those in the Taiwanese classes. While tests were predominantly used by Taiwanese EFL teachers as tools to monitor students' progress and to keep attainment records, less formal exams or tests were used in CFL classes in England. However, oral or written quizzes were used by teachers in England as reviewing practices. In Ms Tang's class, for example, oral or written quizzes were usually used as tools to monitor students' progress, but sometimes were practiced in a relaxed atmosphere through games or competitions between students.

In short, while textbooks and note-taking are commonly found in Taiwan and England as mediational tools for EFL/CFL teaching and learning, the 'pace' (*jìn-dù* 進度) and 'seriousness' (*rèn-zhēn* 認真) of the lessons were very different in defining students' everyday learning processes at school. As a core subject and with a prestigious social status in Taiwan, English is taken very seriously throughout secondary years with rather tight schedules that are textbook oriented and note-taking is highly encouraged, inevitably engendering extra drill practices, revision using workbooks or reference books and routine quizzes or tests to monitor students' progress with the scores earnestly taken by the school and parents as a record of academic performance. In England, on the contrary, the pace of teaching Chinese is more relaxed for beginners and the learning schedule will not become serious until they progress to GCSE level, with textbook use appropriately modified by some teachers in order to avoid scaring those who are beginners or those who have just started on the GCSE Chinese course, as Ms Byrne suggested.

Comparisons of Pedagogies across Cultures

This section provides an overview and cross-cultural comparison of classroom interactional styles across the four schools in Taiwan and the four schools in England. These observational data were drawn from observations of approximately 28 hours in each of the eight Taiwanese classrooms over a period of four months from September to December 2004, and then approximately 28 hours altogether in the two state school classrooms in the summer of 2013 and 2014, and in the two independent schools over a period of two months from October to December 2015. At the outset, general patterns of instructional practice in each country will be discussed. Differences in pedagogic instruction across the classrooms will be examined and compared next by focusing, in turn, on how teachers used students' everyday culture in their interactions, as in the case of

EFL teachers in Taiwan, and on how teachers' cultural backgrounds may impact on their pedagogic instruction, as is the case in England.

Comparing instructional forms across cultures

In general, the instructional process in Taiwanese EFL classrooms relies on textbook and grammar-oriented teaching and learning. Three interactional patterns were detected that were common to all eight classes in Taiwan, as shown in Table 5.7. In England, apart from the dominant use of English as the classroom language, different interactional patterns from those in Taiwan were detected that were common to all classes, namely, an activity-oriented pedagogy which is thinking-based and indirect interactional patterns of classroom control that represent the broader British culture in which each student is respected as an individual learner.

Grammar-oriented pedagogy in Taiwan: The case of Ms Sun

A grammar-oriented pedagogy was observed in all Taiwanese classes. In Ms Sun's class (Class D) as an example, it was the first afternoon class session (13:30–14:15) after lunchtime siesta. The teacher was at the blackboard and students were in their seats facing her. At the outset, she asked some sleepy students to go and wash their faces before beginning the lesson. In this lesson (Lesson Three: I Have To Wear It), Ms Sun was teaching vocabulary items, such as 'right' and 'best' while students were jotting down on their notebooks what had been written on the blackboard. Most of the teacher's grammatical delineation and explanation was done in Mandarin Chinese (termed 'M' in the following extracts).

Extract[1] 5.1:

1 T:	(Besides being a noun meaning 'right hand side', 'right' can be an
2	adjective meaning 'correct'. [...] or an adverb meaning 'right there'-M)
3	((Writing on board)) Right here/ right there.
((Teacher was lecturing by pointing to what has been written on board while some students are still taking notes silently.))	
4 T:	(Finished?-M)....(Are you all ready now?-M)
5 Ss:	Unintelligible ((Some students are still taking notes.))
((The next few turns are spent in lecturing about the word 'best' by the teacher.))	
6 T:	(It's an adverb meaning 'zuì'. Write it down! It's an adjective
7	meaning 'zuì-hǎo-de'- M) 'the best'. Like 'the best students' or 'the
8	best class'. So, 'best' (has two properties -M)
	((Teacher turns to the board writing and talking without microphone))
9	(The first kind- adjective: best means 'zuì-hǎo-de' 'the best'. But be
10	aware that a prefixal 'the' has to be attached to 'best'....What does it

	mean by- M) 'the best'?
11 Ss:	Unintelligible ((Some students are still taking notes.))
12 T:	I am the best. We are the best. 'the' (must be added to-M) best.
13	(Moreover, 'best' is an adverb in the text which means something is
14	someone's favourite. -M)
((Teacher turns to the board writing and talking simultaneously with ascending voice.))	
15 T:	I like baseball best. I like basketball best.
16	((Waiting for note-taking)) (Have you all done?-M)
17	You are the best student. So, the best (can be added with a noun-M).

The teacher was intent on explicitly instructing the class on points of grammar and illustrating them well by writing patterns and examples on the board. As can be seen in Lines 1 and 2 of Extract 5.1, the grammatical properties of the new word 'right' were elaborated and written on the board for students. The class then moved on to another new word 'best'. Besides points of grammar regarding the new word 'best', as shown in Lines 6 and 7, the phrase 'the best' was also underlined with exemplary sentences (Line 12). Ms Sun then elaborated further by stating that a 'noun' could be added (Line 17). The entire teaching process was carried out by the teacher providing explicit instruction about grammatical rules along with students' note-taking. This can be viewed as a form of 'rote learning' – literally translated 'recite to death' (sǐ-jì 死記), aimed no doubt at gaining better scores in exams. As in Ms Sun's classroom, grammar-based pedagogy was found across the four schools. As noted earlier, high scores were valued in language exams and this appeared to encourage the grammar-oriented pedagogy observed. The grammatical explanation was predominantly given in Chinese and was usually accompanied by teachers writing on the board and students taking notes.

A general form of 'rote learning' was evident across all four Taiwanese schools, aimed at gaining better scores in exams. Chapter 7 provides a more detailed discussion concerning the issue of rote-learning and the 'paradox of the Asian learner' (Watkins, 2007), in particular, from cross-cultural comparative perspectives.

Table 5.7 General classroom instructional process in Taiwan and England

Taiwan	England
• Grammar-oriented pedagogy (knowledge based) • Chinese as the dominant instructional language • Direct and indirect interactional patterns of classroom control	• Activity-oriented pedagogy (thinking based) • English as the dominant instructional language • Indirect interactional patterns of classroom control

Activity-based pedagogy: The case of Ms Tan in England

In England, perhaps due to the fact that Chinese language class sizes were relatively small, activity-based pedagogy involving group activities and peer interaction was evidenced across all four classrooms observed. For example, in my first observation of Ms Tan's class on the morning of 1 October 2015 (11:55–13:10), the class (eleven Year 11 students) were reviewing the Chinese characters they had learnt at the outset.

Extract 5.2:

1 T:	…the degree of something…I will give you 8 sentences and have a discussion with
2	each other. You must talk to someone and say something to find out the rules, ok?
3	I will give you three minutes 三分鐘 (sān fēn-zhōng), 好了, 開始 (hǎo-le, kāi-shǐ)
[…]	
((In the next few turns, students are giving their answers actively.))	
4 T:	…so imagine when you speak English… when you describe someone is handsome,
5	how many ways of showing the degree of handsome?
6 Ss:	帥…很帥…非常帥…. (shuài… hěn-shuài…fēi-cháng-shuài…)
7 S4:	好看! (hǎo-kàn)
8 T:	Very handsome. ((Ms Tan gives immediate translation in English.))
9 S5:	太帥了! (tài-shuài le)
10 T:	Incredibly handsome.
11 S6:	帥死了! (shuài-sǐ-le)
12 T:	So handsome that I cannot bear… ((chuckling!))
13 Ss:	((chuckling!))
[…]	
((Some students are looking at the clock on the wall. It's nearly the end of the class.))	
14 T:	Ok, …you want to play 'Hot Chair[2]'?
15 Ss:	Sure! … ((chuckling!))
16 T:	Any volunteer…please take a seat on the Hot Chair. ((A girl is sitting on the chair.))
((In the next few turns, students are enjoying the game time – 'Hot Chair'.))	

In Extract 5.2, following a review of the Chinese characters that students had learnt before, Ms Tan offered the class a 3-minute peer discussion regarding the grammatical use of 'degree of objective'. During the discussion, students were excitedly exchanging ideas with each other. Ms Tan walked around the classroom and responded to students' individual queries when necessary. For example, they were discussing the Chinese subjective word – (shuài 帥), (hěn-shuài 很帥) and (fēi-cháng-shuài 非常帥) (Line 6). When students uttered with various degrees of 'handsome' in Chinese, Ms Tan would follow immediately with the English translation. Then, about 10 minutes before the end of the class, Ms Tan asked the class if they wanted to play 'Hot Chair' again, the class appeared to be delighted. Ms Tan tended to use this game at the end of a class as a reviewing practice if time permitted. Since all students were often excited about playing it, 'Hot Chair' appeared to be a form of indirect classroom control, a type of classroom interactional pattern discussed in the following section.

Direct and indirect interactional patterns of classroom control

The degrees and kinds of classroom control varied across classrooms. As Kleine (1982) put it, what we call 'teaching styles' represent points on a continuum between dichotomous variables, like 'direct' versus 'indirect', 'authoritative' versus 'democratic' and 'teacher oriented' versus 'student oriented'. These dichotomous terms, although imprecise, provide general markers as to how classroom interactions take place. Two crude types of classroom control were identified, direct and indirect, in terms of which the eight teachers in Taiwan and the four teachers in England are roughly characterised. Table 5.8 shows that five Taiwanese teachers can be characterised as 'direct' although degrees of both types of classroom control were found in the practice in each classroom.

Direct Classroom Control: In our observed Taiwanese classrooms, disciplinary discourse such as (*zuò-hǎo* 坐好) (sit properly), (*bì-zuǐ* 閉嘴) (shut up), (*kuài-yī-diǎn* 快一點) (hurry up) and (*bù-yào pā-zhe* 不要趴著) (wake up) were generally used by teachers to remind students of proper behaviour. For example, in Mr Yuan's class (Class E) at Hakka Rural School, direct disciplinary discourse was frequently used. A flavour of life in this classroom is given by my field notes, written after the third visit in October 2004, where some low achieving students fooled around outside the classroom even after the school bell had gone.

> There were still a few students playing outside.... It was like an episode of 'chasing ducks'…to settle them into the classroom. During the course of a 10 minute test, the '3 big wigs' (the most notable, underachieving

Table 5.8 Comparison of classroom control in Taiwan

School	Urban				Rural			
	Urbany		Suburbany		Hakka Rural		Mountainside	
Class	A	B	C	D	E	F	G	H
Teacher	Mr Lin	Ms Wu	Ms Huang	Ms Sun	Mr Yuan	Ms Mei	Ms Lin	Ms Lu
Direct	✓	✓		✓	✓		✓	
Indirect		✓				✓		✓

troublemakers in this class) face prostrated on their desks throughout the whole session. (Field note, 1 October 2004)

Certain forms of punishment, both verbal and physical warnings, could be identified as further forms of his authoritative power and control. Several classroom disciplinary terms like (*fá-xiĕ* 罰寫) (writing extra assignment as punishment) and (*xiū-lĭ-rén* 修理人) (corporal punishment) revealed punitive practices still salient in some Taiwanese secondary schools though corporal punishment was considered illegal. This culturally embedded custom of punishment within schools is still enforced by some teachers and, mostly, approved of by parents, due to overall pressure for academic achievement, despite recent calls from human rights groups for it to be banned.

As in Mr Yuan's class, the other four classes (A, B, D and G) were characterised as having direct forms of classroom control of students' thoughts and actions. Among them, Ms Wu (Class B in Urbany) and Ms Lin (Class G in Mountainside) were found to have the most direct form of classroom control or disciplinary discourse. These stood in strong contrast to practice observed in classes in England that could be characterised as indirect forms of classroom control of students' thoughts and actions, which I will turn to later.

Indirect Classroom Control: In contrast to the five teachers who employed direct classroom control, three teachers – Ms Huang (Class C), Ms Mei (Class F) and Ms Lu (Class H) – relied mainly on indirect modalities. Ms Huang was sophisticated in maintaining the flow of her pedagogy in the face of her high-ability students' somewhat aggressive responses. My field note, written after visiting her class on the afternoon (15:20–16:05) of 17 September 2004, conveyed the impression of discovering an English teacher very adept at exercising emollient classroom control.

> This high-ability class was labelled 'talented student' (*zī-yōu-shēng* 資優生) recruited through academic selection. They were active participants in class in many ways, such as taking notes simultaneously and having quality peer and teacher-student interaction in learning English.... According to Ms. Huang's narrative account and my observations, this class was keen to create or aggressively respond to any innuendo or jokingly risqué reference to juvenile relationships, forming a unique classroom culture among those studied. Ms. Huang was not embarrassed by such 'witty', if unsubtle, banter but, rather, recognised the 'sub-culture' from which they sprang in her humorous responses. (Field note, 17 September 2004)

Ms Mei, as noted earlier, was a Hakka daughter-in-law who employed 'sympathetic' and 'authoritative' modalities to engage both students' emotions (e.g. when they were looking tired) and pedagogic flow in maintaining an intimate, teacher–student relationship. In particular, her frequent use of the Hakka language during pedagogic instruction seemed to forge good relationships, as detailed later. Ms Lu, like Ms Mei, also made use of her indigenous Paiwan identity as a form of social connectedness. More sympathy and a sense of co-membership seemed to be available in her class.

In England, most of the classes observed were characterised by indirect classroom control. Students in Britain, as a Western culture, are more respected as individuals than their Taiwanese peers (see Table 5.9). In Taiwan, perhaps thanks to our Confucian cultural heritage, teachers are generally respected by students as the source of authority. More conditional regard for adult and teacher authority in British culture and greater respect for student autonomy appeared to lie behind more forms of teacher discursive dualism that encompassed 'sympathy' and 'authority' to engage both students' emotions (e.g. when they were confused) and pedagogic flow in maintaining more intimate teacher–student relationships – as seen in Ms Mei's class in Taiwan – were regularly found in all the classes observed in England.

For instance, as seen earlier in this chapter, Ms Byrne (St Peter's School) was welcomed by her students as 'laid-back', meaning a nice, friendly teacher willing to offer individual help whenever students needed it. When asked if Ms Byrne could be classified as a 'strict' teacher, one of the student interviewees commented:

> She is like... she is not exactly 'strict'... but... she is more 'friend' than 'teacher' to us... we call her 'Hey, Miss! what's up? Miss' ((raising voice pitch))... not like 'Hello, Miss' [lower voice pitch]... yeah... 'Good morning' ((lower voice pitch)).... She is more our friend than anything....

Similar to Ms Byrne, Mr Blake (King's School) also had a rather 'liberal' and 'laid-back' teaching style, and would not use disciplinary tones on students. One student, who had been in Mr Blake's junior class (Year 7) and was now in Ms Tan's class compared the two teachers, saying that 'I feel that they are both really good.... I...yeah, I like Mr Blake's teaching... it was fun. ...he was laid-back but he taught very well'.

In sum, comparisons of all eight classrooms in Taiwan revealed similarities in instructional style driven by the need to maintain high

Table 5.9 Comparison of classroom control in England

	State		Independent	
School	Highland/Bath High	St. Peter's	King's	King's
Class	I/J	K	L	M
Teacher	Ms Wang	Ms Byrne	Mr Blake	Ms Tan
Indirect	✓	✓	✓	✓

examination scores that is typical in Taiwanese school culture. Pedagogic wwwpractice was dominated by the three patterns previously outlined: grammar-oriented pedagogy; Chinese as the dominant language; and both direct and indirect interactional structure. The interactional patterns characterising classroom control intended to ensure that students undertook the 'teacher's agenda' (Mehan, 1979) revealed direct and indirect forms, the former involving additional disciplinary discourse, especially in classes with 'big wigs' or 'black sheep'. In contrast, the latter tended to involve discursive dualism that encompassed sympathy and authority as indirect classroom control, like the four teachers observed in England.

It is worth noting that among the three Taiwanese teachers who were identified as employing indirect classroom control modalities, two of them (Ms Mei and Ms Lu) were also found to incorporate students' everyday culture in classroom teaching. In England, Ms Tan was also found to incorporate both students' everyday culture and her native culture in China within their instructional discourse. These findings from both Taiwanese and English classrooms are indeed a matter of interest which I will turn to next.

Pedagogical instruction:
Using students' everyday culture in England and Taiwan

In England, for example, again in Ms Tan's class on the morning of 1 October 2015 (11:55–13:10), the class were undertaking a listening comprehension quiz after reviewing the Chinese characters they had learnt at the outset. This listening comprehension quiz seemed to be welcomed, rather than hated by students. Ms Tan showed the class several Chinese sentences using the electronic whiteboard and read them in Chinese. Students were asked to write down the meanings in English in their own exercise book (red exercise book) and exchange for peer scoring. The red exercise book was the students' notebook where they jotted down notes and it was sometimes used as answer sheets in a quiz.

Extract 5.3:

1 T:	Take out your red exercise book and I'll read out sentences…write down in English.
2	Ok…好(hǎo)! um…I'll speak Chinese.
3 S1:	This's a test?
4 T:	No,… quiz.
5 S2:	You need to speak slowly…((chuckling!))
((The next few turns are spent in giving the quiz by the teacher who read the four Chinese sentences twice and slowly.))	
6 T:	好了…第一題…我打算…明年冬天…去倫敦…學英文 ((repeat twice))
7	(hǎo-le, dì-yī-tí…wǒ dǎ-suàn…míng-nián dōng-tiān…qù lún-dūn…xué yīng-wén)

8 T:	第二題…去英國以前我準備了很多好看的裙子 ((repeat twice))	
9	(dì-èr-tí… qù yīng-guó yǐ-qián wǒ zhǔn-bèi-le hěn-duō hǎo-kàn de qún-zi)	
10 T:	第三題…我比較喜歡歐洲的農村…因為它不僅很安靜，而且很漂亮	
11	((repeat twice)) (dì-sān-tí…wǒ bǐ-jiào xǐ-huan ōu-zhōu de nóng-cūn…yīn-wèi	
12	tā bù-jǐn hěn ān-jìng…ér-qiě hěn piào-liang)	
13 T:	Last one,…如果你想去英國讀書你就得學英文…而且要多和英國人聊天	
14	((repeat once))… (rú-guǒ… nǐ xiǎng-qù yīng-guó dú-shū… nǐ jiù-dé xué yīng-wén…	
15	Ér-qiě yào-duō-hé yīng-guó-rén liáo-tiān…)	

((Ms Tan showed answers in English on the whiteboard and had students exchange their red exercise books for correction.))

In Extract 5.3, all of the four questions in Ms Tan's routine review quiz are relevant to students' cultural backgrounds – Britain. For example, the first question in Line 6 is about learning English in London (我打算明年冬天去倫敦學英文 – I plan to learn English in London next winter). The third question in Line 10 is about the beautiful landscape in the European countryside (我比較喜歡歐洲的農村, 因為它不僅很安靜, 而且很漂亮 – I like the countryside in Europe because it is not only quiet but also beautiful). The last question in Line 13 is again about the British cultural context with which students are familiar (如果你想去英國讀書你就得學英文…而且要多和英國人聊天 – If you want to stay abroad in Britain, you have to learn English). Ms Tan appeared to use students' recurring everyday cultural activities in order to contextualise the learning of Chinese. Although at times the other three teachers in England used illustrations from students' everyday experience, such as referring to going to a Chinese restaurant and ordering food, Ms Tan frequently used such pedagogy.

In Taiwan, as illustrated in Table 5.10, Ms Mei from Hakka Rural School was found to refer to both Taiwanese and ethnic Hakka everyday culture while the Hakka language was also used by Ms Mei, though she was not an ethnic Hakka teacher. As an indigenous Paiwan, Ms Lu from Mountainside School demonstrated similar interactional styles as Ms Mei's, drawing frequently on everyday Paiwan culture involving the use

Table 5.10 Interactional styles of sharing everyday culture in Taiwan

	Hakka Rural		Mountainside	
Class	F		H	
Teacher	Ms Mei		Ms Lu	
Languages used	Chinese/English	Ethnic language	Chinese/English	Ethnic language
Sharing Taiwanese culture	✓			
Sharing ethnic culture	✓	✓	✓	✓

of the Paiwan mother tongue. The following extracts illustrate typical features of their interactional styles.

Ms Mei, the Hakka daughter-in-law

In Table 5.10, Ms Mei at Hakka Rural was able to incorporate everyday Taiwanese culture and, in particular, explicitly share both her students' Hakka ethnicity and mother tongue in classroom teaching, drawing on this joint cultural understanding to bridge between students' school and outside school knowledge.

Sharing Taiwanese culture: In her class on the morning (08:15–09:00) of 30 September 2004, Ms Mei and her students were tackling a textbook dialogue related to different foods in Taiwan. The dialogue was carried out between two boys (Tom and Ben) in a Chinese restaurant. Tom came from America and was visiting Ben who lived in Taiwan. At the outset, Ms Mei asked her students to read the dialogue together. She carried out a little review on what had been taught about the dialogue the previous day. After following up with illustrations and practice of sentence patterns, she asked students to answer questions about Taiwanese food that might be of most interest to foreigners.

Extract 5.4:

1 T:	(What is the foreigners most favourite drink in Taiwan?-M)
2	I have mentioned last time.
3 S1:	'zhēn-zhū nǎi-chá'? (pearl milk tea)
4 T:	Hello? (What is their favourite? –M) ((not satisfied))
5 S2:	'bǎn-tiáo'? (Hakka noodles)
6 T:	(If so, they must be visiting Hakka village.– M) It's true, (but what if
7	they come to Taiwan? –M)
8 S3:	((excitingly)) 'mài-dāng-láo'?(Macdonald)
9 T:	((a suspicious looking)) (You think it is Macdonald? Is that so? – M)
10	Or maybe beef noodles in the night market? What else?
11 S4:	'chòu dòu-fu' (stinking tofu)
12 T:	It's one of their favorite food. (So, you can treat foreign friends to the
13	night market for 'stinking tofu'. They might be feeling... – M) 'Uh~~~!'
	((Teacher frowned humorously.))

Ms Mei asked students about food and drink in Taiwan with a preplanned goal to lead students to think of common Taiwanese popular foods that might interest foreigners. In Lines 3, 5 and 8 of Extract 5.3, she did not accept the answers offered by students as relevant. However, 'stinking tofu in traditional night market' (Line 11), popular with both local people and foreigners, was finally welcomed. Her concluding remark: 'you can treat foreign friends to the night market for stinking tofu' (Lines 12 and 13) and a little humorous facial expression highlighting this popular, smelly but delicious Taiwanese tofu revealed her efforts to bridge between students' in- and outside school knowledge. Her guidance of knowledge construction and epistemic control was carried out in a rather implicit way. Students' initial answers of 'pearl milk tea', 'Hakka noodles' and 'Macdonald', all appealing foods in Taiwan, were not welcomed but neither were they explicitly rejected. The final response of 'stinking tofu', which seemed to fit her agenda, was then agreed and used to create a point of continuity connecting school and non-school experiences. A joint understanding of 'what is the foreigners' most favourite food in Taiwan?' as an element of everyday Taiwanese culture was, by such means, shared by both parties through the use of both the Chinese and English language.

Sharing Hakka language: The following extract focused upon a series of questions regarding Hakka students' cram school experience. Ms Mei and her students were dealing with the textbook dialogue between June and Coco whose focal topic was their different experiences of wearing school uniforms. At the outset, a few turns were spent on how cute these two girls looked in their school uniforms. Ms Mei then initiated questions in the Hakka dialect.

Extract 5.5:

1 T:	Coco and June are in Coco's school. Hello! Where are they?
2 Ss:	(In Coco's school.-M) =
3 T:	= They are in Coco's school. ((Teacher repeats in Mandarin.))
4	Very good. June says first. (They start to talk-M) You look so cu::te!
5	(How does she look?-M)
6 S1:	'*kě-'ài*'. (Cute) =
7 T:	((repeats)) = '*hǎo-kě-'ài*'. (So very cu::te.)
8	((Hakka dialect)) '*yī-kēyī-lái-yǒng-léi?*' (How does she look?)
9 Ss:	((repeat in Hakka dialect)) '*ān-děng-yīxiā*' (So very cute!)=
10 T:	((echoes in Hakka)) = '*ān-děng-yīxiā* ' (So very cu::te!)
11 Ss:	((Respond with laughter when hearing their mother tongue.))
12 T:	(Looks very cute-M) ((Teacher reads and writes on board.))
13	Ok, read together. You look so cute=
14 Ss:	=You look so cute.

Ms Mei's active involvement in learning the Hakka culture and dialect led her to speak Hakka on occasions or to ask students intentionally for the Hakka translation of newly learned English vocabulary. In Line 8 of Extract 5.4, Ms Mei took advantage of her acquired Hakka dialect in asking the question again: '*yī-kēyī-lái-yǒng-léi?*' (How does she look?), triggering a few taking of turns between the two interlocutors in Hakka, the students' mother tongue (Lines 9 and 10). Ms Mei regarded this pedagogical strategy helpful to empower students as they might perceive themselves as capable of giving her new linguistic knowledge rather than merely being receivers of learning English. The emerging empowerment resulting from the teacher sharing with students' understanding and experience of the Hakka language, arguably, made possible a co-constitution of intersubjective meanings between interlocutors.

Sharing Paiwan ethnic culture: Ms Lu was a native Paiwan teacher who had first language capacity in sharing Mountainside students' indigenous mother tongue and relevant cultural customs. She used such shared knowledge and identity in classroom instruction that drew on joint cultural understanding to bridge between students' school and outside school knowledge, as shown in Extract 5.6.

The lesson observed in Ms Lu's class was on the morning (10:10–11:00) of 8 September 2004. She was at the blackboard and students were in their seats facing her. Ms Lu and the students were tackling new vocabulary. At the outset, Ms Lu asked the students to read all the vocabulary items together, and then reviewed some new words learned in the previous lesson. While introducing the word 'family', she led students to connect the previously learned word 'reunion', thus generating the phrase 'family reunion'. She then initiated the question: 'When do we indigenous people have family reunion?'.

Extract 5.6:

1 T:	Family reunion=
2 Ss:	=Family reunion ((Students repeat loudly together three times.))
3 T:	(How do you translate it?-M)
4 Ss:	'jiā-tíng tuán-jù' (family reunion) =
5 T:	=Ok, 'jiā-tíng tuán-jù' ((repeats while writing on board))
6	Ok, when do we indigenous people have family reunion?
7 S1:	(On the wedding day.-M)
8 S2:	(And on the day they get engaged.-M)
9 T:	(On wedding day, the day they get engaged and what else?-M)
10 S3:	On 'qīng-míng jié' (Chinese Tomb-sweeping Day[3])
11 T:	What about our 'wǔ-nián jì '? (Paiwan Five-Year Ceremony)
12 Ss:	(Yes, we do. -M)
13 T:	(None of the villagers are sober, right!-M)
14 Ss:	((Students smile with apparent understanding.))
15 T:	(What about our 'Community Athletic Competition[4]'? -M)
16 Ss:	(Yes.-M)
17 T:	So we have 'family reunion' on these events.
	((The next few turns are spent in learning another vocabulary; 'rice'.))

18 T:	Next one, 'Rice'=
19 Ss:	=Rice. ((Students repeat together three times.))
20 T:	(Does anyone of you plant 'rice' at home? -M)
21 Ss:	No
22 T:	You are right. (We don't grow rice here. We only eat millet. -M)
23 Ss:	((Students are hilariously chatting over home plants and food.))

In Line 6, the 'we' statement seemed to set the scene for initiating common ground upon which teacher and students could comfortably interact. In Lines 11 and 15, two specific Paiwan cultural events, the 'Paiwan Five-Year Ceremony' (see also Chapter 3) and the 'Community Sport Competition', were both evoked as joint knowledge that allowed students to reflect upon and conceptualise the new phrase 'family reunion'. The invocation of the 'Paiwan Five-Year Ceremony' as an example of a cultural activity of the Paiwan tribe, led me to write in my field notes after this observation that I had gained the impression that Ms Lu had hit upon a highly valued cultural activity in which Paiwan family members returned home for family reunions and religious purposes.

> Paiwan's Five-Year Ceremony ('Maleveq' in Paiwan dialect) is a unique cultural event in Paiwan. It's the most important ritual held every five years during which families will get together celebrating the Return of Gods and Ancestors while, at the same time, drinking their home-brewed millet spirit (*xiǎo mǐ-jiǔ* 小米酒) to their heart's content. As this ceremony will be held this year, Ms. Lu seems to have raised a timely issue in the right season. (Field note, 8 September 2004)

The 'Community Sport Competition', another Paiwan cultural event, was also used by Ms Lu to bring together students' understanding of their home community in which sporting prowess was highly valued. For decades, this has been an important annual cultural occasion when family members come home. Both were used by the teacher to arrive at a point of intersubjectivity whereby students effectively reflected upon and conceptualised the new phrase 'family reunion'. Growing 'rice' at home which followed not only introduced the term but enabled Ms Lu to ask: 'Do any of you plant rice at home? (Line 20). Following students' 'No' response, Ms Lu immediately elaborated such shared cultural knowledge by saying: 'We don't grow rice here' (Line 22), again bridging students' home and school experiences.

Sharing Paiwan mother tongue: Besides sharing her students' culture in classroom interaction, Ms Lu used the Paiwan dialect, as in introducing the vocabulary item 'grow', thus initiating another question trying to connect students' home and school experiences.

Extract 5.7:

1 T:	'grow'=
2 Ss:	='grow' ((Students repeat together three times including its past tense.))
3 T:	(For example, what do you 'grow' at home now?-M)
4 S1:	((speak Paiwan dialect)) '*Vasa*'...
5 S2:	'*Vaqu*'. ((Other students utter different plants in Paiwan dialect.))
6 T:	So '*vasa*' is carrot. ((Teacher repeats in Paiwan dialect and elaborates it.))

In Line 3 of Extract 5.7, Ms Lu initiated the question: 'What do you grow at home now?'. To my surprise, one student automatically replied '*Vasa*' (carrot) in Paiwan dialect (Line 4). As indicated in Line 6, Ms Lu immediately took advantage of her Paiwan identity by elaborating '*vasa* is carrot' using Paiwan dialect. In relating how she felt while using the Paiwan language in teaching English, Ms Lu said:

> I tend to use our mother tongue quite often... just to make my class relax. It seems that 'a sense of intimacy' (*qīn-qiè gǎn* 親切感) could be created by using our shared Paiwan language although I am not definitely sure if this strategy helps in any sense... it may help to promote their English learning.

Although Ms Lu did not intend to use their shared mother tongue to enhance students' cognitive development, improvisation of this kind and its appeal to shared understanding and experience of the Paiwan language seemed to connect students' home and school knowledge effectively. It could be argued that achieving 'a sense of intimacy' entails not only a sense of co-membership but also a state of intersubjectivity, meaning when interlocutors find a common ground that allows shared meaning to take place.

Following Vygotsky (1987), Rogoff (1990) has referred to the state of 'intersubjectivity' as 'bridging'. In fact, a slightly different form of bridging seemed to emerge in the Chinese classrooms in England – 'sociolinguistic bridging', which I will discuss further in the next section.

Emerging 'sociolinguistic bridging' in England

As mentioned earlier, students considered Ms Tan (King's School) a very good teacher who 'approaches lessons seriously but makes it interesting by adding variety so that we don't get bored, essentially' (comment by Year 11 student Jade). Apart from having an activity-based pedagogy, Ms Tan also liked to encourage students to challenge each other during the process of classroom discussion and presentation if they had better or additional thoughts. In her own words, '...you have to fight back... if you have better ideas' was a frequent reminder before and during the discussion. Therefore, students appeared to be empowered to constantly exert their critical and creative thinking capacities. One of the capacities was the way in which some students seemed to be able to 'link' their new learning of the Chinese language to their old/existing knowledge of British culture and language.

For example, in the morning class of 5 November 2015, Ms Tan and the class (Year 11) were reviewing Chinese characters they had learnt in previous lessons. When the class were discussing the Chinese term '防晒霜' (sunscreen), one student, Steve, took advantage of his existing knowledge of Western culture where many people enjoy sun-bathing and helped his acquisition of the new Chinese vocabulary – '晒' (hot or exposed under the sun). He conceptualised this Chinese character '晒' as having two parts, namely '日' (the sun) and '西' (the West). This was, indeed, creative enough for students to develop a new understanding of the target language from learners' existing cultural knowledge. In fact, this has pedagogic implications because once teachers' pedagogies are based on students' needs and understanding of the Chinese language, teachers will be able to accelerate students' language learning (He & Jiao, 2010).

It could also be argued that there are potential 'cross-sociolinguistic similarities' between English and Chinese that have facilitative effects for language learning (Singh & Han, 2014). For Shea (2008), this means teachers may encourage learners to

> ...actively analyse how the structures and sound systems of their native language compare to their target language. Where they align, learning can be jumpstarted. Where they do not, differences can be analysed and potentially rendered less intimidating. (Shea, 2008: 701)

In other words, if teachers recognise students' native language as cultural resources, value the cultural and sociolinguistic experiences students bring to the classroom and share a commitment to connecting with individual learners on a personal level as well as at an instructional level, the learning of a new language such as Chinese can be facilitated.

In sum, a comparison of Ms Mei's and Ms Lu's classroom interactions revealed similarities in interactional styles in sharing students' everyday culture, the former incorporating both everyday Taiwanese culture and the Hakka mother tongue and ethnic culture, the latter exercising her indigenous mother tongue and cultural knowledge in order to achieve 'a sense of intimacy' with students within their pedagogic practice marked by indirect classroom control. Access to students' ethnic knowledge and minority dialect was found to be an important sociocultural resource that aided English learning in Taiwan even when the dominant classroom language was Chinese. In England, similar classroom interactional styles of using students' everyday culture or teacher's own background culture were also detected, such as in Ms Tan's classroom. Although no ethnic cultures were used by the Chinese teachers in England, the emerging form of 'sociolinguistic bridging' in the CFL classrooms in England is intriguing and worth our attention. It could be argued that teachers in such contexts with this shared cultural and sociolinguistic knowledge may effectively achieve intersubjective meanings with their students, even when the teacher is not sharing the same ethnicity or mother tongue with the students (e.g. Ms Mei at Hakka Rural School and Ms Tan at King's School). The emerging finding of a new pedagogy – 'inclusive pedagogy' – also has implication for teacher education, which I will discuss further in Chapter 7.

Chapter Summary

In this chapter, we have examined the institutional and material cultures in school settings in Taiwan and England in order to understand how they structure or regulate students' English/Chinese learning. The EFL and CFL teachers' backgrounds, including their personal English/Chinese learning and teacher training experiences, have been explored and found to have an impact on their pedagogic styles, exemplified, for example, in Ms Tan's case. Then, an exploration of similarities and differences in interactional styles between schools in Taiwan and England has revealed that, in Taiwan, a general pedagogical pattern of knowledge-based grammar teaching was detected as opposed to the activity-based pedagogy in England. The Taiwanese 'rote-learning' style, which is largely used to ensure students' high exam grades, bears with it a negative meaning for students and parents. However, from a comparative perspective across cultures, it has been considered by many as 'effective' among Asian students, as opposed to many of their international peers, in knowledge and skill testing such as PISA, an interesting point which will be discussed in Chapter 7.

In addition, comparisons of classroom pedagogy among the four social groups in Taiwan heighten awareness that learning takes place not only within classrooms but is also embedded within broader school locales and ethnic cultures. Teachers who employed students' ethnic culture or mother tongue in dialogical interactions between teacher and students were found to be able to create a sense of co-membership between them and facilitate students' English learning. This form of cultural bridging in classroom pedagogy was mostly associated with the 'indirect' type of classroom control, engendering affective meaning-negotiation in the process of classroom life. In Chinese classrooms in England, each Chinese language teacher observed appeared to employ both activity-based pedagogy and indirect classroom control modalities in engendering students' cognitive and affective development. Moreover, the emerging sociolinguistic bridging in the Chinese classrooms in England was interesting and worth our attention. The issues of cultural/sociolinguistic bridging in classroom pedagogy will be discussed further in Chapter 8.

Last but not least, in order to avoid falling into the trap of being 'cultural-centric' which attributes everything to culture, we are aware, for example, that teachers' personalities are also important factors that may regulate their teaching styles. With this in mind, we are also aware that all those material cultures that mediate pedagogy and cultural/sociolinguistic resources which shape learning have to be examined without individual personalities or experiences being ignored. This 'participative appropriation' (Rogoff, 1990) on the personal plane of analysis is what I will turn to in the next chapter.

Notes

(1) Transcription conventions, modified from Silverman (1993), are indicated in the Appendix.
(2) 'Hot Chair' was a popular language game in Ms Tan's class. One student was invited to sit on a chair in front of the classroom facing the class. Then a Chinese term, usually a vocabulary item just learnt, was shown on the electronic whiteboard. The class were encouraged to describe it in Chinese without saying out loud the exact term so that the student on the Hot Chair could try hard to guess and speak it out in Chinese.
(3) Chinese Tomb-sweeping Day falls on 5 April when people tend to use it as a family reunion.
(4) The annual Community Athletic Competition is also regarded as another day for family reunions.

6 Language Learning and Identity: Communities of Practice

In Chapter 4, we investigated the broader sociocultural settings of learning English in Taiwan and Chinese in England at the level of 'community activity', and teacher–student interactions in classroom settings in Chapter 5. In exploring patterns of classroom pedagogic behaviour in Taiwan, ethnic language and cultural legacies were seen to play pivotal roles in the construction of intersubjective meanings, through bridging school and out-of-school knowledge within classrooms. While some similar interactional forms were detected in Chinese classrooms in England, major differences were also uncovered in relation to a more 'thinking-based' pedagogy as opposed to a more 'grammar-based' approach to teaching English in Taiwan. In this chapter, empirical findings concerning Rogoff's (1990) third, personal plane of analysis in the investigation of how learning takes place within sociocultural settings, are presented. We explore how individual students' active social positioning involving membership identities emerged both within English as a foreign language (EFL) and Chinese as a foreign language (CFL) learning 'communities of practice' (Lave & Wenger, 1991; Wenger, 1998), particularly with reference to different social and ethnic groups in Taiwan and state/independent schools in England. Within our theoretical framework of communities of practice, individual students' learning trajectories are characterised as 'central' or 'peripheral'.

As argued in Chapter 2, sociocultural and situated theories of cognition pose challenges to traditional views of learning theory and recognise learning as not taking place in a social vacuum but within sociocultural processes. Mapping such human mental processes of learning entails recognition of 'the essential relationship between these processes and their cultural, historical and institutional settings' (Wertsch, 1991: 6). This notion of situated learning is nicely captured by Lave and Wenger (1991) and, in particular, Wenger's (1998) notion of 'communities of practice'. Students may be viewed as acting members within language learning communities of practice where they constantly negotiate the meanings of their experiences on a continuum at whose extremes they may either move towards full participation or non-participation. Those who are able to build a membership identity through meaning negotiations within such communities of practice become empowered as central participants.

In this study, there is a call for an even broader scope of communities of practice that accounts for the relationship between students' mental processes and their cultural, historical and institutional settings. In light of Scribner and Cole's (1981) 'practice account of literacy', a functional and context-sensitive approach is needed to investigate English learning within Taiwanese society and Chinese learning in England where 'communities of practice' are conceptualised as not limited to concrete social settings, such as classrooms, schools or cram schools, but also involve practices in various kinds of material circumstances and in relation to 'cultural artefacts' (Cole, 1996), such as street English/Chinese signs, computers and TV. Students who appropriate resources or cultural capital offered by their locales in participating schools are seen as more likely to become more competent and central participants in English/Chinese learning communities of practice. Others who fail to get access to such cultural resources tend to position themselves or be positioned as less than full participants in English/Chinese learning communities of practice. Their 'marginality' (Wenger, 1998) or non-participation may emerge as an outbound trajectory to peripheral participation. Among our 16 Taiwanese student interviewees, 11 were characterised as central participants and 5 as peripheral. In England, 15 students were interviewed, of whom 14 were characterised as central participants and only one as peripheral. The characteristics of their different English/Chinese learning trajectories are outlined in this chapter.

Mapping English Learning Trajectories in Taiwan

Learning is a sociocultural process involving the 'mutuality' (Rogoff, 1995) of its individual and social aspects. The following discussion foregrounds the mapping of individual learning trajectories, seeking to answer the fundamental question of why students learn differently, even though they attend the same school, are taught by the same teacher and have access to similar cultural resources. In answering such questions, these learning trajectories are firmly located within broader English or Chinese learning communities within Taiwanese or English society. As 'central' or 'peripheral' participants in their foreign language learning communities of practice, individual students may appropriate cultural resources provided either by various features of their locales or by classroom interactions.

Learning English in communities of practice: The individual cases

During the course of fieldwork in Taiwan, already referred to in the preceding chapters, 16 students (8 girls and 8 boys) were interviewed (see Table 6.1), all having first been encountered during the course of

Table 6.1 Characteristics of students interviewed in the four Taiwanese schools

School	Students	Gender	Ethnicity	Encouragement	Participation
Urbany	Helen	F	Mainlander	Mum/Dad	Central
	Ken	M	Holo	Mum/Dad	Central
	Carol	F	Holo	Mum/Dad	Central
	Howard	M	Mainlander	N/A	Peripheral
Suburbany	Yvonne	F	Mainlander	Mum/Dad	Central
	Eddie	M	Holo	Mum/Dad	Central
	Julia	F	Mainlander	Mum	Central
Hakka Rural	Wendy	F	Hakka	Mum	Central
	Chris	M	Hakka	Mum/Dad	Central
	Fay	F	Hakka	N/A	Peripheral
	Sharon	F	Hakka	Mum/Dad	Central
	Mark	M	Hakka	Mum	Peripheral
Mountainside	Vincent	M	Paiwan	Mum	Central
	Jack	M	Paiwan	N/A	Peripheral
	Dave	M	Paiwan	N/A	Peripheral
	Vanessa	F	Paiwan	Mum/Uncle	central

classroom observation. The process of selecting and accessing them for interview involved taking into account teachers' knowledge of them, my observations, students' and parents' questionnaire responses and their academic attainment. For example, after a period of one month, each of the eight classroom teachers provided a list of those students they considered to be 'central', high achieving or motivated learners, and possible 'peripheral', low achieving or struggling learners, in their English classrooms. Demographic information, including whether family members helped or encouraged them to learn English, was also accessed from students' personal and parents' questionnaires, along with their attainment in English at the first school monthly exam as providing evidence of academic performance. Of the 16 eventually interviewed, 11 (7 girls, 4 boys) were central and 5 (4 boys, 1 girl) were peripheral participants.

Urbany School: The distinctive school vision of Urbany School concerning the promotion of bilingual education ran alongside its more generic goal, shared with many other urban schools, of helping students to achieve academic success. Within it, as shown in Table 6.1, Helen, Ken and Carol were viewed as central participants achieving high attainment in English, while Howard was peripheral, not only rejecting learning English in class but also resisting English by, for example, confessing to ripping off the school's bilingual signs on occasions. A comparison of the three central participants revealed that all were from affluent families. Table 6.2 indicates that, in terms of parents' education level, Helen's father was college

Table 6.2 Familial characteristics of Urbany School interviewees

School	Student	Parents	Ethnicity	Education	Occupation	Engagement
Urbany	Helen	Father	Mainlander	University	Business	✓
		Mother	Holo	Senior High	Business	✓
	Ken	Father	Holo	University	Business	✓
		Mother	Holo	College	Teacher	✓
	Carol	Father	Holo	University	Engineer	✓
		Mother	Holo	University	Employee	✓
	Howard	Father	Mainlander	University	Business	
		Mother	Holo	Vocational	Domesticity	

educated and Ken's a university graduate, as were both Carol's parents. Helen's father was in business as an employer, Ken's was also in business and used English daily at work and Carol's father was a computer engineer. All were aware of the future importance of English and encouraged their children by, for example, arranging for them to attend cram schools and practice English at home. Howard's parents had also achieved high educational levels, his father was a business manager who was good at English and like Ken's father, had considerable foreign travel experiences, according to Howard. However, in contrast to Ken's intensive English practice at home with his father, the lack of parental encouragement may have contributed to Howard's non-participation in English.

In urban areas, there is an overwhelming culture of academic competition and cram schooling. Differences in students' access to English in everyday life appeared to contribute to the 'urban–rural' divide referred to in Chapter 1. While among urban groups, Mainlander students demonstrated higher propensities than their Holo peers to access English learning through various cultural resources, it could be argued, however, that ethnic variations did not seem to stand out. Inter-marriage between Mainlander (predominantly military men moving to Taiwan in 1949) and Holo (local Taiwanese women) social groups has been common in the post-war era. As illustrated in Tables 6.2 and 6.3, the parents of Helen, Howard and Julia in Suburbany clearly exemplified this particular inter-marriage pattern. In these cases, urban culture cut across ethnic lines and seemed to minimise the ethnic difference in English learning. In addition, Helen and Ken were in Mr Lin's class and Carol and Howard were in Ms Wu's class. Both teachers' classroom control (see Chapter 5) was characterised as 'direct', with similar interactional patterns involving grammar-oriented pedagogy and Chinese as the dominant language. Given this similarity in dialogic interaction between the two classroom settings in bilingual Urbany School, students' participatory appropriation of various familial opportunities appeared to play key roles in defining who became central and peripheral participants in English, a matter I will turn to later in more detail.

Table 6.3 Familial affordances in Suburbany School

School	Student	Parents	Ethnicity	Education	Occupation	Engagement
Suburbany	Yvonne	Father	Mainlander	Post G.	Navy Officer	✓
		Mother	Mainlander	University	Teacher	✓
	Eddie	Father	Hokkien	University	Engineer	✓
		Mother	Hokkien	University	Employee	✓
	Julia	Father	Mainlander	College	Employee	
		Mother	Hokkien	University	Business	✓

Suburbany School: Suburbany School promoted elite education and high academic success. As indicated in Table 6.3, Yvonne, Eddie and Julia were viewed by their English teacher – Ms Huang – as high attaining, central participants in English, while James, initially invited, but not finally interviewed because of shortage of time, rejected learning English, though he was competent in other school subjects.

Eddie was the highest achieving boy among all those interviewed, having passed the intermediate level of the General English Proficiency Test (GEPT) in 2005, equivalent to senior high student level. Again, a crude comparison of the three central participants revealed that they all came from affluent families with considerable cultural capital. Yvonne's and Eddie's parents had achieved the highest education level as university graduates, Yvonne's parents both working as civil servants, giving them a relatively high social status. Julia's parents were both college educated, while James' parents' had not gone beyond high school level. All of the three central participants enjoyed parental encouragement and the opportunities afforded by family affluence involving, for example, home practice, cram schooling and foreign teachers. Yvonne had rich, foreign, cultural experiences which her father's education level and, more importantly, military career as a navy officer, made possible. Indeed, her early encounter with English through foreign teachers and cultural experiences may have created tensions between her past learning history and observed classroom behaviour, addressed in more detail later.

James, a peripheral participant, experienced little exposure to English at home and lacked parental encouragement. As revealed in his mother's questionnaire, her rather short encounter with English, only in junior high school, went with her rather low valuation of the importance of English for children. As with Howard at Urbany, James' only contact with English was in the classroom listening to his teacher, writing schoolwork and taking notes. English was being learned only because it was a 'school subject' and not for its importance for academic study or future career. His only English practice outside the classroom appeared to be asking for help from high achievers in order to solve problems in school 'exams'.

Yvonne's and Eddie's ethnic background indicated distinctive differences between 'pure' Mandarin and Holo families, both affluent, reflecting the classic anthropological differences between 'political' Mandarin and 'business' Holo outlined in Chapter 3. Yvonne's family exemplified the case of second-generation Mainlander families as Mandarin, urban dwellers engaged in either military or civil servant careers, which bestowed a middle-class socio-economic status on them and ensured that their children had access to many cultural resources in learning English. The family backgrounds of Eddie and Julia, whose mother was chiefly engaged in her schooling, in contrast, exemplified the 'business' Holo model reflecting historical interest in trading and business of the past 300 years since immigration from south-eastern China. Economic realities related to competing in global commerce have undoubtedly accelerated the rising tide of learning English among Holo people engaged in business, while tending to bypass parents, such as James', both Holo but with lower high school education levels.

On the interpersonal plane, Yvonne and Eddie were both in Ms Huang's class and Julia was in Ms Sun's class. Ms Huang's pedagogic style involved an indirect form of control, while Ms Sun's was more direct, as referred to in Chapter 5. Given her relatively experienced pedagogic practice and the high-ability nature of her class, Ms Huang appeared to be able to establish an English learning community of practice for her elite students that contributed positively to Yvonne's and Eddie's central participation. Her sympathetic pedagogic style provided Yvonne with everyday encouragement which helped her gain a learning identity characterised by an 'in-bound trajectory' (Wenger, 1998), addressed later in this chapter. On the other hand, as with both teachers at Urbany, Ms Sun displayed 'direct' classroom control, her 'grammar-based' pedagogy particularly matching the dominant culture of valuing high scores in elite Suburbany. Her style created tension for Julia's early involvement in learning English, caught between her past foreign teacher experience and the current grammar-translation method. A specific form of teacher–student intersubjectivity, discussed later, alongside her home practice with her mother, as noted earlier, seemed to contribute to Julia's central participation.

Hakka Rural School: Hakka Rural was located within a cluster of Hakka villages, the 'town of PhDs' (see Chapter 3) with an intake of nearly 90% Hakka ethnic students. The school vision focused on cultivating 'cognitive competence'. In this school, Wendy, Chris and Sharon were high achieving, central participants in English, and Fay and Mark were peripherals who had difficulties learning English. Like other central participants in urban groups, a crude comparison suggested that Wendy, Chris and Sharon were also 'haves' in terms of familial resources, though not as affluent as their urban peers. Table 6.4 indicates, in terms of parental education level, that Sharon's parents were both college graduates.

Table 6.4 Family characteristics of interviewees in Hakka Rural School

School	Student	Parents	Ethnicity	Education	Occupation	Engagement
Hakka Rural	Wendy	Father	Hakka	College	Business	
		Mother	Hakka	Senior High	Business	✓
	Chris	Father	Hakka	Senior High	Business	
		Mother	Hakka	Senior High	Domesticity	✓
	Fay	Father	Hakka	Senior High	Unknown	
		Mother	N/A	N/A	Unknown	
	Sharon	Father	Hakka	College	Employee	
		Mother	Hakka	College	Employee	✓
	Mark	Father	Hakka	N/A	Unknown	
		Mother	Holo	N/A	Unknown	✓

She was the school's highest achieving student in Year 8. Mark had parental encouragement, familial resources and parental education levels (father: college level; mother: senior high school level) as rich as those of Wendy. Both Mark's parents, however, worked in urban Kaohsiung during weekdays so he lived with his grandmother, which appeared to pose certain constraints that contributed to his peripheral participation. The major distinction between these two students' English performance appeared to lie in their differential access to cultural resources. Wendy's 'mother–daughter' intersubjectivity, in contrast to Mark's grandparent child-rearing style, appeared to be important influences in defining their participation. According to students' questionnaires and interview account, a crude comparison of the parental encouragement and engagement afforded to Wendy, Chris and Sharon revealed similarity in maternal care over their schoolwork at home. The strong gender roles of traditional Hakka women in both domestic and agricultural labour appeared to be reproduced in new contexts, as will be seen in Wendy's account of her interaction with her mother. Mark's mother was not ethnic Hakka but she provided him with encouragement and cram school learning although he still failed to do well. He stated that he did not know his parents' educational level and their careers were not stated.

Wendy, Chris and Fay were in Ms Mei's class and Sharon and Mark were in Mr Yuan's class. As indicated in Chapter 5, Ms Mei demonstrated indirect classroom control and was able to access students' mother tongue and Hakka culture to achieve intersubjective meaning with her students. Wendy, the local English-speaking contest champion, appeared to benefit from such student–teacher intersubjectivity, as will be seen below.

Mr Yuan exercised direct classroom control and his disciplinary discourse reminded students about proper classroom behaviour. It was probably because of this modality of classroom control that Sharon, the highest achieving girl in school, remained 'silent' for most of her interview concerning Mr Yuan's classroom interaction. Her silence raised some doubt as to how far classroom learning alone accounted for students' academic performance in such a class. When asked 'what makes you learn English well so far?' Sharon said:

> Practice... going to cram school. It does not mean going to cram school is better than other methods. It is because I can get more 'practice' (liàn-xí 練習). So I can listen to the school lesson twice from cram school teachers.... The cram school teacher will help me with 'test items' (tí-mù 題目) on the paper.

It could be argued that such cram school 'practice', mirroring the Hakka collective culture's emphasis on academic study, may have contributed to Sharon's central participation in learning English, albeit decontextualised, as practices in most Hakka cram schools were far from the 'practice account of literacy learning' proposed by Scribner and Cole (1981).

Mountainside School: Mountainside's distinctive school vision, aiming to nurture the 'body' (tǐ-néng 體能) for athleticism and sport rather than academic success, stood in contrast to intentions and practices in the two urban schools and Hakka Rural School, which aimed to cultivate the 'mind' (xīn-zhì 心智) for academic success. As shown in Table 6.5, Vincent and Vanessa were characterised as high achieving central participants in English, while Jake and Dave were peripheral students who encountered difficulties learning English. As in other schools, the former pair were 'haves' in terms of family cultural capital, although, again, not as affluent as their urban counterparts and both Vincent's and Vanessa's mothers were senior high graduates but had secured relatively affluent careers as a clinic cleaner and crèche caretaker, respectively, which played pivotal parts in helping their children get access to English. Moreover, Vanessa's father was a vocational school graduate, equivalent to senior high school level. Both of the peripheral participants' parents had

Table 6.5 Familial characteristics of interviewees at Mountainside School

School	Student	Parents	Ethnicity	Education	Occupation	Engagement
Mountainside	Vincent	Father	Paiwan	Junior High	Peasant	
		Mother	Paiwan	Senior High	Clinic cleaner	✓
	Jack	Father	Paiwan	Junior High	Labour worker	
		Mother	Paiwan	Primary	Domesticity	
	Dave	Father	Paiwan	Primary	Mechanic	
		Mother	Paiwan	Junior High	Domesticity	
	Vanessa	Father	Paiwan	Vocational	Military	
		Mother	Paiwan	Senior High	Caretaker	✓

no more than primary or junior high school education. Jack's parents worked as temporary labourers, while Dave's father worked at home as a car mechanic. Jack enjoyed parental encouragement even though they had little experience or contact with English themselves. Jack claimed that he wanted to participate in the national athletic team in the future.

In terms of ethnicity, the parents of all students' interviewed at Mountainside School were indigenous Paiwan. In comparison with other social groups within Taiwanese society, the interplay of their indigenous culture and their emphasis on athletic prowess, alongside problems engendered by a widespread pattern of grandparental child-rearing and alcohol dependency arising from a drinking culture, contributed to a disvaluing of education. Such a cultural ensemble played a part in shaping students' learning, creating a younger generation disillusioned with learning English and other academic work. Vincent's and Vanessa's parental encouragement and engagement were particularly exceptional within this community, as was their valuing of English learning.

Vincent, Jack and Dave were in Ms Lu's class. Vanessa was in Ms Lin's class. Ms Lu, the Paiwan teacher, relied on indirect classroom control and her ability to access students' Paiwan mother tongue and culture helped her to achieve intersubjective meanings with her students. In interview, when asked how he felt about Ms Lu's classroom interaction and the use of the Paiwan mother tongue, Vincent indicated that 'I think I can comprehend better when Ms Lu used Paiwan mother tongue in her teaching'. Ms Lin, the Holo teacher, employed direct classroom control, particularly when annoyed by students' overtly aggressive verbal behaviour in class. As Vanessa pointed out in her account of Ms Lin's classroom interaction with students, 'I just take notes. I think she follows the textbook mostly'. With her seeming lack of intersubjectivity with students and her inability to value the specificity of indigenous culture, Ms Lin seemed to have difficulty achieving their rapport. It could be argued, however, that Ms Lu's ability to achieve intersubjective meanings might not alone account for her success in supporting students' learning. Various planes of analysis are needed here to understand the agencies and processes involved, including the resources provided by the locale and whether and how far students are able to find sociocultural tools that would help them to access English. For example, cram school attendance appeared to contribute to Vincent's and Vanessa's central participation in learning English, while Jack's inability to engage in cram school learning because it was unavailable locally together with his parents' lack of aspiration seemed to contribute to his relative disengagement.

Central participants in learning English: Stories unveiled

The preceding, crude comparisons are intended to provide a picture of similarities and differences in the resources available to help students access English. More detailed investigation and explanation are still needed to explore who became central or peripheral participants, even though they may attend the same school, interact with the same English teacher or are provided with similar cultural resources. In the following in-depth personal accounts, in exploring the understanding of meaning negotiation processes, I will compare pairs of central participants in each school by foregrounding one of them. The pairs – Helen and Ken in Urbany, Yvonne and Eddie in Suburbany and Wendy and Chris in Hakka Rural – were in the same class; Vincent and Vanessa in Mountainside School were in different classes.

Urbany School: Helen and Ken

In Mr Lin's class, Helen and Ken, who enjoyed somewhat similar familial opportunities and cultural capital, were among those students who always concentrated. While sharing the same Taiwanese, urban, competitive culture and school bilingual ethos, Ken achieved more highly than Helen in English, though both were central participants. Helen experienced a more 'winding' trajectory than Ken, caught by a tension between her past English learning history, including experiences of foreign teachers and her present decontextualised school and cram school learning, leading to a value conflict. Ken, in contrast, enjoyed an exceptional father–son relationship that appeared to encourage his participation in English.

Helen, an English-lover, was a third-generation Chinese Mainlander and the elder of two children. She demonstrated enormous interest in learning English in comparison with her peers. During my fieldwork in Urbany, she was particularly interested in my English learning experience in Taiwan and study abroad. When asked why she liked English so much, she said:

> I do not know exactly why I particularly like English since childhood. Seems like I am very 'close' (*qīn* 親) to English.... Perhaps it is because English is important for communication and the way to know different people around the world.

Following my briefing on the study to students and an explanation to them about informed consent on my first field visit to her class, Helen came to greet me saying 'hello' with a beaming smile of welcome. The following field note illustrates some of the questions she raised on that day which seemed to indicate her desire to study abroad in the future.

> Helen is very interested in why and how I learned English well. She asked me if I received family support before going abroad for advanced academic study... relevant queries involving the process of how I went

abroad, the approximate expenditure and why I chose to study in the UK, not other countries such as the U.S. in particular. She also asked me... if English would still be an international language in the near future. She appears to be very keen to know everything from me about learning English. (Field note, 23 November 2004)

Her initial interest in my presence foreshadowed her becoming an interviewee. Her apparently fluent daily use of English, both in and out of school, was evident from her questionnaire responses. For example, when asked if she had helped anyone because she knew English, she wrote 'I helped my mum with reading some English instruction on the medication because she did not comprehend it'. Helen appeared to be proud of being able to help family members, contending that 'it is more convenient to read objects written in English', indicating a somewhat 'practice approach' to literacy (Scribner & Cole, 1981).

Parental support: As shown in Table 6.2, Helen's parents worked in business and encouraged her to learn English, which they regarded as important for her future career and beneficial when going abroad. Helen encountered English in her kindergarten year, known as a 'nursery English class' (*yòu-yòu bān* 幼幼班), an affiliate class in kindergarten where children interact with foreign teachers through language games for a few hours per week. Such arrangements are gaining popularity among urban, Taiwanese parents, who accept the adage that 'learning English, the earlier the better'. Helen became an 'early bird' in learning English, though she did not seem to recall much of what she learned at this stage. Her formal English learning started at an American language institute in Year 4 of primary school and built on her initial 'early bird' interest. She recounted an episode of providing help with English to others for the first time in Year 5, describing her excitement as follows:

> I had two English teachers; one is a Taiwanese and the other is an Australian.... I had an opportunity to translate something for that Australian teacher in English.... Her understanding of what I said really impressed me and incited my interest in English.

This early out-of-school English learning with foreign teachers had both engendered her growing interest in learning English and foreshadowed her value conflict with it that emerged soon after beginning at Urbany School.

With similar family cultural capital to Helen, Ken, a Holo student and elder of two children, was the highest achieving boy in his class. He was provided with even more parental engagement in terms of home practice than Helen, as well as having an early encounter with learning English in Year 1 of primary school (English summer camp) and a specific relationship at home with his father, whose business career involved competent English usage in daily interaction with customers. Ken was inspired by his father's verbal encouragement and home practice which together generated what was tantamount to a domestic community of practice. As he said of his father:

> English is one of his best subjects. I remember he listened to the English magazine Studio Classroom when I was little. He said 'English is an international language therefore English is very important. We need to use it all our lives'.... My father has to use English to communicate with foreigners as his business career...sometimes his colleagues will ask him for help with translation because of his good English.

Home practice began in Year 4 when Ken's father bought him Kenyon and Knott (KK) phonetic symbols and videos, recognised by Taiwanese parents and teachers as the first and crucial stage of learning English, though many students are defeated by the abstraction of the phonetic symbols before really learning any English. This is not helped by the rote learning approach encountered in schools. Ken's father had been one of this sequence's victims, claiming to have suffered from not learning KK phonetic symbols well. Ken reported that:

> My daddy told me to learn KK phonetic symbols in order to recite vocabulary 'easier' (*qīng-sōng yī-diǎn* 輕鬆一點) because he used to use 'Chinese phonetic symbols' (*zhù-yīn fú-hào* 注音符號) which was very tiring.

Apparently, because of this somewhat unhappy learning history, Ken's father was keen to scaffold his son with KK phonetic symbols and teach him how to pronounce words. After learning KK, as the second phase of his home practice, Ken learned to recite vocabulary, his mother, a primary schoolteacher, joining in by Years 5 and 6: 'Mum cut off those vocabulary memory cards from reference books in order to let me recite'. Sometimes, his father would copy additional words for him to memorise, such home practice making it possible for Ken to accumulate about a 500 English word bank by Year 6 through memorisation. It was not easy but, with such parental resources, Ken went on learning, even though he felt the 'difficulty' of reciting vocabulary and 'hated' English at the outset.

In Year 7 in Urbany School, Ken started to learn from the English magazine *Live ABC* as part of Urbany's bilingual policy. He felt it a little 'tough' (*chī-lì* 吃力) to read this magazine at first. English learning in primary school had been easier and more relaxed than at junior high level. Familial support again helped Ken through hard times: 'my father accompanied me reading and explaining words and sentences page by page at the outset'. Ken was initially able to follow it in a slow but steady manner and started to gain more interest:

My English has been getting better... English is not as hard as I imagined. The summer after Year 7, my father asked me to recite the basic 1000 words for junior high students. So currently I have finished the 1000 and am ready to recite another 2000 words.

With such systematic home practice, Ken became a central participant in English learning communities of practice, both at home and school. Though Ken's home English practice was predominantly based on reciting vocabulary in his primary school years, comprehension of the school English magazine in junior high was made possible through daily interaction with his father. Processes of home 'apprenticeship' and 'guided participation' facilitated Ken's active 'participatory appropriation' (Rogoff, 1995) and led to his central participation without a cram school.

Appropriation of school bilingualism: Urbany's bilingualism enabled Ken to access the English magazine and practice at home with his father which contributed to his further comprehension and consequent growing interest in learning English. In contrast, Helen's learning trajectory appeared to be more winding and imbued with value conflict at junior high school. While Urbany's bilingual vision aimed to provide students with a strong environment for learning English, it deterred Helen who felt that English was no longer 'real' and 'fun' because there were no foreign teachers and no real-life English conversations in class. What was taught was predominantly grammar oriented, both at school and at the traditional cram school. Helen expressed her dissatisfaction as follows:

> I feel that, though we have English signs... which may help a bit, it is not an authentic 'whole English' environment... it [bilingual setting] is good for visitors from 'outside'... In general the school bilingual environment is looking good from an outsider's point of view. In comparison with other schools, we do have more English materials... and school newsletters which are at least half English.

A 'participatory appropriation' perspective (Rogoff, 1995) suggests that present actions are not isolated events but extend through past and future. Helen's experience of 'real-life' English learning with a foreign teacher in her early childhood left her caught in tensions between her past learning history and present school discourse. One of the tensions resided in her understanding of the inevitable constraints and limitations of Urbany's bilingual practice. Its discontinuity with her personal, foreign teacher experience appears to be at the heart of her conflict. Her early English learning experience had been interesting. In contrast to her active and reciprocal engagement with foreign teachers, Helen did not consider Urbany's bilingualism to be something 'authentic' or to provide a 'holistic' English environment. The bilingual approach seemed to her to be aimed at promoting the school's reputation and furthering annual recruitment rather than providing meaningful ways to accelerate learning. The English signs posted around the school campus seemed to her to be decorations serving as propaganda. Though not without complaint, Helen recognised the advantages to be gained from reading them, confessing that 'I can learn something about how to say some technical terms about playing basketball in English'. Her understanding of 'authentic' was linked to her desire for more active participation. In her view 'We have English signs but they do not talk', revealing her longing for a 'holistic' English environment which was not possible in Urbany School, despite its daily bilingual broadcast, half English and half Chinese.

A closer look at Helen's interaction with Mr Lin indicated similar tension within the classroom. In talking about her classroom learning in relation to how much English her teacher spoke in class, she said:

> He [Mr. Lin] uses more English when you are in our classroom... I had better go to cram school following foreign teachers because they cannot speak Mandarin therefore I have no choice but to speak English.

All of our participant English teachers confessed that they spoke more Chinese than English in the course of their pedagogic practice. The culture of valuing high scores and what was regarded as prerequisite to attaining them, grammar-based teaching, made Chinese the instructional language of their classrooms. It seemed that my appearance in at least one classroom incited the teacher to speak more, though still rather limited, English.

Cram school learning: Ken, backed by plentiful parental resources, was among the three highest achieving students who did not attend cram school. Others, like Helen, had to engage in it to secure what they sought as appropriate academic attainment. Despite its grammar-based pedagogy, cram school practice could be viewed as an invaluable after-school activity whereby students accessed a particular form of English. However, not everyone who attended cram school became a central participant. Some were positioned or positioned themselves as moving away from the centre of the community towards the periphery. Helen described how some students became disillusioned and formed identities of non-membership that demonstrated resistance and repulsion:

> Many classmates go to cram schools... Most students are asked by parents to go for cram school learning. Some of them go there because their parents are 'tough' (*xiōng* 兇)... they will not go home until the cram school closed at 10 or 11 pm. Some of them are completely inattentive.

Because many students were forced to engage in non-voluntary after-school learning activity, they became disengaged and viewed cram schools as 'shelters' to get away from demanding parents. An identity as a non-participant in cram school marks an outbound trajectory from English as a community of practice and, arguably, encouraged students to become 'inattentive'. Helen, however, was able to build a membership identity through negotiating meaning within cram schools. Her attendance allowed her to imagine her future as an active English speaker and this may have accounted for her academic competence. My later email correspondence with Helen indicated that she was working on her English in order to pass the intermediate level of the GEPT. She wrote in English:

> Now in senior high school, I join an English club and is (am) ready to take part in an English competition.... I am (was) interested in 'English' before. But now, I am interested in their (foreigners) culture, and English can help me to know them more. (Email correspondence, 20 September 2006)

Suburbany School: Yvonne and Eddie

In Ms Huang's high-ability class in Suburbany School, Yvonne and Eddie were among those elite students who were central participants in learning English, and both had affluent family backgrounds, albeit of different kinds. Although they experienced the same elite education and Ms Huang's indirect classroom control pedagogy, Eddie achieved more highly than Yvonne in English. As with her peer discussed in the previous section on Urbany School, Yvonne's forward trajectory in English was less straightforward than Eddie's. Yvonne was caught in tensions and struggles between her past learning history, present discourse and the imagined future that implicitly guided her present learning actions. Eddie, a single child, had been provided with elite education since primary school, had become a central participant in English and had a clear view of his future success. It is worth noting that a cross-cultural comparison of students' learning experiences between 'high-ability classes' in Suburbany School in Taiwan and in King's School in England could be useful for our understanding of their appropriation of their schools' elitism and 'forward thinking' school visions, a matter which I will turn to later in this chapter.

Yvonne was a third-generation Chinese Mainlander and second child in her family. I came to know her because I had worked at the same school as her mother, a pre-military establishment only 10 minutes away from Suburbany. As a boarding school, it was equipped with various facilities, including an ample library where students and many teachers spent time both for leisure purposes and academic study. A unique staff residential area with some 100 families adjacent to the school campus was particularly distinctive and was where Yvonne's family and mine lived. As colleagues as well as neighbours, I came to know Yvonne's family well, making it possible for Yvonne to become one of my interviewees. During the course of my fieldwork, I was particularly impressed with Yvonne's hard work and the engagement of her parents in arranging their children's education. I frequently encountered her in the pre-military school library, finding her either reading 'textbooks' alone or accompanied, sometimes tutored, by either or both of her parents.

In contrast to Yvonne, Eddie was a Holo student and the highest achieving of all central participants in the four schools, passing the higher-intermediate level of the GEPT in 2005, roughly equivalent to non-English major university graduate level in Taiwan. I was particularly impressed with his brave and adept use of English in his oral report during my English teaching[1] of his class in the summer of 2004, prior to my formal fieldwork. His English pronunciation was not as good as other top students but sounded relatively knowledgeable in terms of phraseology and the way he delivered ideas. In contrast to his peers, most of whose reports were copied from the web, Eddie's appeared to be original and resourceful.

Parental support: As shown in Table 6.3, both Yvonne's and Eddie's parents were university graduates. Yvonne's father, a navy military officer, held a higher degree and, more importantly, had lived abroad in many countries during the course of his military career, training and postgraduate study. Such extensive, foreign, cultural experiences had led him to view English as an important tool in job mobility, travel, self-actualisation and assisting children's learning. Both he and his wife were 'civil servants' (*jūn-gōng-jiào* 軍公教) with middle-class incomes and social status. In our regular encounters in the pre-military school library or on campus, he liked to refer to Eddie and other high English achievers in Yvonne's class, and how their family support had contributed to their success. Commenting on family impacts on children's English achievement, he said:

> I think parents play a crucial role in children's English learning and academic achievement.... Parents have to 'create' (*yíng-zào* 營造) an environment by sending their children to study abroad (e.g., in summer vacation) on a regular basis or engage children in learning English from foreign tutors.... Parents have to make such efforts 'intentionally' in order to help children learn English.

He believed that sending children to study abroad on a regular basis to obtain foreign cultural experience or having them learn from foreign tutors was effective. He hoped that someday Yvonne would reach an equivalent level to her high-ability peers, such as Eddie. As Yvonne put it, 'Dad likes to tell me who are really sharp in my class and asks me to work harder in order to catch up with them'. She complained that her father tended to push her to 'compete' with high achieving peers and asked her to 'desperately recite' (*pīn-mìng-bèi* 拼命背) vocabulary daily. Regardless of such complaints, Yvonne was aware that the support offered by her parents was strong in comparison to her non-elite peers. She had encountered English through living abroad at the age of three during her father's postgraduate study in New York. She started her first English learning in Taiwan in Year 2 at primary school and had been abroad more than 10 times to 15 countries. Both parents encouraged Yvonne to do well in English because of its importance to career and travel opportunities. Given this, Yvonne regarded English learning as not only a required school subject but also a way of actualising her intention to study abroad.

In comparison to Yvonne's abundant foreign cultural experiences, Eddie appeared to be much shyer. Neither he nor his parents had been abroad, though they intended in future to do so. As the highest English achiever, however, Eddie demonstrated an exceptional autonomy and competence in English. As with Yvonne, Eddie had encountered English at a relatively early age at kindergarten, albeit not happily due to his resistance to learn. As a gifted student in a high-ability class in primary school, Eddie had been brilliant at achieving academic success in all his schoolwork except English. He became concerned about his relatively poor English in class and decided to spend more time improving it: 'In year 5, I found my classmates were very "strong" (*qiáng* 強) in English in contrast to me. So I would say it was my "classmates" who raised my aspirations to improve my English ability'. In addition to his self-motivation, Eddie received considerable family support and resources. For example, Eddie's parents would often take him to bookstores as one of their major leisure activities as a family. Constant exposure to libraries helped him to acquire easy access to books, making reading an important pastime. In our interview, Eddie's father described their family reading ethos as follows:

> We provide lots of books for him at home... children are like 'sponge'. Parents provide 'water' ready for them to take in.... I like to take him to the bookstore and encourage him to purchase any book he likes, as the old saying goes 'opening books benefits you' (*kāi-juàn yǒu-yì* 開卷有益).

In Eddie's family, books were used by his parents to encourage intellectual development. His enculturation into the family reading culture seemed to contribute to his progress in achieving higher levels of English.

Appropriation of school elitism: Suburbany School's vision which emphasised its elite character generated enormous academic pressure. Yvonne and Eddie both went through a highly competitive process of academic selection involving only a 2.5% pass rate before reaching Ms Huang's high-ability class, as had most of their classmates. In terms of English, more than 10 had passed the elementary level of the GEPT and about 6 the intermediate level. These students were highly competent in listening, speaking, reading and writing skills in English. For them, academic competition and mounting pressure to achieve were inevitable facets of school life. Yvonne described her emotional state as follows:

> We were asked to write down our self-introduction... a classmate handed in hers which was a few pages long... I found myself unable to comprehend some of the words when she read them aloud for the class... I was indeed shocked by her 'sophistication' (*jīng-liàn* 精煉) using English.

The shock of being comparatively incompetent in English led her to work hard, as evidenced through classroom observations and her presence in 'our' pre-military school library. As well as her personal perception of the gulf between herself and others, she also felt she lagged behind in her English reading skills. In Year 7, she had initial difficulties in reading *Let's Talk in English* (*dà-jiā shuō-yīng-wén* 大家說英文), a popular local English magazine in Taiwan, begun in 1962. It served as a compulsory basic-level English language learning text used by many junior high schools including Suburbany. To her dismay, some of her classmates were already reading *Studio Classroom* (*kōng-zhōng yīng-yǔ jiào-shì* 空中英語教室), an advanced-level English magazine issued by the same publisher. Yvonne confessed that 'I felt a little bit scared' by such a discrepancy between herself and those high achievers. Yvonne's emotional perturbation served to motivate her even more to achieve.

Appropriation of dialogic interaction: Among the prestigious resources afforded to high-ability classes in Suburbany were 'famous teachers' (*míng-shī* 名師) and extra learning sessions on Saturdays taught by foreign English teachers. Access to these resources appeared to assist Yvonne and Eddie in becoming central participants. A grammar-based pedagogy characterised a generally decontextualised English learning experience in the classroom and seemed to have been counterbalanced by the presence of foreign English teachers in Suburbany School. Given her past learning history, Yvonne was particularly interested in attending foreign teachers' classes and appreciated the more interactive pedagogic modalities. However, she was not satisfied with the whole-class teaching method employed by her current foreign teacher. Six of the highest English achievers, including Eddie, with intermediate level GEPT accreditation were allocated to a different classroom for advanced lessons with another foreign English teacher who had higher pedagogic qualifications. The formation of this group, of which Yvonne was not a member, reinforced her perception of her relatively 'low' social situation and exacerbated her discontent with whole-class teaching and pedagogic style.

Yvonne's perceived 'lower' social position and, hence, dissatisfaction led her to attend a much smaller class of four students taught by a new foreign English tutor who was paid for by the four students on a weekly basis. She felt more comfortable with this because it provided greater opportunities to practice speaking and more opportunity to write in English. Moreover, Yvonne's participation in Ms Huang's daily English class appeared to be pivotal in shaping her learning identity. Ms Huang's indirect and humorous manner, emollient classroom control and verbal encouragement particularly inspired Yvonne who said:

> She always 'encourages' (gǔ-lì 鼓勵) students. She amplifies every student's 'merits' (yōu-diǎn 優點)... whenever Ms. Huang asked me to read in front of the class, she would praise me by saying 'your English pronunciation is very good'.

Such praise made it possible for Yvonne to acquire a more positive self-identity. Yvonne felt that she had made much progress in writing and reading English. She recalled that she used to be able to read only 'simple and small' novels. Now she could manage reading 'thicker ones'. The growing sense of competence allowed her to imagine future success in learning English. This image of the future, arguably, served to organise her own thoughts, manage her own feelings and direct her own actions to fit in with this imagined, 'becoming' self (Holland *et al.*, 1998).

Hakka Rural School: Wendy and Chris

Wendy and Chris were central participants in Ms Mei's class in Hakka Rural School. They had similar learning trajectories and had been encouraged by their mothers, were sent to cram school and were supported by their Hakka culture which emphasised academic study. Ms Mei used indirect classroom control techniques in lessons. Wendy achieved slightly higher than Chris and enjoyed a high level of interaction with her mother and Ms Mei at school.

Wendy, an ethnic Hakka and elder child, was among the most diligent students in Ms Mei's class and it was on her recommendation that I came to know Wendy and learned that she had been very enthusiastic in participating in English competitions within and outside school. During the course of classroom observation, I was particularly impressed with her diligence, especially in taking notes, as many good 'Chinese students' tend to do in class. Wendy had participated in the local English-speaking contest in 2004 and was titled as rural, regional champion. Unfortunately, she was defeated in the suburban, Kaohsiung county competition, though she had spent some time rehearsing her scripts with Ms Mei during class breaks. She described her dismay as follows:

> I went to join an English speaking contest.... I felt their English was 'beautiful' (piào-liang 漂亮) and more native-like.... Most of the competitors were from Fengshan area (i.e., suburban Kaohsiung). The champion spoke very 'beautiful' English in particular.

When she entered suburban regional levels of the competition she became aware of a limitation common to rural students. In comparison with those students who spoke 'beautiful' and native-sounding English, she regarded her accent as 'a bit weird' (*guài-guài-de* 怪怪的). Rural students had little access to foreign English language teachers and therefore did not hear native English accents. Wendy expressed disappointment and 'envy' with respect to her urban peers.

Chris also started his English learning in a local cram school in Year 3 and then moved to a nearby suburban township cram school where foreign teachers were available in Year 4. Encouraged by his cram school, he took part in the elementary level of the GEPT. He failed by one point and expressed his determination to 'try again next January (in 2005)'. However, many peripheral participants were also cram school goers, like Mark in Mr Yuan's class, in Hakka Rural School, so that a closer look at students' appropriation of various types of family cultural capital or other cultural resources like cram school experience is required.

Parental support: Wendy and Chris experienced similar learning experiences in cram school. Wendy's parents were both Hakka and worked together at home running a frozen food company as a small-scale, family business. Compared to urban students whose parents were able to provide ample resources, such as foreign travel (e.g. Yvonne in Suburbany School) and foreign teacher experience (e.g. Helen in Urbany School), Wendy's family cultural capital was relatively moderate:

> They did not 'push' (*yāo-qiú* 要求) me to study English.... They did not ask me to go to cram school until school started teaching English (in Year 3).... They told me that English will be very 'important' (*zhòng-yào* 重要) in the future.... I did not 'hate' (*tǎo-yàn* 討厭) English, so I went to a cram school.

In Wendy's account, the word 'push' highlights the fact that many Hakka parents tend to engage their children to go to cram school. Wendy's parents clearly articulated the importance of learning English and she reported that they checked daily on her school and cram school work. To encourage her to work hard, they reminded her of the importance of learning for the sake of her own future prospects rather than for them. As Wendy also reported, her mother said 'if you work harder now, you will not have to live a tough life in the future'.

Wendy was particularly encouraged by her mother to become a schoolteacher, collectively recognised as one of the best careers for girls in Taiwanese society and especially within the Hakka community. Wendy's interaction with her mother was an important resource. Her mother, for example, 'helped me order English magazines... told me to try my best and see how far I can go (i.e. taking GEPT)'. This was exceptional because not many high achieving Hakka students, including Sharon in Class F, aspired to take the GEPT English language proficiency exam. Interestingly, Wendy's mother typified the unique dual gender roles of Hakka women, mentioned in Chapter 3. According to students' questionnaires, three times as many Hakka mothers (33%) were likely to encourage their children to learn English than fathers (11%). This 'mother–child' interaction exemplified not only a unique Taiwanese cultural trait of 'men exterior and women interior', but mirrored the continuing roles of Hakka women in taking multiple responsibility for domesticity, children's schoolwork and assisting with family businesses, the modern counterpart of traditional agricultural work.

Cram school learning: Like many of their Hakka counterparts, Wendy and Chris had gone to cram schools every day after school since their primary years. Wendy had begun in Year 5 and reported that English had been taught predominantly through grammar-based texts and placed emphasis on getting ahead of the lessons scheduled in the textbook. This gave a certain competitive advantage to the pedagogy and fitted well within local Hakka culture, pleasing many parents:

> We were asked to learn vocabulary and tackled school textbook content. We started to learn Year 7 textbook content in Year 5.... I did not 'encounter' (*jiē-chù* 接觸) listening practice until attending Year 7 in Hakka Rural because it would be evaluated in school exams.

However, due to this competitive spirit, Wendy had to learn 'Year 7 textbook content in Year 5', which was exactly two years ahead of the schedule. Under such conditions, it would be interesting to speculate how many Hakka students became 'inattentive' (in Helen's word) because of the fast pace of lessons.

Mountainside School: Vincent and Vanessa

Mountainside School students had no cram schools within their local community during my fieldwork in 2004. Some central participants with appropriate family resources accessed those in a nearby township, like Vincent and Vanessa, both indigenous Paiwan students with similar English learning trajectories. Vincent and Vanessa were hard working, concentrated in class and had the highest English attainments. Both also had exceptional parental encouragement and engagement in learning English. In Mountainside School, they were the 'haves', though on quite a different scale from students elsewhere, such as Helen, Yvonne and Eddie in urban or suburban schools. Moreover, their learning experiences were embedded in a broader, athletically oriented indigenous culture, which seemed to influence the very different trajectories from those of the central participants from other social groups in Taiwan.

Vincent, a timid boy and a single child in a Christian family, was the quietest boy in Ms Lu's class. During the course of my classroom observation, I found Vincent special not only because of his good academic performance but because of his relative timidity as an indigenous boy in contrast to other peers who tended to be outgoing and sometimes verbally aggressive in English classes. Unlike others, known for their athletic prowess, he was not particularly conversational and talked slowly in our interview and in our field encounters. His personal disposition seems to be reflected in his English learning processes which were 'slow but steady', a learning style nicely captured by his claim that 'while learning new things, I tend to get used to it slowly (*màn-man shì-yìng* 慢慢適應)'. Vincent was not particularly interested in learning English when he started it in Year 3 in a cram school located in a Holo township 30 minutes from Mountainside. He recalled experiencing 'a little rejection perhaps' because he was too timid to study with other non-indigenous 'strangers'. Out of curiosity, however, he gradually found interest and wanted to progress. Vincent's mother commented on his development as follows:

> He has the tendency to feel 'timid' (*bù-hǎo-yì-si* 不好意思) at anything at the first try… indigenous kids mostly belong to 'restless' (*hào-dòng* 好動) and 'agile' types. I think his classmates are far more agile than him. But Vincent is working harder than any other peers.

Given Vincent's timidity and limited conversation, his mother's description is useful here for mapping Vincent's learning trajectory. According to her, while Vincent tended to be 'shy' when encountering new tasks, he would not give up once familiar with them. His initial reluctance over cram school attendance suggested that he was not used to encountering non-indigenous children outside the Paiwan community. Vincent was not used to those 'plain dwellers' (*píng-dì-rén* 平地人) because he said the Holo kids had a slightly different complexion from his. Her mother's encouragement in saying 'just give yourself a go and have fun!' eventually enabled him to progress.

Vanessa was another high achieving girl student in Ms Lin's class. In comparison with her 'verbally aggressive' indigenous peers, she was rather diligent and concentrated. Consistent with the indigenous propensity for singing, dancing and athletic prowess, if not stereotyped, Vanessa liked singing English songs very much: 'I like listening to English songs…. I also learn English from listening to songs'. Vanessa believed that singing English songs helped her to improve her listening ability and contributed to her successful accreditation at the elementary level of the Cambridge English as a second language for speakers of other languages (ESOL) examination earlier and the elementary level of the GEPT in 2005. Vanessa longed to go abroad and her 'curiosity' combined with her determination to get regular access to English songs provided her with aspirations, as she explained:

I have a 'strong aspiration' (*hěn-xiàng-wǎng* 很嚮往) (i.e. going abroad). I feel the scenery in foreign countries is more beautiful than Taiwan. I want to go for a look, perhaps it is partly out of my 'curiosity'.... English is an international language and it is better to use English to communicate with foreigners.

Vanessa recognised that English was 'an international language', and a tool to communicate with people around the world. However, her personal aspirations did not seem to entirely account for her central participation in the English communities of practice. The rural location of Paiwan community seemed to have constrained students' English learning. The support that she and Vincent gained from their families appeared pivotal in shaping their English learning trajectories.

Parental support: Vincent's and Vanessa's mothers, both senior high graduates, provided their children with encouragement and were actively engaged in their learning. Both were interested and helpful in responding to my questionnaire survey and in interviews. Vincent's father and Vanessa's mother were high school classmates and both families were well acquainted with each other. Vincent's mother worked as a cleaner in a clinic in a nearby Holo township which made it possible for her to give Vincent a routine ride to cram school. 'We hope he can learn one more language so we let him learn English as early as in Year 3', his mother suggested. Her dedication to the cram school routine lasted for five years until Vincent began at Mountainside School, and only stopped because Vincent became exhausted as she explained:

> We have no cram schools particularly for English learning... the only way is to send them to Chao-zhou (the nearby Holo township)... some parents tend to regard it a 'waste of time' sending children around.

Most other Paiwan parents could not take their children to cram school because there was no bus. In comparison with other indigenous parents, Vincent's mother's involvement with her children's education was exceptional. Most Paiwan people had little access to English in daily life in contrast to the heavily Westernised, modern, Taiwanese urban cities. Very little opportunity was available for Vincent to practice English either at home or in the community. However, Vincent watched English TV programmes and read at home, in addition to his cram and formal school work. He was provided with English storybooks and magazines to read at home, though sometimes his mother did feel like sending him out to do a little sport, like other boys. With no one at home with whom to practice English, watching English TV programmes became Vincent's next best option. As his mother admitted:

> Sometimes we will block the Chinese subtitles when we are watching English films on TV together ((she chuckles with a little guilt)). Sometimes we feel 'sorry' (*kě-lián* 可憐) for him because he has to learn something even when watching TV at leisure.

The action of blocking 'the Chinese subtitles' could mean very different things in different social contexts. For some groups, it may provide an effective way of helping children to learn English. However, for indigenous groups, this somewhat arbitrary action seemed to have clashed with a comparatively 'easy-going' lifestyle (see Chapter 3) in this rural village albeit Vincent would normally translate happily upon request, according to his mother.

Mother–child intersubjectivity: Vanessa's mother worked as a caretaker in a local crèche. She was herself interested in learning English and knew that it was important for children's future. The following field note indicates this and the 'curiosity' of indigenous children.

> It is a hilly kindergarten, ten minutes' walk away from Mountainside School…. Vanessa's mother reveals that, for marketing reasons, they have invited a local Taiwanese English teacher to teach English on a weekly basis. As a caretaker, she has opportunities to learn with children, which suits her interest in learning English. During the break all the children ran out playing in the tiny yard…. She introduced me to some curious kids telling them about my role as an English teacher. To say hello, I asked 'How are you?' and 'What's your name?' respectively. To my surprise, they could respond fluently with pronunciation in English (at such a young age) and with gleaming smiles. (Field note, 21 November 2004)

Given her mother's personal interest in learning English and recognition of its importance, Vanessa was encouraged to attend a cram school for English as early as Year 3. In another cram school from Year 4, Vanessa followed its interior English accreditation system, starting at Level A. However, her experience was not all plain sailing. Tuition cost NT$6000 dollars (about £150) per three-month term, engendering financial strain which her father worried about and used to oppose her attendance when she reached Level B in Year 4. She poignantly remembered:

> My father is a somewhat 'traditional' (*chuán-tǒng* 傳統) man who takes money very seriously, but my mother values my schooling…. (she chuckles) So I have been stopped from going to cram school for a while. But my mum helps me move on.

Vanessa eventually continued her cram school learning following her mother's successful negotiation with her father, though tension about it continued to exist within the family. Her desire to learn English out of curiosity helped her to get through difficult times at home, as she said firmly: 'For me, I think English is interesting as a foreign language. I am so curious about this language that I like it very much. I think I should move on'. With this aspiration, Vanessa reached Level F in the cram school and was entitled to take part in the elementary level of the GEPT in 2004, eventually achieving it in January 2005.

Peripheral participants in learning English: Different stories uncovered

In comparison with the individual learning trajectories of the central participants in the four schools, attention is now turned to the peripheral participants in continuing to try to clarify why some students achieve differently from others with whom they attend the same school, interact with the same English teachers or have access to similar cultural resources. We see these peripheral participants as positioning themselves or being positioned as moving away from the 'centre' of their English communities of practice. Some became disillusioned and disengaged from English. The experiences of the peripheral participants, such as Howard (Urbany School), Mark (Hakka Rural School) and Jack (Mountainside School), contrasted greatly with the central participants. Though the sample of students interviewed was small and thus findings are limited, it is interesting to note that the peripheral group contained five boys and only one girl, suggesting gender differences in attitudes towards English (see Table 6.6).

Urbany School: Howard, the astray sheep

Howard was one of the many students put off by English in Ms Wu's class in bilingual Urbany School and perhaps the most unusual peripheral participant – the 'astray sheep' (in my own words) wandering around the border of the English learning communities of practice. He was a third-generation Mainlander and the eldest child in a family of three, a 'have'

Table 6.6 Peripheral interviewee participants in four schools

School	Student	Gender	Ethnicity	Teacher	Scores	Participation
Urbany	Howard	M	Mainlander	Ms Wu	30	Peripheral
Suburbany	James	M	Holo	Ms Sun	20	Peripheral
Hakka Rural	Mark	M	Hakka	Mr Yuan	36	Peripheral
	Fay	F	Hakka	Ms Mei	29	Peripheral
Mountainside	Jack	M	Paiwan	Ms Lu	24	Peripheral
	Dave	M	Paiwan	Ms Lu	18	Peripheral

Note: English scores (1–100) were accessed from the first monthly school exam in 2004. Although each school used different test sheets, they followed similar curriculum schedules.

from an affluent family background. His parents had relatively high education levels. There was a striking similarity between his and Ken's father because they were both university graduates in business careers. Both were competent in English as managers who frequently travelled abroad. However, unlike Ken, Howard did not seem to have been given opportunities to actively benefit from foreign travel. He also did not attend cram school.

Bilingual Urbany School sought to provide rich cultural resources and a strong English learning environment. For Howard, however, English at Urbany and other aspects of the school setting did not seem to attract his attention. During observation, Howard's attention either wandered or he dozed off, whereupon Ms Wu usually tried desperately to remind him to sit properly and pay more attention. There were even times when she was nearly 'driven crazy' by Howard and other 'astray sheep' as when they playfully sat in the wrong seats in class. As Carol, Howard's high achieving classmate, put it, 'Howard does not like Ms Wu because he does not like English'. In the following interview (see Extract 6.1), Howard's brief description of his learning experience revealed his deeply held beliefs that informed his actions in school. Most peripheral participants were not as eloquent as their central counterparts in articulating their seemingly poor English learning experiences, though Howard was their most eloquent representative. In cases such as Howard, Mark (Hakka Rural School) and Jack (Mountainside School), interviews predominantly took place on a 'turn-taking' basis in Chinese involving rather short responses.

Extract 6.1:

1 Interviewer:	Could you describe your English learning experience?
2 Howard:	In Year 4, I started learning English … taught in school.
3	I felt 'bored' (*wú-liáo*) because I did not understand it.
4	I felt it was troublesome to recite things ((i.e. alphabetical
5	letters and vocabulary))
6 Interviewer:	Is there anyone at home encouraging you to learn English?
7 Howard:	No. They just said to me 'English has to be learned well'.
8	They did not push me.
9 Interviewer:	What about now in Ms. Wu's class?
10 Howard:	I still fail to comprehend English. I do not follow what she
11	says in class. So I do not like to listen to her.
12 Interviewer:	So, have you thought of why you learn English…?
13 Howard:	I don't know. Perhaps it is used at school… or school subject.
14	People say it is more convenient to use [English].
15	But I feel it is 'very troublesome' (*hǎo-má-fan*).
16 Interviewer:	But do you know people also say it is because English is an

17	'international language'.
18 Howard:	Yes, my father says so because he is a business manager...
19	He often travels abroad...so he is good at English.
20 Interviewer:	I know parents who are good at English tend to help their
21	children with English... Maybe your father has been too busy.
22 Howard:	I don't know. He is good...but he does not teach me.
23	He is going abroad again tomorrow.

Howard seemed to have a very specific view of learning English. For him, English was not perceived as something important or helpful in terms of future benefits but as a 'school subject' (Lines 2 and 13). In contrast to Ken's abundant English home practice and clear explanation of its future importance, Howard seemed to be provided less with encouragement than an abstract order, even mere lip-service: 'English has to be learned well' (Line 7), without follow-up activities. Lack of home practice in English and cram school attendance suggested the fact that English was not particularly valued at home. Howard seemed to have developed a deeply rooted belief, with associated frustration, from his elementary school years that English had to be learned through memorisation (Lines 3 and 4). He expressed his frustration when he said it was 'very troublesome' (Lines 4 and 15). In the classroom, Howard's rejection of learning English was clear. He said 'So I do not like to listen to her' (Line 11). He complained: 'I cannot recite vocabulary...even after someone tells me how to memorize words by using a phonic-based approach, I still cannot do.... English is so difficult for me!'. When asked if he wanted to learn English provided he were given the opportunity, he said:

> No... because I cannot learn it well. I used to try reciting vocabulary but in vain even after writing down that word for a hundred fifty times!... I did so as some people told me but I still could not make it through reciting.

Learning English through memorisation, which dominates pedagogic approaches in Taiwan, was problematic for him. Howard's frustration and rejection of English learning gave rise to his deviant behaviour:

> I feel it is 'meaningless' (*méi-yì-yì* 沒意義).... I fail to learn it by rote. I was allocated here in this school only because I live within this school catchment ((he was not attending Urbany voluntarily)).... When I feel 'all English again' ((a feeling of hatred)), I will rip those bilingual signs off and dump them into the bin.

Howard's 'marginality' (Wenger, 1998) as a member of bilingual Urbany's English learning communities of practice was maintained as an active resistance to the rote learning pedagogy he experienced. He was not alone in this in Urbany School. His English and home-teacher, Mr Lin, pointed out how some other students perceived the bilingual signs:

> I think it is helpful for high achievers if they see and learn.... But for many, the English environment appears to have no 'connection' (*xiāng-guān* 相關) with them. Take my class for example, the signs next to the toilet are immediately torn down when posted.

To those peripheral participants in Urbany School, the bilingual environment tended to represent something 'imposed' or privileged institutionally that contradicted their home values or personal beliefs. Mr Lin's description of such anti-English behaviour helped to explain Howard's attitude and revealed conflicts between home and school and between aspects of the school system.

Howard's experience of rote learning also contradicted Urbany School's stated emphasis on promoting an interactive English learning environment. Howard was so caught up by his past learning history that he still strove to 'memorise' rather than 'practice' English in terms of the opportunities afforded by his school. The overt signs of bilingualism and practice seemed to enrage him. Moreover, Howard attended Urbany School not because of its bilingual environment but 'only because I live within this school catchment'. These words highlighted his involuntary enrolment in Urbany School and added to his alienation. Howard, as a peripheral participant, was positioned and also positioned himself as moving away from the 'centre' of the English learning community of practice. His repulsion of learning English and the meaningless bilingual environment made his peripheral participation understandable.

Hakka Rural School: Mark, the trapped sheep

Mark, a peripheral participant in Mr Yuan's class in Hakka Rural School, was one of the many 'trapped sheep' (in my own words) willing but failing to learn English. In contrast to Howard, Mark demonstrated initial interest in English, possibly because of his mother's encouragement. With such encouragement, he was sent to a cram school for English lessons, like many other Hakka students. Mark reported some everyday English practice at home when playing with his computer (using email and chat rooms), listening to music and perceiving some things written in English at home, in school and on the street. This differed from many other peripheral participants in the four schools who not only demonstrated school failure academically but also claimed to lack everyday English practice at home and community activity level.

Even with maternal encouragement, cram school learning resources and relevant everyday English practice, Mark eventually 'fails to comprehend' (*tīng-bù-dǒng* 聽不懂) English and withdrew from the cram school after six months. The following interview highlights Mark's dismay and portrays his learning identity as a trapped sheep, still trying to find a way out of his quandary.

Extract 6.2:

1 Interviewer:	Could you briefly describe your English learning history?
2 Mark:	I started learning English in Year 6….We were all playing
3	most of the time…so I could not follow the lesson when I
4	attended Year 7 in junior high school.
5 Interviewer:	Which part did you fail to understand?
6 Mark:	I could listen…but failed to write it out. ((i.e., in exams))
7 Interviewer:	In Year 6, did you learn anything like alphabetic letters?
8 Mark:	Yes, only English letters.
9 Interviewer:	Anything else, such as spelling or …
10 Mark:	No.
11 Interviewer:	Was it a foreign English teacher or local one?
12 Mark:	Local.
[…]	
13 Interviewer:	So you did not follow…as long as you were in year 7!
14 Mark:	Yeah…I went to cram school, but still 'did not
15	comprehend' (tīng-bù-dǒng).
16 Interviewer:	Did your parents encourage you to learning English?
17 Mark:	My mother did so, but I still 'tīng-bù-dǒng ' ((chuckles!))
18	My mother was bothered and did not know how to 'solve'
19	(jiě-jué) this problem.
20 Interviewer:	Do you know if your parents know English?
21 Mark:	… I don't know. ((chuckles!))
22 Interviewer:	Have you ever practiced English (for fun) with friends?
23 Mark:	No. ((chuckles!))
24 Interviewer:	…with your family members?
25 Mark:	I guess not.
26 Interviewer:	Do you have any relatives who know English?
27 Mark:	Yes, but they seldom come back here…

Mark seemed to point to a fundamental curriculum gap in learning and teaching English between primary and junior high school level in Taiwan. For example, there is a growing concern over the problems of primary–junior high school transition and how to ensure continuity in pedagogical practice in EFL between the two social settings (e.g. Lin & Byram, 2016). As Mark says, '…in Year 6… We were all playing most of the time… so I could not follow the lesson when I attended Year 7' (Lines 2 and 3). Consistent with the Grades 1–9 national curriculum, 'playing' is highly valued in primary schools; however, this is not the case in junior high. As Mark pointed out, he could 'listen' but 'failed to write it out' (Line 6), representing his prior knowledge of 'play' and audio-based English practice as being denied by junior high school teachers and school culture.

The low status of oral (audio-based) activity in junior high was nicely captured by Abreu's (1995) word 'taboo', referring to teachers in her Brazilian sugarcane farming study who devalued children's home mathematics as inferior to that of the school. Oral English seems to be devalued as written English (e.g. grammar-translation methods and written exams) is distinctly privileged in junior high school. As illustrated in Chapter 5, 'grammar rules' involving discrete linguistic patterns are predominantly taught and highly valued in junior high classrooms. Given little time for oral practice, students learned English through memorisation and were constantly assessed in order to test out their knowledge and competence in English. The following account exemplifies the inferior status of oral English, as perceived by students, not their teacher. Dismayed by her students' reluctance, Ms Mei complained that

> I am often provided with free sample GEPT magazines with CD-ROMs from publishers which I like to give out to students as gifts.... I told them not to feel 'under pressure'... just 'give yourself a go'. Some mid-ability level students will try it for fun but some high achieving students will not because they fear the difficulty.

In fact, Ms Mei perceived the importance of both oral and written English practice and had tried to bridge the gap between them. As she says, 'I tried very hard indeed', even stating their market value: 'They cost two hundred dollars... take them if you are willing to try'. Students' passive response and hesitation usually disappointed her, causing her to speculate that maybe English was viewed by Hakka students as synonymous with a written 'test' (*kǎo-shì* 考試), leading to rejection of free audio English practice. This speculation exactly mirrored Fay's quandary as another peripheral participant in Hakka Rural, as she confessed 'When I think of English, I think of test, followed by hatred and then leave it alone'.

In Mark's interview, it is worth noting that he was provided with an opportunity to engage in traditional, typically grammar-based cram school practice. In the Hakka 'town of PhDs', excessive emphasis on 'academic study' (*dú-shū* 讀書) and, mainly traditional, cram school going seem to intensify the value asymmetry between the two kinds of approaches as social organisations of practice. Mark's participation in traditional cram school justified his non-participative membership identity: 'I went to cram school, but still did not comprehend' (Line 14). Moreover, the declaration, 'I do not understand grammar and all other stuff... even after I have asked questions from former English teachers' revealed in his questionnaire response also mirrored his troubled situation arising from grammar-based learning. The lack of interaction with friends or family members (Lines 20–27) concerning everyday English practice did nothing to assuage, indeed it contributed to the circumstance of his learning problem that remained unresolved (Lines 18 and 19).

Mountainside School: Jack, the athletic dreamer

Jack, a peripheral participant in Ms Lu's class in Mountainside School, was one of the many 'athletic dreamers' (in my own words) who were hoping to become future athletes perhaps as a way out of poverty. Like many other indigenous students, he demonstrated initial interest in learning English in an 'open-minded' and 'curious' manner, like Vincent and Vanessa, in terms of the audio-based approach valued in primary school. Jack also shared their dream of going abroad, albeit through different endeavours. However, in comparison with Vincent and Vanessa's family resources, Jack appeared to be teetering, neither engaged in cram school learning nor demonstrating everyday English practice at home or at community level. The following interview extract may provide a schematic picture as to why he became a peripheral participant. As with Vincent, his relative inarticulacy concerning English learning experience made it more than incumbent upon me to ensure that I did not over-direct his response.

Extract 6.3:

1 Interviewer:	Could you briefly describe your English learning history?	
2 Jack:	I started in Year 5 in elementary school…	
3 Interviewer:	How do you feel your learning at that time?	
4 Jack:	Very happy!	
5 Interviewer:	Can you describe what you were learning?	
6 Jack:	I cannot remember… it was a long time ago.	
7 Interviewer:	It's fine. Did you have some games or interactive teaching?	
8 Jack:	Yes, we did.	
9 Interviewer:	Did you like such learning at that time?	
10 Jack:	Yeah.	
11 Interviewer:	…any difference between when you start learning and now?	
12 Jack:	I started to dislike it when I got to Year 7.	
13 Interviewer:	Why is that?	
14 Jack:	…because I did not understand…what is 'verb' (dòng-cí)…	
15 Interviewer:	You mean grammar and sentence patterns.	
16 Jack:	Yes.	
17 Interviewer:	Do you have any idea about grammar such as verbs?	
18 Jack:	They are more difficult to recite (bù-hǎo-jì) …	
19	I can recite it today but will forget it tomorrow…	

[...]	
20 Interviewer:	Do you have any opportunity practicing English at home?
21 Jack:	A little writing...few days before the school exam, I will start
22	writing and 'reciting hard' (*měng-bèi*)!
23 Interviewer:	Recite vocabulary, sentence patterns and grammars...?
24 Jack:	More or less...mainly vocabulary...
25 Interviewer:	Do you know the importance of learning English?
26 Jack:	Going abroad ... to USA.
27 Interviewer:	So do you hope to go abroad in the future?
28 Jack:	I don't think I will unless I become a 'national basketball player'!

In Extract 6.3, Jack appeared to have a 'very happy' (Line 4) time learning English in primary school years and enjoyed learning (Lines 9 and 10). The 'asymmetrical relationship' (Abreu, 1995) of primary and junior high school practices emerged that when he attended the latter; 'I started to dislike it when I got to Year 7' (Line 12) due to more grammar-based learning (Lines 15 and 16). Like Howard, Urbany School's 'black sheep', who felt compelled to but failed to learn vocabulary by rote, Jack appeared to feel a similar quandary; English grammar 'are more difficult to recite' (Line 18). His only English practice at home was to recite 'vocabulary' (Line 24) a few days before the school exam by 'writing and reciting hard' (Line 22) as a basic effort to secure minimum scores from the vocabulary test. When asked if he perceived the importance of learning English, Jack pointed out his dream of 'Going abroad... to USA' (Line 26), yet immediately reflected upon his own constraints and regarded such a dream as impossible. He knew there was a way out of this impasse, saying 'I don't think I have the chance unless I become a national basketball player' (Lines 27 and 28). Based on his interest in playing basketball and the school cultural system of promoting athletic performances, with various bursaries as encouragement, Jack had been provided with a form of cultural 'scaffolding' (Woods *et al.*, 1976), such that he could project himself as being a future national basketball player. It could be argued that, if 'going abroad' was Jack's ultimate goal, being an athlete was probably the most effective way of realising it rather than changing his peripheral participation trajectory in English learning. A closer look at this cultural scaffolding of sport and athleticism within the Paiwan community indicated that Jack was not alone in being inspired in such a direction. Jack's aspiration echoed many of those of his indigenous peers, symptomatised overt, athletic, rather than academic, let alone, English, learning communities of practice.

Mapping CFL Learning Trajectories in England

In England, both central and peripheral participants were detected in learning Chinese as a foreign language, although most of the

Table 6.7 Characteristics of students interviewed in the four schools in England

School	Students	Gender	Encouragement	Participation
Highland	Amelia	F	Mum/Dad	Central
	Ellie	F	Mum/Dad	Central
	Tabby	F	Mum/Dad	Central
	Rebecca	F	Mum/Dad	Central
	Kira	F	Mum/Dad	Central
	Megan	F	N/A	Central
St Peter's	Erica	F	Mum/Dad	Central
	Candy	F	Mum/Dad	Central
	Michele	F	Mum/Dad	Central
	Jenny	F	Mum	Central
	Rosa	F	Mum	Central
King's	Steven	M	Mum/Dad	Central
	Angela	F	Mum/Dad	Central
	Holly	F	Mum/Dad	Central
	Tom	M	Mum/Dad	Central
	Jenifer	F	Mum/Dad	Peripheral

student interviewees were central participants sitting the General Certificate of Secondary Education (GCSE) at King's School and at St Peter's School (see Table 6.7). Unfortunately, given greater time constraint on my fieldwork in England, access to students' parents for interview was impossible, so that the following descriptions of individual students' Chinese learning in communities of practice will largely draw from student questionnaire data, class observation and teachers' and students' interview accounts. To focus our discussion, I will foreground central participants, such as Steven and Angela (Year 11), then Jenifer (Year 8), the only peripheral participant to be interviewed, at the independent King's School. Jenifer revealed that she was trying to move forward through studying harder and her case was not comparable to those Taiwanese peripheral participants who either tended to 'give up' or be 'trapped' in English learning communities of practice, a matter of difference which I will turn to later in this section.

Learning Chinese in communities of practice: The individual cases

During the course of fieldwork, 16 students (14 girls and 2 boys) were interviewed, all first encountered during the course of classroom observation either in 2013 or 2015 in the four schools in England. As in Taiwan, after a period of one month, their classroom teachers recommended a list of those who they considered to be central and possible peripheral participants in their classrooms. Demographic information was also accessed from students' personal and parents' questionnaires, though attainment in Chinese was only provided for Mr Blake's class at King's School as evidence of students' academic performance. As with the sociocultural study undertaken in Taiwan, the process of selecting and accessing students to be interviewed involved taking into account teachers' knowledge, my observations, students' questionnaire responses and their academic attainment. Of the 16 students eventually interviewed, 15 (13 girls, 2 boys) were central and only 1 (girl) a peripheral participant. Jenifer, in Mr Blake's class, was characterised as 'peripheral' rather than central because she scored only 56 (1–100) in the school regular semester exam in 2015. I hoped, as did Mr Blake, that in the course of her interview I might learn how her Chinese learning might be helped appropriately.

Central participants in learning Chinese: Angela and Steven from King's School

King's School: Angela, the hard-working girl

Angela and Steven, like their nine other classmates in Ms Tan's class, were all classified as central participants in Chinese learning communities of practice. Like many of her peers at King's School, Angela's parents had a high education level and high-profile jobs. Her mother had a bachelor's degree in the arts and worked as a flight purser for an international airline. Her father had a bachelor's and master's degree in law and worked as a senior police officer. I was curious as to whether her mixed heritage, with her mother from an Asian ethnic background, had shaped her family cultural capital that helped her access Chinese. However, Angela noted that her high-ability performance in the Chinese language was by no means largely the cause of this cultural heritage. She said:

> I wouldn't say that my mixed heritage was largely the cause of the inspiration for my Chinese learning as my mother spoke Thai and had taught me basic sayings and words from when I was about 5. This by no means affected the speed of my Chinese learning. Sometimes I have used Thai pronunciations to help with the memorisations of the Pinyin on some characters, but for the majority of my learning my mixed background was not a very large factor.

Despite the fact that Angela's parents were very supportive of her learning and believed that 'it is fundamental to have a basic understanding of the language (i.e. Chinese)', she attributed her excellent performance to her appreciation of the 'difference' of Chinese from other European languages, such as French, which are mostly 'phonetical alphabets'. She thought 'the Chinese characters and the drawing aspect and learning are completely new stuff and actually... I feel that... I'm kind of obsessed into it and then I enjoy it so much'. It could be argued that it was largely due to her positive attitude towards learning the Chinese language as a 'new and different' subject that she became a central participant. At the interpersonal plane of analysis, her close social interaction with Ms Tan, her Chinese instructor, could not be ignored. Although Angela had never felt like 'it was the teaching that led to a bad mark', she had enjoyed Ms Tan's teaching and said, 'Ms. Wang… was really really nice and…. Overall I am quite happy with all of the teaching methods I have been exposed to throughout my learning journey'.

Angela believed that it had to be a student's individual responsibility and effort to achieve academic success, rather than blaming failure on others, such as teachers. She had begun attending King's School in Year 9 in 2013 and started learning Chinese in Year 9 in a class that had commenced it in Year 7 and she had, after extra hard work catching up in the summer of 2014, eventually climbed to the top of the class in academic performance. When reflecting on the highs and lows of her Chinese learning journey so far, she said:

> I think the real highs for me when learning Mandarin were seeing really good exam results even in my first year of learning, I was scoring way up in the 90%'s and making very few errors, I once got 99.5% in my end of year exam and it was these scores that gave me confidence in my learning and that knowledge that I can do well in learning this language. The only low points were probably the frustration at not being able to memorise the vocabulary, especially in tests where you know the answer but you can't remember it!

King's School: Steven, the creative boy

Steven, like Angela, was not only a central participant in his Chinese learning communities of practice but was also observed to be a very creative and diligent student in class. Steven, like Angela, could be classified as a 'have' in terms of parental encouragement and arrangement as family resources. His mother attended university and his father went to an art school. Both his parents started work in media, his mother as a production manager for a television company and his father having a graphic design company before starting a new business more recently. Steven used to take part in the school's foreign travel programme to Beijing, China, and was inspired by this foreign cultural experience, although he would not be 'taking Mandarin further than GCSE level'. In talking about his aspirations in learning Chinese, he said:

> In terms of my own aspirations, I am not actually taking Mandarin further than GCSE level; however I would love to revisit it later in life. After visiting Beijing a few years ago, I was inspired to reach a level of fluent

conversation. I have always believed it is a great skill to be multilingual, and one that is sought after by international companies. It seems I perhaps have a future in engineering, so maybe learning Mandarin will be very helpful if I work overseas in the future. (4 December 2016)

Rather than confine his aspiration to Chinese learning at the academic level, Steven seemed to have projected his future career as an engineer while working abroad where Chinese proficiency could be an advantage. Attending a fee-paying, independent school, he seemed to have enjoyed the learning resources provided in making Chinese a compulsory subject. These included invited speakers and lecturers for various subjects in order to 'give another insight to the subject and take it deeper than the basic learning level'. He said:

> The teachers at our school seem to make extra effort with class resources, spending time making detailed PowerPoints and handouts to aid our learning. Besides this we often have speakers and lecturers in for various subjects to give another insight to the subject and take it deeper than the basic learning level. I believe for the most part, lectures are something that is only offered at private schools like King's School.

In addition to the resources provided by his family and the school, Steven appeared to have enjoyed the classroom teaching of Chinese. The teachers at his school seemed to 'make extra effort with class resources'. We have already seen this exemplified in our discussion in the previous chapter in the case of Ms Tan's 'thinking-based' pedagogy, through which Steven's class would have been encouraged to do creative thinking when it came to learning Chinese characters:

> For 30 minutes, students were given opportunities to teach/learn at the same time during group work session. It's thought-provoking because students were encouraged to challenge (to 'fight back if you have better ideas' in Ms. Tan's words) the teaching of their peers. This form of learning by thinking/teaching 'sī-kǎo-zhōng xué-xí / jiào-xué xiāng-zhǎng' (思考中學習/教學相長) is exactly what can be seen in today's class. Students were empowered to teach and learn through challenging tasks via discussion. For example, Steven, the most active male student; when he is describing the word – sun screen 'fang-shài shuāng' (防晒霜) to his classmates, he described the word – 'shài' (晒- literally means 'burning') by saying that 'the sun – "rì" (日) and the West – "xī" (西) is that when the Westerners tend to have "white" skin, so they are venerable to the sun beam. Therefore they need sun scream to protect their skin'. Of course, some students challenged him that not all Westerners are 'white'… but this indeed helps other peers to memorise this phrase and characters effectively. (Field note, 5 November 2015)

In fact, Ms Tan's class was very innovative in linking new Chinese words with what had already been learned in very student-centred, thought-provoking and effective ways.

Parental support: As with Yvonne and Eddie from 'high-ability classes' in Suburbany School in Taiwan, both Angela's and Steven's parents had high education levels and either extensive foreign cultural experiences (Angela's) or ran a business (Steven's) which may have led them to view Chinese as an important tool in future job mobility or academic aspirations. Comparing these four students' family cultural capital, the similarity of parents with middle-class incomes and social status appear to stand out as one of the significant factors that contribute to their children's being central participants in learning English/Chinese.

Appropriation of school elitism: As mentioned earlier, our cross-cultural comparison of students' English/Chinese learning experiences between the 'high-ability classes' in Suburbany School in Taiwan and in King's School in England has allowed us to understand students' 'participatory appropriation' (Rogoff, 1995) of their schools' elite elements and 'forward thinking' school visions. There was an interesting overlap of elite characteristics between Suburbany School and King's School. All four students went through a highly competitive process of academic selection before attending high-ability classrooms. All of the students were provided with dedicated and experienced 'famous teachers' (*míngshī* 名師), Ms Huang and Ms Tan. And while in terms of English and Chinese proficiency level, students at both schools were not only of above average competence in listening, speaking, reading and writing skills in English/Chinese, but academic competition and mounting pressure to achieve success were also inevitable facets of their school lives.

Appropriation of school vision: We have highlighted the language learning trajectories of some highly successful central participants impelled by the 'visions' of their respective schools. In 'forward thinking' King's School, the intentions that imbued its 'cultural scaffolding' directed teaching and learning, as in the case of making Chinese compulsory, in ways that deeply affected students' school life. While at Taiwanese Suburbany School, many students were compelled to pursue language and academic excellence and, somewhat in contrast, in Mountainside School, sport and athleticism, Angela and Steven, at King's School, were not alone in not just being encouraged to achieve A level, like their school peers elsewhere, but rather A* (*plus*) as the target for all students here.

The peripheral participant in learning Chinese

As indicated in Table 6.7, among those 16 students who were interviewed, only 1 girl (Jenifer) was characterised as a peripheral participant. Her lone presence should not be taken as an indication that British students learning Chinese are doing better than their Taiwanese peers in learning English. Many British students encounter difficulties in learning Chinese and end up dropping out (e.g. CiLT, 2007). Jenifer was one who struggled but was determined to overcome her difficulties in the journey of learning Chinese. She was both brave enough and delighted to accept my invitation to share her stories.

King's School: Jenifer, the struggling girl

Jenifer, in Mr Blake's class, was one of the students who struggled with learning Chinese. Like many students at King's School, she was doing three foreign languages simultaneously, in her case Chinese, Spanish and Russian. She had been learning Chinese since Year 7 for two years but seemed to encounter more difficulties in learning it than others. She said:

> Chinese is a lot more difficult.... because I've been doing it for longer hours and I'm kind of getting behind because I moved to a new class as well... kind of behind... yeah... I'm kind of behind a lot then ((wry smile!))... I learned it only for 2 years... try to catch up.

According to Jenifer, the main problem for her was that she moved from a beginner's class to a more advanced one and started to feel left behind. One aspect of learning Chinese that seemed to trouble her most was speaking, as Chinese is a tonal language, different tones indicating different meanings even with the same Pinyin:

> ...speaking has different tones and learning... you know the tones of the words... and how different tones means something completely different... that's really hard.... it's just... I didn't realise how important the tones were, so I didn't really learn them as much at the beginning when I should have. ...so now I struggle with different tones.

Another source of trouble for her seemed to be how to comprehend the Chinese characters, although she loved writing them. According to Jenifer, 'I struggle with it a lot because a lot of characters and different radicals can make the characters all the same,... um... yeah.. ((looking frustrated))'. She said she had tried to memorise the characters and did a lot of school work at home, but still felt it was 'really hard' because there were lots of stroking orders in writing Chinese. She said:

> Um... I do a lot of memorisation, such as the website, and I try to write lots of characters from the same language we learn from the school, so um... and I spoke to Mr. Blake that I have struggled with Mandarin... um... like at home, go over things like in class and do my prep orally... also trying to revise things and... yeah, it's really hard, but I really want to build it up.

Jenifer seemed to have done a lot to try to sort out this academic problem without having possible recourse like cram school attendance, contact with a language tutor (*qǐng-jiā-jiào* 請家教) or reaching for the helping hands of parents who know English, to which students in her position in Taiwan have resorted. In England, not many parents, including Jenifer's, know Chinese. Nevertheless, regarding her parents' encouragement for her to learn Chinese, Jenifer said that, 'my parents love that.... My parents think that's really a good idea, yeah, they think it's brilliant'. They knew Jenifer's struggle and did try to offer her some help. For example, Jenifer said that 'yeah, like my mom knows I struggle with that, so she likes to make me do... she makes me go on to the computer and practice... but she cannot really help me because she doesn't know Chinese... ((wry smile))'.

In sum, Jenifer was still trying her best to carry on learning Chinese even though she knew very well that it was hard especially when she got 'so much homework and try to do three languages and... a lot of stress...'. Yet, despite her struggle with speaking tones and writing characters, she was provided with enough social scaffolding, including her parents' encouragement, the caring support of her schoolteacher, Mr Blake, and the 'forward thinking' school vision and ethos that make Chinese compulsory, to project herself into future career perspectives and was willing to carry on. In her own words about learning Chinese:

> I think it's like an upcoming language... I think it will be really big soon... because China's like developing and there are so much going on right now.... I think soon you will be able to be forced not speaking a bit... if you got the options like all the facilities in Mandarin... lots of people like my friends are really going for it, so even though it's hard... they even know I struggle with it.... I really will get to GCSE... because it's a cool language.

Identity, Value and Learning English/Chinese

Certain issues appear to have emerged from our investigation of the interplay between these central or peripheral participants' mental processes and their cultural, historical and institutional milieu in Taiwan and in England. The following discussion will take up the issue of student identity formation in relation to imagined futures and current actions and trajectories in learning English in Taiwan and Chinese in England.

Identity as imagined futures

Holland *et al.* (1998) argued that human beings have habitual liking for entering into imaginary worlds, which can inspire new actions. Inspired by Vygotsky and Bourdieu, they pointed out that

> Vygotsky gave central place to collectively developed signs and symbols as the media by which children's mental and emotional faculties were culturally formed. He paid special attention to the role of tangible objects, made collectively into artifacts by the attribution of meaning, as tools that people use to affect their own and others' thinking, feeling, and behaviour. Through habitual use these cultural tools become resources available for personal use, mnemonics of the activities they facilitate, and finally constitutive of thought, emotion, and behaviour. Describing how children develop the ability to enter into an imagined world, Vygotsky speaks of a 'pivot', a mediating or symbolic device that the child uses not just to organise a particular response but to pivot or shift into the frame of a different world. (Holland *et al.*, 1998: 50)

Indeed, many of the human activities that engage energy and interest tend to have an imaginative component. It is this competence that makes possible the 'figured world', 'a social and cultural realm of interpretation in which particular characters and actors are recognised, significance is assigned to certain acts, and particular outcomes are valued over others' (Holland *et al.*, 1998: 52).

Through a cross-cultural comparison between young people learning English in Taiwan and learning Chinese in England, a common theme of 'studying abroad' (in Taiwan) and 'doing business' (in England) as an imaginary future worlds or 'figured worlds' (Holland *et al.*, 1998) of some kind has emerged from the data, particularly among the relative 'haves', in contrast to the locally bounded 'have-not' worlds. Provided with rich cultural capital by their locales, some central participants seemed able to envision a self-identity, such as Julia's at Suburbany School of studying abroad, and Steven's at King's School of doing business, an ambition in value symmetry with the social organisation of practices of their home and school. Next, I will describe a case from Taiwan – Julia, one of the central participants in Ms Sun's mixed-ability class in Suburbany School, as an example, to demonstrate how family and school cultural capital and her identity of the imagined future contributed to her central participation in the English learning communities of practice.

Suburbany School: Julia, the xenophile

Julia was a third-generation Mainlander and the elder of two children. Although her academic achievement was not as high as the other elite students, Yvonne and Eddie, in Ms Huang's class, Julia was high achieving and showed exceptional interest in learning English from foreign teachers. I observed Julia to be active and verbally responsive in class. She enjoyed Ms Sun's instruction, liking English so much that she tended to seize every chance to participate in dialogic interaction with her. Like some other central participants, such as Helen (Urbany) and Yvonne (Suburbany), she did not particularly enjoy grammar and textbook-based school learning, which was not in line with her previous experience with foreign English language teachers who had used colloquial expression rather than grammar-based styles of interaction. Julia was provided with early English learning resources, encountering English in Year 2 at a 'crèche' (*ān-qīn-bān* 安親班), a popular after-school setting for primary school students. Her formal and cram school English learning both started in Year 3 in primary school and she first encountered foreign English teachers in the latter. Julia particularly enjoyed communicative approaches to learning English, claiming that 'I feel like speaking English with foreigners which is a lot of fun...I still attend class (in a non-traditional cram school) with foreign teachers where we can undertake open dialogue'.

On-going foreign teacher experience: Julia's experience with foreign English language teachers was striking and positive. An English outing held by her cram school in Year 3 probably accounted for Julia's initial explosion of interest in learning English. She retold her first experience speaking English with excitement:

> There were many foreigners and we had to speak English in order to buy what we wanted.... So I spoke the first English word in my life, asking for 'a cup of coke'.... I made it which really excited me. So I feel like speaking English with foreigners which is a lot of fun.

Julia still attended a cram school class with a foreign teacher where she could continue with 'open dialogue'. The following interview extract described the tension of the value asymmetry between her personal beliefs and Suburbany school culture:

> I prefer 'real-life' (*shēng-huó-huà* 生活化) English to 'textbook' learning. The textbook is too 'tedious' (*tài-sǐ-le* 太死了)! ((repeats twice)) I do not like learning from the textbook.... I remembered when Ms Sun asked if we wanted to learn English with a foreign teacher. I felt it 'valuable' (*hǎo-bù-róng-yì* 好不容易)... but the idea was 'rejected' (*pái-chì* 排斥) by the majority of the class because they complain about the tuition.... I like a foreign teacher's class. I felt it was lots of fun.

Julia's longing for 'real-life' English was highlighted by her disappointment at her classmates' rejection to pay for foreign teachers. She was evidently caught in a tension between her past learning history through communicative approaches and the current 'grammar-based' learning at school. As in Mark's case as a peripheral participant in Hakka Rural School who could listen but 'failed to write it out', and Ms Mei's complaint about her Hakka students' rejection of her offer of English audio CD-ROMs, Julia's preferred communicative approach to English learning activities claimed only low status in junior high school. However,

Julia still enjoyed greeting foreign teachers in English during break in the school corridor: 'I get excited when seeing foreign teachers and want to greet them in English.... I feel it is natural to greet foreigners'.

Julia seemed to have developed coping strategies to balance her current school learning and her preferred way of enjoying English. She understood the importance of following lessons in Ms Sun's class.

Appropriation of intersubjectivity: Julia's negotiation of subjective meaning and identity formation rested on cultural capital involving dialogical interaction with both Ms Sun at school and her mother at home, which facilitated her English learning. Ms Sun, a young female teacher who also graduated from Suburbany School, saw Julia as a 'shadow/reflection' of her past in terms of learning English, a ready aspect of Suburbany alumni 'co-membership' (Cazden, 1988). While revealing that Julia was not among the highest English achievers in her class, Ms Sun claimed that Julia maintained enormous interest in English, just as she had done in the past:

> Julia is like me when I was in junior high school because I was also interested in English.... Though she is not on the top list, she used to express to me that she wanted to take GEPT. She did maintain her interest throughout.... I did not focus on school materials but on 'listening' to the English TV programs.... Julia also likes to watch such English TV programmes.

This dialogically constructed intersubjectivity between them, arguably, played a pivotal role in Julia's subjective construction of 'becoming' a girl at least not rejecting English, as Ms Sun used to be. Through their semiotic mediation in everyday classroom activities, Julia was gaining something implicit from extended common understanding of shared learning activities. As she put it in her interview, 'I will not reject what I have to learn from the teacher'. At home, her mother's unique engagement and encouragement in her English learning appeared to be just as crucial:

> Mum said to me that my English sounds very 'charming' (*hǎo-tīng* 好聽) ((chuckles))... When she is watching TV for learning Japanese, she will ask me to repeat that Japanese and reply by saying 'why do you pick up so fast'. Mum feels that my English and Japanese pronunciations are both charming.

Julia was evidently delighted that her foreign language 'talent' was highly valued at home, where her mother's verbal approbation exactly paralleled Ms Lu's, the indigenous Paiwan teacher at Mountainside School, when she attended cram school in her junior high school years. As Ms Lu recalled:

> I found I could do better and easier than my friends because my English pronunciation sounded better... teachers tended to compliment my pronunciation... that was why I had much interest in learning English.

It is intriguing to discover such similarity between Julia and Ms Lu which helped explain how Julia was empowered in the process of imagined 'becoming' through dialogically constructed intersubjectivity. Besides receiving verbal approbation, Julia would sometimes be consulted by her mum on English vocabulary; 'We will tease each other in simple English... though not lengthy words'. Her mother also subscribed to and read the same magazine, *Let's Talk in English*. Since Julia's English was generally better than her mother's, she said 'we will ask each other some questions' regularly in learning English at home, which was indeed a further, distinctive reinforcement in sustaining her English learning interest.

A dream of 'becoming': While Julia revealed that 'Mum thinks my English is good and deserves making more efforts to keep it moving forward', she also said that she suggested that 'we can travel abroad and have fun if we have the chance'. Studying abroad was exactly Julia's dream, knowing very well that it took good English to do so. She claimed that 'I will still major in English if I study abroad.... I can learn English well, so I will try hard to make it better'. With such an imagined future world in mind, she incorporated events that might facilitate it in her daily activities, particularly watching TV programmes:

> I feel that the DJs of the 'tourist programs' on TV are particularly good in English and are 'lucky' enough to travel around different countries.... Playing and learning at the same time (*biān-wán biān-xué* 邊玩邊學) would be a great idea. I want to go for it because I feel it is fantastic to study and enjoy exotic views simultaneously.

Although she had never been abroad, she was confident in saying, 'I feel like learning English well and have the chance to go abroad', positioning herself in an imagined future, serving to organise her own thoughts, manage her own feelings and direct her own actions to fit the self she hoped to become. As she said in a more assertive tone, 'now I feel English is fine for me... I know I will take part in GEPT... so I need to move on'. Indeed, according to her email message to me in English a few years later in 2007, Julia was attending a local public high school and had been working hard on her English. Most importantly, she still remembered her 'dream':

> I have just attended the Intermediate test of the GEPT. I hope I would pass the test. (Good luck to me!) I am studying hard in English, and I am a student of.... Do not worry about me. I'll study harder for myself and my dream. (Email received on 25 February 2007)

Just as 'studying abroad' seemed to be a supreme goal directing Julia's mediated actions and efforts as an English learner, so other 'central participants' were impelled by other imaginary future trajectories, as with Steven at King's School in England. Some students not identified as 'central participants' also imagined very different futures for themselves, for example, at Mountainside School, as 'sporting coaches', 'studying in athletic academies' or Jack's imagined future of becoming a 'national basketball player'. For most of those lacking appropriate cultural capital or resources as mediational tools, such as Julia possessed, simply projecting themselves forward as English language speakers was not possible, particularly those from homes where low or even 'zero' value was given to English learning, such as those of Howard (Urbany School) or Dave (Mountainside School).

Chapter Summary

In this chapter, I have attempted to delineate the broader scope of communities of practice that account for relationships between students' mental processes and their cultural, historical and institutional settings, conceptualising English or Chinese language learning as 'communities of practice' not limited to concrete social settings, such as classrooms, schools or cram schools. Students appropriate the cultural capital and other resources offered by their locales in their school participation, whether as central or less than full participants in English/Chinese learning communities of practice. In Chapter 7, I will carry out further synthesis and cross-cultural comparisons of EFL learning in Taiwan and CFL learning in England with reference to the global and neo-political framing of foreign language learning and discuss emerging issues of linguistic and cultural globalisation, potential social inequality due to language competition and social gender identities in learning the two target foreign languages.

Note

(1) I was invited by Eddie's English teacher (Ms Huang) to teach one class session, as a way of both contributing to the class and building a rapport with them.

7 Synthesis and Cross-Cultural Comparisons

In previous chapters, three planes of analysis in the investigation of how learning English/Chinese as foreign languages takes place have been explored within specific sociocultural settings, so as to uncover individual students' active social positioning involving membership identities emerging within communities of practice. In this chapter, we pursue further synthesis and cross-cultural comparisons of English as a foreign language (EFL) learning in Taiwan and Chinese as a foreign language (CFL) learning in England with reference to similarities and differences of structural or institutional forces that impact on learning these two foreign languages including, for example, global and political framing of learning the two foreign languages, elite social status, student motivations and teaching/learning styles and emerging social inequality in learning them. Particular attention is paid to emerging gender gap issues revealed in participant students' English academic performance in Taiwan. These issues are in the context of different socialisation processes experienced by girls and boys and associated, different, value-asymmetric social expectations of gender roles within Taiwanese and English societies.

In comparing across cultures, constant awareness is required of contextual similarities and differences. For example, even though both Taiwan and England are 'in the same boat', officially keen to engage young people in learning English/Chinese as strategic foreign languages in order to maintain the nations' economic competitiveness in an era of rapid globalisation, the vessels are of quite different sizes, impelled by different forces and on rather different trajectories. Mason (2007: 192) reminds us that in the design of comparative educational research, 'researchers should… bear in mind the objective of comparing across cultures only what is comparable', that in doing research we need to avoid a typical focus on local and surface events that are 'merely symptomatic of deeper and more powerful structural forces, especially economic and political factors' (Mason, 2007: 181). Therefore, 'context' should be explored, not as limited to 'local and surface events', but as reaching out to the wider context of rapid globalisation and its impact on foreign language education in England and Taiwan.

Similarities in Learning and Teaching English/Chinese

Global and political framing of learning and teaching English/Chinese

At the outset, the global and political framing of learning English and Chinese tends inevitably to be seen as having much to do with the phenomenon of linguistic and cultural globalisation. Globalisation involves a process of international integration arising from the interchange of world views, products, ideas and other aspects of culture. In 2000, the International Monetary Fund (IMF) identified four basic aspects of globalisation: trade and transactions, capital and investment movements, migration and movement of people and the dissemination of knowledge. In the last few decades, the whole world has been experiencing major economic, demographic, societal and technological change. This has greatly increased the popularity of English, which has become the lingua franca of the whole world. Furthermore, in a world that is becoming 'smaller' and 'flattened' (Friedman, 2005), learning English for strategic purposes has become a form of 'political correctness' in countries like Taiwan. Even in non-English language averse countries like Britain, a sense of the consequences of the neglect of foreign language learning may be affording some signs of a turning in official, business and personal recognition that learning the language of national trading partners (like Chinese) may be increasingly intimately linked to economic earning potential, both personal and national.

Our findings and discussion from Chapters 1 and 3 demonstrated an intimate interaction between 'global' and 'political' planes of analysis. For example, part of Taiwan's political reality resides in language divisions and oppression having historical roots among its differing ethnic groups. Economic imperatives have dominated the last half century of national existence in Taiwan. An explosion of interest in and pressure to learn English has underpinned social policy changes in many countries around the world. This has included in many national public school systems, the introduction of the downward extension of the starting age for learning English and the introduction of national English proficiency accreditation systems (e.g. the General English Proficiency Test [GEPT]), as is the case in Taiwan and many other Asian countries, such as Japan and China. In Taiwan, the Grades 1–9 curriculum required by the MOE since 2001 institutionalised English learning as early as primary level Grade 5 (age 10) and extended it to Years 3 and 4 in 2005, with many schools using their autonomy to extend it even further to Years 1 and 2 to meet parental expectations. To further encourage the study of English, the official GEPT accreditation system for learners at all levels of proficiency was introduced in 2000. Successful candidates are awarded certificates of achievement which have rapidly become one of the most important basic admission and graduation criteria for both senior secondary and higher education. Record numbers of participants have entered the GEPT each year, and developing better English ability has become an overt pressure upon young people in Taiwan at every school level.

Interest in learning Chinese and about its associated culture has increased along with the historically unparalleled growth in significance of China in world business in recent decades. Chinese has entered the curriculum in England and other European countries, such as France, as well as Anglophone countries such as Australia and the USA. The vast growth of Confucius Institutes worldwide has exemplified this trend of learning the Chinese language and culture. As noted in Chapter 1, according to the annual development report of the Confucius Institute 2017, there are in total over a thousand Confucius Institutes/Classrooms in countries (regions) in Asia, Australia, America and Europe. Britain claimed to have the largest number of 186 Confucius Institutes/Classrooms in Europe (see Figure 1.2). The geopolitical shift of China as the new superpower in world business appears to be stirring the learning of Chinese. A survey by the British Council (2013) indicated that the Chinese language has climbed to fourth place, right after the traditional 'big three' foreign languages (French, Spanish and German) in British schools, as the recommended strategic foreign language that people in Britain need to learn in order to maintain Britain's economic status in the business world. Perhaps closer to the reality of what is happening in the British and English school systems is that emerging political and economic imperatives are beginning to nudge some young people to learn CFL despite the fact that there has been historically limited provision for and a degree of cultural aversion towards learning foreign languages on a predominantly non-compulsory school curricular basis.

Elite social status in learning English/Chinese?

While achieving proficiency in both languages in Taiwan and England, there are emerging aspects of elite social status and creates many social issues in terms of language learning identities and social inequalities, that have more or less in common and matters of concern worthy of discussion. A major difference between the two foreign language learning situations lies in the fact that English is compulsory for young people in Taiwan but learning Chinese in England as yet involves only a tiny minority of students.

In Taiwan, learning English is for everyone and seems like a form of 'national movement' (*quán-mín yùn-dòng* 全民運動), as mentioned in Chapter 1. Young students, who appear to be good at English and who may already come from families with favourable social positions, tend to experience an enhanced sense of superiority, given the general belief that better English means better opportunities. Lin and Byram (2016) have noted that English has prestigious status because

...people in Taiwan tend to assume that anything involving English must be good. In Taiwan, learning English as an international language has become vital to its economy in terms of providing access to the world community, and is viewed as one of the keys to success in Taiwan's economic globalisation and modernisation. Being able to speak English carries considerable prestige and it is generally believed that speaking better English fuels upward mobility in terms of occupation and social status. (Lin & Byram, 2016: xv)

In England, in contrast, though public policy places a degree of emphasis on foreign language learning, it can by no means be said that learning Chinese in schools is seen as the key to national success. However, students in the study reported here who chose to learn Chinese, like their aspiring counterparts in Taiwan, also tended to have a 'sense of superiority' and felt proud, not least as beneficiaries of the doubtful historical myth in Britain that 'only intelligent students can do languages better'. For example, in the two-week Chinese taster lessons I taught at St Mary's in 2013, I was informed by the school language head that the 60 students had been invited to attend because they were top ability set students. I was unsure if either she thought that only high-ability students could do languages better or that she was politely trying to tell me that their motivation and enthusiasm were such that I would not have to worry too much about classroom management with such students. Indeed, all of the students proved to be highly motivated and visibly enjoyed Chinese language and culture learning. In writing about their experiences, most of them reported that they enjoyed Chinese because learning it is 'interesting', 'exciting', 'challenging', although some felt it 'difficult'. One girl student revealed her high expectations in learning Chinese as a new language, saying:

> When I found out I was going to be having Mandarin lessons I was really excited because I knew it was a really useful skill to have... Also, I was excited that we were getting a change from learning French and German...we were getting the opportunity to have Mandarin lessons taught by a Mandarin teacher who speaks it as his first language. Me and all my friends were intrigued to what learning the language would be like and how good we would be at it.

At the end of the first week learning Chinese under my instruction, she said, 'I have found it a very interesting and rewarding experience. Learning a new language is a fantastic feeling as it gives you a real sense of achievement and you know it is a great skill to have'. In fact, some of the students also felt 'privileged' to be 'offered' to learn it in school. One of the boy students revealed this sense of privilege. He said:

When I found that we were being offered two weeks of Mandarin Chinese I was immediately excited! I know that Mandarin is a very important and popular language worldwide, so therefore felt privileged to learn it in school as part of our curriculum. The first thing I thought of when someone mentioned the language 'Mandarin' was the beautiful and interesting symbols and tones which it includes.

After years of teaching Chinese in different schools in England, Ms Wang seemed to know very well about students' feeling proud once they were selected to learn Chinese. When she had taught at Highland School, she felt it would be good to take advantage of students' feeling 'privileged' while being selected to learn Chinese, though her desire to channel high-ability students to do so was not supported by her school head, as we saw in Chapter 5. She believed, approvingly, that it was

> another school's policy is to allow top two percent students to select Chinese. Other foreign languages such as German, French, Spanish and Japanese can be chosen by students from any sets… only top two percent can choose Chinese…. So, soon after choosing Chinese… students start to feel they are really 'good' (*liǎo-bù-qǐ* 了不起)…. If they were selected at the outset, they would have the sense of 'pride' (*jiāo-ào* 驕傲). (29 June 2014)

She also reported that there seemed to be an emerging belief among young people in England that learning Chinese could be considered 'freaky'. Ms Wang confirmed this phenomenon to be 'normal', becoming a new form of 'peer pressure'. She said:

> …people say we are 'freaky' to learn Chinese. But this is quite 'normal' (*zhèng-cháng de* 正常的)…. In the first class when teaching at another school, I would ask students, 'you are here today because… you don't want to learn an easy language'…. But that 'freak' is something negative. When he/she said 'freak', under that context, is negative… because of peer pressure… kind of feeling that 'yeah, you're learning Chinese!' ((a sense of jealous… why you!)) It really takes academically able students to learn Chinese well…. Why select students?… some of them found they could not follow at the end of the day… that's why we ended up having only six clever girls in that class… three or four of them are gifted students. They're all very high-achieving students themselves so that they can 'cope' (*yǒu bàn-fǎ* 有辦法). (29 June 2014)

Her teaching experiences at Highland School left her with a sense that learning Chinese required 'academically able' students and that where it was not compulsory, teachers had to struggle with relatively small class sizes and experience difficulty in retaining students. Dropout was stressful and frustrating to both classes and their teachers and might be prevented by recruiting only academically able students. Being called 'freaks' while learning Chinese was a kind of peer culture or pressure particularly evident when students, who were not academically able but wanted to try out learning Chinese, tended to be 'mocked at' (*cháo-xiào* 嘲笑). She continued to say:

> Yeah, unless you yourselves are really good academically… you are high-ability students (*zī-yōu-shēng* 資優生), meaning you are top-set in every subject. So, 'no doubt' (*lǐ-suǒ-dāng-rán* 理所當然) you can learn Chinese well. But if you happen to be not that good… just because you are very interested and really want to learn Chinese… but you just end up getting classmates teasing you, which is 'really annoying'(*hěn tǎo-yàn* 很討厭)…. Your peers can be those who do not have as good academic level as you and they will 'tease you' (*wā-kǔ* 挖苦)… this is not nice really. (29 June 2014)

In Ms Wang's view, students who were not selected might challenge, somewhat out of jealousy, and say 'why not me?'. One way to express their feelings was to annoy peers who appeared to be more academically able and were selected to learn Chinese. Calling those who learned Chinese 'freaks' suggested more than one set of meanings for such name-calling. For one thing, it took students extra time and energy to comprehend this new language, beyond those required by other European languages more linguistically similar to English. Those who chose to learn it had to be both brave and willing to take the challenge. In some students' eyes, it was crazy because these 'freaks' had to make twice the effort learning Chinese as a GCSE A-level subject. For others, it could be just a matter of 'jealousy' (*suān pú-táo* 酸葡萄) for, given the growing importance and popularity of Chinese, those who were learning this rather different/difficult foreign language were sometimes labelled 'good/smart'.

If such views characterised the case of the state school – St Mary's, where only 60 top ability set students were allowed to attend the Chinese classes I taught in the summer of 2013, in which some of the top ability set 'lucky' students reported making other school peers feel jealous, the issue of learning Chinese in St Mary's as 'freaky' was perceived differently by students at St Peter's School. At group interview, the five girls who were sitting GCSE Mandarin appeared to have a different take on being called freaky. When asked if their friends considered them freaks while learning Chinese, they confirmed 'yes, freaky…, but not in a bad way'. One of them revealed that her friends just said that '…why do you choose it? …and it's more like…wow! it's amazing!' Since studying Chinese was new to all students at St Peter's School, their friends were, indeed, quite impressed by the way that the five girls in Ms Byrne's Chinese class were trying to do something new and different. As Erica, the highest achiever among them went on to say, she 'definitely feels proud of it... it is quite hard... a language to learn':

> ...when I was preparing for the writing exam.... I have been writing out my sentences while listening to the tape about examples in Chinese. ...I just like writing and then my friends... they came to me... they just said like 'so cool, how can you do that!' and I just said to them 'I like it just not that hard when you done...

The other four girls in Erica's class were also feeling proud of doing Chinese GCSE and did not take it too seriously when friends called them 'freaky', knowing that it took extra time and energy to master this new and different language from other European foreign languages with which they were already familiar. Ms Byrne encouraged them in Chinese class with the notion that in learning Chinese 'it takes a really long runway for the plane to take off... but as soon as you get up... you will roll up... and enjoy the different view of the world'.

Differences in Learning and Teaching English/Chinese

Comparing motivations in learning English/Chinese

Students in both Taiwan and England, while perceiving learning English or Chinese mainly as one among many school subjects, usually also saw their similar geopolitical significance as languages in world business. Moreover, in Taiwan it was well established that English proficiency meant more opportunities for upward job mobility and social status, leading to greatly heightened pressure upon young people. Pressure from future job perspectives had engendered a belief in 'learning English the earlier the better', fuelling a 'national movement'. Heightened academic pressure for young people to learn English at school motivated them to get 'good exam scores' (*hǎo chéng-jī* 好成績) and fuelled cram school attendance as part of many young people's everyday lives. In England, our much more limited picture of learning Chinese is somewhat different between state and independent school students.

Motivations and experiences in learning English

In the previous chapters, we conceptualised how resource disparity among the four Taiwanese social groups may empower or constrain students' English learning. In Table 7.1, among their 'reasons' for learning English, students reported overall that it was as a 'school requirement' (mean: 73%), followed by 'travel abroad' (mean: 58%). Holo and Mainlander students disproportionately reported studying English because it could be used 'for future jobs' (62% and 61%, respectively). In contrast to other social groups, 'white-collar Mainlanders' demonstrated

Table 7.1 Students' reasons for learning English

Reasons	Urban			Rural	All students
	Holo	Mainlander	Hakka	Indigenous	
1. School requirement (%)	77	75	81	57	73
2. Travel abroad (%)	59	68	49	57	58
3. Use it for future jobs (%)	62	61	37	32	48
4. Make foreign friends (%)	40	54	26	45	41
5. Enjoy studying languages (%)	31	39	27	47	36
6. Study abroad (%)	25	50	26	38	35
7. Achieve a qualification (%)	30	57	21	23	33

the highest percentages in all categories, except 'school requirement', where Hakka students, in line with the historico-cultural imperatives of their culture, exceeded them in this respect. Regarding the reason 'enjoy studying languages', which indigenous respondents rated most highly, it arguably bears close relation to their Western cultural and religious identities (see Table 4.8 in Chapter 4). However, these indigenous students' relatively low rating of to 'achieve a qualification' (23%) or for 'use for future jobs' (32%), in common with Hakka respondents, while standing alongside relative lack of parental encouragement and engagement as familial resources, no doubt reflected their accurate perceptions of their relation to labour market structures.

Dynamic motivations and experiences in learning Chinese

The reasons that young people adduced learning Chinese in England appear to be more dynamic. At King's School, which had made Chinese compulsory in the formal school curriculum, almost 88% of students reported that they would want to learn this school subject irrespective of its compulsory status. As indicated in Table 7.2, 72% also reported that they 'enjoy this subject' and more than half 'enjoy studying

Table 7.2 Students' reasons for learning Chinese

Reasons	Percentage
1. Enjoy this subject	72
2. Enjoy studying language	54
3. Be able to travel aboard	49
4. School requirement	48
5. Achieve a qualification	47
6. Use it for future jobs	42
7. Make friends with foreigners	26
8. Attend an elite university	16

language' (54%). No more than half (48%) considered being forced to study Chinese merely as a 'school requirement', as opposed to 73% for their Taiwanese peers. Besides, it is also interesting to see that nearly half of the respondents recounted that they learn Chinese for the purpose of 'travelling aboard' (49%). This is consistent with their overall high frequency of travelling abroad and thus enjoying foreign cultural experiences largely made available through parents' arrangements, and apparently in sharp contrast with the more instrumental reasons of the Taiwan students.

Moreover, these students appeared to be aware of the 'usefulness' of Chinese for their future career, evincing awareness that it was going to be one of the main languages used in business within the next decade, along with English: 'it already is the second most widely spoken language in the world apparently', as one student said. Another student explained that 'not only is Chinese language and culture fascinating, I also thought that Chinese is very helpful as a language in later life, especially when it comes to trade or business, where China is a key country' (see Table 7.3). These views are consistent with the findings from the question students were asked: 'has knowing Chinese helped you in any way?', which 66% confirmed positively. Some considered Chinese interesting, useful in business and 'looks good on CV', likely to be helpful in their future application to elite universities such as Oxford or Cambridge.

Table 7.3 Reasons for learning Chinese

Categories	Students' accounts
Useful	'The initial attraction... be attributed to the utility of the language, and learning Mandarin would theoretically improve employment possibilities... work in China or with Chinese people.... I began to enjoy learning the language itself'.
	'...not only is Chinese language and culture fascinating, I also thought that Chinese is very helpful as a language in later life, especially when it comes to trade or business, where China is a key country'.
	'It is different and interesting compared to the normal languages... like French and Spanish. Learning it will help me get the job I want when I am older'.
Different	'...not many people get the chance to learn Mandarin and I thought it'd be really good to do. It was something different and I prefer it to Spanish, French and Latin which were also compulsory'.
	'It is not one of the standard languages offered at schools which made it intriguing, and the culture in China is so drastically different to ours that I was curious to learn more'.
Interesting	'It is an interesting new language which is very different from the usual languages we learn at school... it gives us a wider range of language and culture, and will help us to broaden our horizons'.
	'Languages interest me and Mandarin is a particularly interesting language. Having previously only studied English, Welsh and French, Mandarin was exciting and intrigued me'.
Other	'Because our teacher was really good and really enthusiastic'.
	'I love the language and the culture that goes along with it'.

It was intriguing to discover that, from students' own words, they enjoyed Chinese because it was very different from other European languages such as 'Spanish, French and Latin which were also compulsory'. Perhaps it is this difference in terms of the linguistic structure and associated cultural elements in Chinese that intrigued students. For example, one student revealed that 'it is an interesting new language which is very different from the usual languages we learn at school… it gives us a wider range of language and culture, and will help us to broaden our horizons', as shown in Table 7.3. Another student even said that Chinese is interesting and different because '…I was bored of the other languages I was doing and I wanted a change'. Last but not least, students enjoy a subject because they like the teacher and enjoy her/his teaching and this was certainly the case in King's School, as one student explained; 'because our teacher was really good and really enthusiastic'.

For those elite students from King's School, I was intrigued to see whether their school's 'forward thinking' vision in making Chinese compulsory had scaffolded perceptions of learning Chinese as the road towards elite universities such as Oxford or Cambridge. In an interview with four students from Ms Tan's class, I asked them if attending elite universities was one of their motivations in sitting the GCSE Chinese. Their responses were mixed. For example, Angela agreed with the idea that Chinese could be beneficial but there was something more. She pointed out that:

> I agree, but I don't think it's just that… it's not just about grades. I think it's also the culture experience as well because you also learn about different lifestyles… stuff like that… and it's just another way of learning something different….

In tune with Angela's thoughts, another boy student, Sam, added that

> Yeah,… sort of similar… I don't think… in my life like in the job I'm going to speak Mandarin for daily basis… but I really like the Chinese characters…. I just like how it is so different. It is not like learning something…. I can go to any other classroom learning about projective equation (science subject)…. I'm having 9 lessons of science a week going… obviously they are different… different areas but a lot of them are sold like the same… like science concept… so it's nice coming to Mandarin class learning about something unlike French… it doesn't use our alphabets… just the other side… completely new different ideas… so obviously I'm still very hard-working… it's not for grades… it's not like a coming in to assess or work… it's definitely a change from a normal sort of academic work.

As we saw in Chapter 5, Ms Tan's classes were observed to be very dynamic, involving thought-provoking and interactive pedagogy which seemed to be suited to these academically able students. In Sam's words, learning Chinese is 'definitely a change from a normal sort of academic work'. In other words, these independent school students, like some of their peers from state schools, envisaged Chinese learning not only as a means to high scores in the GCSE required for elite university entry, but also seeing it as a challenge to themselves in self-actualisation at school or life in the future.

Comparing styles in teaching English/Chinese

Against the mundane backgrounds of the institutional and material cultures in school settings, including, for example, class timetables, textbooks and the use of technology,[1] our investigations suggest that EFL and CFL teachers' backgrounds, including their personal English/ Chinese learning and teacher training experiences informed their classroom pedagogy. Among the differences in interactional styles evident in schools in both studies, the most pervasive general pedagogical pattern was 'knowledge-based' grammar teaching in Taiwan in contrast to 'activity-based' pedagogy in England. The following discussion will consider differences between rote learning in Taiwan and activity-based pedagogy in England and the prospect of an emerging inclusive pedagogy encompassing cultural and sociolinguistic bridging in teaching English/ Chinese in Taiwan and England.

Rote learning vs activity-based learning

Among the various interactional styles in evidence between schools in Taiwan and England, the most interesting difference is the dominant 'knowledge-based' grammar teaching and learning in Taiwan engendering memorisation learning strategies and 'activity-based' pedagogy in England oriented towards latent development of thinking abilities.

In Taiwan, driven to keep up with tight learning/teaching schedules (*găn jìn-dù* 趕進度) and to carry out grammar teaching, teachers tend to use Chinese to explain English grammatical rules, as it is considered to be efficient in saving time and energy. In Taiwan and many other Asian countries, such as China, Japan and Korea, there is a general reliance on rote-learning strategies to memorise content knowledge, requiring long-term dedication, concentration and commitment, in pursuit of high exam grades. Relative success among Asian students in contrast to many of their international peers in testing regimes such as the PISA[2] has, in recent years, led to identifying rote-dependent teaching and learning styles as more 'effective', though the comparisons in PISA have sometimes lacked methodological insights as we have argued in Chapter 1. The Chinese 'rote-learning' style that engenders a learning strategy of 'memorisation' that we report in this study tends to be conceptualised differently by Western teachers and students as a 'surface' approach to learning, and this difference is worthy of our attention.

Watkins (2007) argues that several qualitative investigations of the learning approaches and conceptions of Chinese learners in Hong Kong and China (e.g. Kember, 1996; Watkins & Biggs, 2001) have partially supported the conceptual validity of the construct of deep and surface approaches. However, while these studies concluded that Chinese students tended to view memorisation as relevant to both surface and deep approaches to learning, Western students were more likely to see memorisation as characteristic of a surface approach, indicating a lack of conceptual equivalence in regard to their learning approaches. Research into the so-called 'paradox of the Asian learner' arising from comparisons of student learning across cultures appears to be interesting but controversial. For instance, Watkins (2007: 308) argued that the 'paradox' starts with a seemly simple syllogism:

(1) Asian students use rote learning more than Western students.
(2) Rote learning leads to poor learning outcomes.
(3) Therefore, Asian students have poorer learning outcomes than Western students.

But most comparisons of international performance indicate that the reverse is true; students from Asia, such as those from Singapore, Japan, Taiwan and Hong Kong, usually outshine Western peers in tests of achievement in a range of subjects (Watkins & Biggs, 2001). There is a need to view cultural differences in perceptions of relationships between memorisation and understanding because many Western educators fail to draw a distinction between 'rote learning' – memorisation without thought or understanding, and 'repetitive learning' – learning in order to improve future recall in company with understanding. As Watkins (2007) argued:

> Whereas Western students saw understanding as usually a process of sudden insight, Chinese students typically thought of understanding as a long process that required considerable mental effort. (Watkins, 2007: 310)

Chinese students tend to learn repetitively, both to ensure retention and to develop their understanding through memorisation. Given the foregoing interpretation of student learning across cultures, we understand the importance of making a conceptual distinction between rote and repetitive learning for Chinese students. Our Taiwanese participants who were central learners in their EFL communities of practice are probably best described as displaying repetitive learning modalities, viewing understanding as a long process requiring considerable mental effort, whether in relation to learning English grammar or other aspects of language learning such as speaking, listening, reading and writing practices that also seem to require repetitive learning for mastery.

If we consider the memorisation of grammatical knowledge as one extreme of language learning within Taiwanese cultural contexts, the pedagogy observed in the CFL classrooms in England seems to represent the other extreme – an 'activity-based' teaching modality. Perhaps smaller class sizes and more relaxed learning/teaching schedules in England enabled such interactional pedagogy to be practical and helped to enhance students' motivation and understanding of Chinese. The size of classes has long been taken to underlay differences in interactional styles because the number of students may affect how much time teachers can focus on attending to the needs of individuals rather than those of the group as a whole. However, there has been a long debate on the size of classes and their impact. For instance, Ehrenberg *et al.* (2001) argued that class size has the potential to affect how much is learned in a number of different ways but caution that

> ...changes to the class size are considered a potential means of changing how much students learn. Not only is class size potentially one of the key variables in the 'production' of learning or knowledge, it is one of the simplest variables for policymakers to manipulate. However, the amount of student learning is dependent on many factors. Some are related to the classroom and school environment in which the class takes place, but others are related to the student's own background and motivation and broader community influences. (Ehrenberg *et al.*, 2001: 1)

Moreover, Pedder (2006) also called into question simple one-way relationships between class size and students' learning and suggested that future class size research should incorporate sophisticated qualitative methods in order to adequately understand the complex relationship between classroom processes and student's learning. Since our data are ill-suited to joining the usual terms of the debate on correlations between class size and student achievement, we will move our focus to the emerging 'inclusive pedagogy' (Verplaetse & Migliacci, 2008), which can be seen to have brought about cultural and sociolinguistic bridging in EFL in Taiwan and CFL in England.

Cultural and sociolinguistic bridging in teaching English/Chinese

In our investigations of classroom pedagogy (see Chapter 5), we discovered that those Taiwanese teachers who employed students' ethnic culture or mother tongue in dialogical interactions were able to create a psychological co-membership and enhanced students' EFL learning; while in England, similar classroom interactional use of students' everyday (though not ethnic) culture or teacher's own background culture was also detected in some Chinese classrooms in England. Perhaps most interestingly, an emerging form of pedagogy – using learners' existing sociolinguistic knowledge of English to learn Chinese – was identified in Ms Tan's classroom at King's School, as exemplified in Chapter 5, where her student (Steve) creatively used his existing knowledge of Western culture to scaffold his learning of the Chinese vocabulary – '晒' by conceptualising this Chinese character composed of two parts, namely '日' (the sun) and '西' (the West). Such a 'sociolinguistic bridging' brings about what Singh and Han (2014) proposed – a new angle on teaching and learning Chinese in predominantly English-speaking societies such as Britain, the USA and Australia.

In monolingual English-speaking countries such as Australia, young Chinese language learners have encountered the difficulties of a 'high dropout rate' (Orton, 2008) like their peers in England. Additionally, there are also problems of low intake of local Australian students learning Chinese whereby 'Chinese risks becoming perceived as a "ghetto" language to be taken only by students of Chinese background' (Asian Studies Association of Australia – ASAA, 2009: 6). Therefore, the 'cultural/sociolinguistic bridging' in classroom pedagogy may help stop the stubborn difficulties of learning Chinese in monolingual English-speaking countries. For example, Singh and Han (2014) call for the need to employ 'cultural/sociolinguistic bridging' in classroom pedagogy to solve one key problem of Chinese teaching in Australia – the 'alienation' of beginning learners. They argue that

> …the methods for teaching Chinese, limited the use of English to explanatory, managerial and interactive functions. …the dominance of rigid Chinese-only pedagogies deprives beginning learners of the educational use of their existing sociolinguistic knowledge of English for learning Chinese. (Singh & Han, 2014: 168)

The problematic method employed in those Chinese classrooms is a way of focusing on teaching forms of Chinese that learners are expected to use in China, which is monolingual (Chinese only) and decontextualised, making learning difficult. Following Pennycook's (2010) notion of 'language as a local social practice', they continue to propose that 'the form of Chinese that is taught is integral to, expressive of and responsive to the corpus of local, everyday sociolinguistic activities which beginning learners use recurrently, day in, day out' (Singh & Han, 2014: 170).

The notion of 'language as a local social practice' is exactly in line with neo-Vygotskian scholars' arguments that language learning is close to everyday give-and-take activities – 'the practice account of literacy' (Scribner & Cole, 1981) and as 'everyday' situated practice (Lave, 1988), which we have delineated in Chapter 2. In particular, following Lave's (1988, 1996) notion of 'situated learning theory', we have challenged the conventional assumptions of decontextualised cognition and believe that human minds are socially and culturally constructed whereby learning takes place in ubiquitous, everyday practices. In a similar vein, Singh and Han (2014) found that when Chinese teachers (e.g. from China) who are made familiar with everyday Australian cultural activities and then employ 'cultural/sociolinguistic bridging' in pedagogy, these teachers may help to make Chinese more 'learnable' and less 'intimidating' while facing the particular characteristics of Chinese learning – the 'pain/gain ratio' – a characteristic in learning, for example, Chinese written characters, which requires repetitive writing practice to ensure retention and to develop a sophisticated understanding of Chinese linguistic structures.

While challenging the monolingual (Chinese only) and decontextualised pedagogy in Australia, which makes Chinese learning difficult, our investigations of classroom pedagogy in England revealed that the dominant instructional language was English and no problematic 'Chinese only' pedagogies were observed in classrooms. However, in Taiwan, there is a growing popularity of an 'English only/no Chinese'[3] policy implemented in many English language institutes or cram schools. With the pedagogical and psychological effects of 'cultural/sociolinguistic bridging' in mind, we can argue that without the monolingual 'English only/no Chinese' policy, we may also help to make English learning more contextualised and less 'intimidating' for young Taiwanese learners.

Emerging Social Issues in Learning English/Chinese

Five different languages, the predominant one of instruction, Chinese, the target language – English – and three ethnic mother tongues, Hakka, Paiwan and Holo dialects, were seen to be used in the classrooms observed in Taiwan. In Hakka Rural School, some high-ability students were found to reject speaking their mother tongue because of its low status and seemingly inferior associated cultural valence. At the same time, given the rising tide of learning the Holo dialect (*tái-yǔ* 台語) alongside English for economic success encouraged by the recent political climate in Taiwan, asymmetry and competition among these five languages appeared inevitable. Asymmetrical values attached to languages make it possible for ethnic languages (Hakka and indigenous Paiwan) to be 'jammed' between English and other high status languages (Chinese and Holo dialect) with consequences both for language in practice and emerging social identities in learning English.

In Britain, though not, as we have seen, in any uniform sense among the variety of its historico-national (for example, Welsh) or recently immigrant ethnic communities, the social phenomenon of language competition appears to be somewhat different from that in Taiwan. English is still the dominant language in Britain and the international lingua franca. A similar form of language competition takes place predominantly between English and other social groups' mother tongues, such as the Welsh language in Wales where there is a substantial and growing Welsh medium state school provision and some degree of tension between using English or Welsh in public and everyday life is an ongoing cultural and political issue. In the cases of heritage languages or immigrant languages such as Chinese, Urdu and other immigrant groups' mother tongues, the tendency is still for them to be taught at after-school clubs or weekend schools for the purpose of celebrating social-ethnic group identities.

Resource divide in learning English/Chinese

As we saw in Chapter 1, Taiwan has experienced a long-existing urban–rural divide in the availability of cram schools which has impacted on students' compulsory English learning, though among the four schools which we studied, Hakka social groups' cultural emphasis on education had led to a booming business for cram schools in rurally located Meinung township, leaving Mountainside School and its indigenous Paiwan ethnic group as the only one without access to cram schools because of its remote location. In England, where the overall provision of Chinese is extremely limited, it was, at the same time, four times higher in independent schools than state schools according to a national survey (British Council, 2014). Further analysis of the latter would amount to little more than to draw attention to the limited data which we have on independent and state school differences in the provision of Chinese, to which attention has already been drawn. Therefore, our focus will be on Taiwan.

In Taiwan, cram schools have multiplied sixfold in recent decades, with nearly 70% of elementary children (Years 4–6) attending them right after their formal school day for 1–3 hours. Some are even obliged to attend at weekends, though half express dislike of doing so. The popularity of cram schooling for learning English tends to be attributed to the highly urban, competitive culture within Taiwanese society. As Greenhalgh (1984) puts it, the unique Taiwanese social phenomenon of the 'swarm of bees' (*yī-wō-fēng* 一窩蜂), drawing on a traditional Chinese idiom, meaning following something blindly, leads to many young students being encouraged by their parents to go to cram schools for major, after-school learning practice. For example, cram schooling culture in Hakka Meinung township was closer to urban levels despite the fact that Meinung is geographically a rural township. As high as 61% of Hakka students reported they first commenced learning English in cram schools. As noted in Chapter 3, Hakka people are known for their traditional emphasis on 'academic study', group solidarity and hard work. Hakka students were encouraged to undertake evening revision activities in cram schools even though, sometimes, their efforts were futile. Ms Mei, the English teacher from Hakka Rural School, depicted this cram school-going trend as follows:

> Cram schools can be viewed as the most lucrative business in Meinung. The pushy Hakka parents send their children to cram schools even though it is sometimes unnecessary.... two kinds of students who should not really be there. Those labelled as completely left behind (hopeless). They are forced by parents and simply hang around with friends. The others are high achievement students who go there because of parental encouragement.

While it was Hakka students' good fortune or otherwise to get such ready access to cram schools, a different form of social inequality in learning English seems to have struck them, namely, the emerging language competition within Taiwanese society, a matter of concern I turn to in the following discussion.

Social gender identities in learning English/Chinese

From a sociocultural perspective, learning is viewed as a social practice taking place within various social settings in home and school milieu, involving 'understanding and participation in on-going activity' (Lave, 1996: 9). Research on pre-school children's role-play has suggested that children pay attention to diverse activities from a very early age and that the development of divergent interests and related achievements continues with age (e.g. Murphy, 1999). Different socialisation processes experienced by girls and boys from early childhood are carried forward into formal schooling, entailing 'gendered experience, choices and achievement' (Murphy & Elwood, 1998) in school settings.

The notion of 'gendered experience' as socially constructed can be nicely captured, for example, in Sunderland's (1994) inquiries into English language education in Britain. She argues that many English language teachers have experienced gender differences between boys and girls in the language learning process. She says:

> That English as a Foreign Language, English as a Second Languages and English for Specific purpose (ESP) extended beyond the classroom is evident.... It is evident in those learners' attitudes to English which relate to the historic-political role English has played in their country (if it has) and the sociocultural one it does now, attitudes that inevitably comprise contradictions.... Experience tells English language teachers that this 'beyond the classroom' world has a lot to do with gender. At secondary

school, for example, languages may be taken at higher levels mainly by girls – this is, of course, if girls get to secondary school in the first place. (Sunderland, 1994: 185)

Following Sunderland's (1994) view that this 'beyond the classroom' world has a lot to do with 'gender' in language learning, it is intriguing to discover if there are gender differences in CFL learning in England and EFL learning in Taiwan.

Gender differences in learning Chinese in England?

Although more evidence is needed to suggest gender differences in CFL learning in England, a seeming gender imbalance among student interviewees is worthy of our attention. Of the 16 eventually interviewed students, 15 (13 girls, 2 boys) were central participants and only 1 (girl) a peripheral participant. Girls outnumbered boys in learning Chinese across the four schools observed and in the national survey in 2014 conducted by the British Council. A close look at the 41 Year 10 students' internal school exam results in Mr Blake's two Chinese language classes by gender also revealed an imbalance in their academic achievement. Though it must be borne in mind that these were based simply on their teacher's marking and can carry none of the authority of a standardised survey based on a large sample population, a rough analysis showed girls (22%) appearing to perform better than boys (15%) in the high achieving category, as shown in Table 7.4, and more boys than girls remained at the intermediate and low level of Chinese language performance.

Student interviewees tended to reflect mixed thoughts about this difference. For example, Angela, the high achieving student at King's School upon whom we have focused, thought that it was student 'attitude' that mattered:

> For me, personally I think people who have an eye at recognizing and linking certain points together (Like finding similar characters) and of course a good memory can be good at any language. I do see why Mandarin can be logical, as new characters can be broken down into parts.

Table 7.4 Exemplified gender differences in Chinese exam result

Chinese ability (total out of 100)		Boys	Girls
	(n = 41)	(n = 22)	(n = 19)
High (80–100) (%)	37	15	22
Intermediate (60–79) (%)	34	22	12
Low (0–59) (%)	29	17	12

Note: Internal exam results from the fourth-form (Year 10) group in the autumn term of 2015.

> However, any language is based on memory of vocabulary and grammar structures, so I personally don't think gender is a factor. I feel like girls can learn on par or more compared to boys because I have only 3 years of experience of mandarin and I am performing well in a class of people that have had about 4-5 years' experience, so I think it's more of an attitude to the learning than gender being a factor.

Both she and others in Ms Tan's class considered Chinese to be a logical language (e.g. in terms of its written characters), which could be learned better if students understood that logic. Gender should not be a key indicator because both boys and girls could comprehend that logic well if they worked hard enough. Steven, their high achieving male peer, thought that 'an equal amount of boys and girls do well' in learning Chinese, though he saw more girls struggle with it than boys:

> I mean definitely, there are very talented speakers in Mandarin of both genders but... it seems... I've seen more girls struggle than boys struggle... but an equal amount boys and girls do well, so I think it's apart from being logic.... I mean it's the commitment of a language and... because a lot of learning involved besides the class... you have to keep up, otherwise you will be left behind.

Ms Byrne found that boys tended to achieve better in her senior class (Years 9–11) at St Peter's School:

> ...you know what I've found is that boys love learning Chinese more than girls.... I think it's like 'code-breaking'. Have you noticed that, every time, I would have like for every class... say, 10 boy students, there might be two girls, and every year I had to give the Chinese prize to a boy, because they were the best students, and I used to think 'people are going to think I'm sexist because I never give a girl a prize', but the boys just love, and I think it's to do with code-breaking.

Ms Byrne's experience that boys do better in Chinese seemed to conflict with a general view that more girls are doing languages than boys in England, a similar vein in Taiwan that learning English is also a largely female-dominated territory.

Although there is a lot of research on gendered experience in language learning processes, its results tend to be mixed; thus, more studies are needed in order to examine whether it does become a factor affecting CFL learning. It could be argued that learning Chinese for boys and girls in England should not be generalised about or culturally stereotyped as either a female- or male-dominated territory in an oversimplified way.

Social expectations of gender roles in Taiwan

In Taiwan, if only illustratively, it is intriguing to discover the gender imbalances among Taiwanese student interviewees in learning English. Data from seven girls and four boys who were central participants and four boys and one girl who were peripheral participants (see Table 6.1) suggest emerging gender issues related to different socialisation processes experienced both at home and school, with the context of wider social expectations of gender roles within Taiwanese society 'beyond the classroom'.

For example, the common belief in Taiwan that 'men work outside and women work at home' (*nán-zhǔ-wài nǚ-zhǔ-nèi* 男主外、女主內) has been amply evident in our findings on parental encouragement of students' English learning. The underlying masculine legacy embedded within Taiwanese society can be nicely captured by the exemplary Chinese idioms shown in Table 7.5, which traditionally place females in subordinate roles in everyday activities. A common thread running through these idioms is the asymmetric status of 'men superior and women inferior' across various circumstances involving everyday family life, career choices and education. It could be argued that these traditionally gendered idioms as cultural legacies reinforce masculinity and perpetuate its influence. Therefore, social expectations of gendered roles influence gendered experience, choices and achievement within institutional settings. For example, historically, school subjects at Taiwanese secondary education level are characterised by two major domains: natural sciences (*lǐ-kē* 理科) such as maths and physics, and social sciences (*wén-kē* 文科) such as languages and geography. These two subject areas carry with them distinctive social values that entail masculine/feminine asymmetry that guides parental expectation, which influences and may affect young people's choices of or achievement in subjects.

The generic norm of 'girls social and boys natural science' (*nǚ-wén nán-lǐ* 女文男理) echoes a common belief in 'girls soft while boys hard'. Such polarisation of cultural beliefs leads girls, encouraged by parents,

Table 7.5 Gender imbalance in Chinese idioms

Category	Pinyin	Literal meaning in English and Chinese
Marriage	*láng-cái nǚ-mào*	Intellectual husband and beautiful wife. 郎才女貌
Family	*fū-chàng fù-suí*	Husbands sing whilst wives follow. 夫唱婦隨
Career	*nán-gēng nǚ-zhī*	Men farming whilst women weaving. 男耕女織
Education	*nǚ-zǐ wú-cái biàn-shì-dé*	It is virtue of women to be non-intellectual. 女子無才便是德

relatives and schoolteachers, to engage in subjects, such as EFL, history and geography when they are required to select learning domains in the second year (Year 11) of senior high school.

At a deeper level of local meanings associated with Taiwanese learning culture, 'soft' subjects are held generically to demand much learning by rote and long-term concentration and dedication in order to achieve high attainment. Such long-term concentration and dedication is regarded as 'female territory'. Importantly, girls are expected to be 'quiet' (*ān-jìng* 安靜) and 'compliant' (*shùn-cóng* 順從), female virtues in traditional Chinese culture. Those who can sit calmly indoors and engage in learning 'soft' subjects by rote best fit the moral code of being 'good' (*guāi* 乖) girls. Boys, in contrast, are expected to undertake 'hard' subjects, which have high status within society and activities related to them are valued as practical and beneficial for their successful future careers. Most boys, therefore, are encouraged to be, for example, outgoing, engaging in scientific discovery or physical fitness for athletic prowess.

This broader sociocultural background, the feminine legacy of soft school subjects, may well have played a part in explaining why more girls (7) than boys (4) are central participants and more boys (5) than girls (1) are peripheral participants in learning English in Taiwan. The values attached to English language learning certainly deserve further investigation, particularly with respect to low or underachieving boys who seem to have to make considerable effort to manage their precarious positions through negotiating crossings into 'alien gender territory' (Ivinson & Murphy, 2007).

The boundary crosser: Vincent's story in learning English

Vincent, a timid boy, was one of the very few central participants in learning English at Mountainside School in Taiwan who provided an important example of crossing into alien female territory. Vincent's crossing has to be interpreted within the broader 'soft–hard' distinction between subjects commonly held within Taiwanese society, rather than from any specifically 'feminine legacy of English', as is well documented in Ivinson and Murphy's (2007) research into schoolboys' outsider identity in learning English. The rising tide of learning EFL in Taiwan has been so overwhelming that it might be expected to cut across gender lines so as to eclipse the influence of a feminine legacy of English, such as has been employed in tackling boys' 'underperformance' in English, well documented in many Western studies (e.g. QCA, 1998).

In Vincent's case, a dominant ethnic culture which valued athletic prowess for boys also has to be addressed when understanding his social gender identity in the process of learning English as he stayed indoors reading or watching TV, keeping away from the assumed 'male territory' of outdoor sports. What was at stake was how he experienced balancing membership identity with his male peers and his subjective interest in learning English, while keeping a coherent gender identity. Jake, an athletic dreamer and Vincent's classmate, described Vincent as 'the only boy who can sit at the table reading for three hours at home', attributing Vincent's good academic work to his ability to 'sit at the table reading' for long hours, an activity alien to boys like him. It could be argued that it was Vincent's parents who made possible his central participation, though the process whereby they did so was not without conflict. Although Vincent's mother did not particularly address gendered differences in doing sport, her account revealed a worrying struggle about Vincent not being sporty, though it advantaged his schoolwork:

> I used to ponder why Vincent does not like sports... we try to encourage him to be 'outstanding' in schoolwork.... But sometimes we will still encourage him to walk out after staying home for the whole day reading or watching TV. I will send him 'out of the door' (gǎn-chū-mén 趕出門) for some exercise.... Indigenous kids are usually 'restless' (hào-dòng 好動) and 'agile' (mǐn-jié 敏捷). I think his classmates are far more agile than him.

Vincent's mother experienced, implicitly or explicitly, tension between masculine/feminine asymmetry played out in indigenous culture, even though she knew the importance of academic study. His crossing into alien female territory by staying home for long hours reading or watching TV again seemed to go against the masculinity of athletic prowess embedded within Mountainside School culture. That he was unusual in doing so attested to the relevance of issues of gender identity to why more boys than girls became peripheral participants in English in learning communities, such as those at Mountainside School in Taiwan.

Chapter Summary

In this chapter, with globalised cultural contexts in mind, we have synthesised and compared EFL learning in Taiwan and CFL learning in England with reference to similarities and differences in sociocultural forces that impacted on learning these two foreign languages. We first discussed the impact of globalisation on foreign language education and pointed out the future need to view foreign language learning from traditional 'knowledge value' as school subjects or 'use value' to 'exchange value' (Kramsch, 2014) or 'intercultural value'. We then identified the common elite social status which emerged in the processes of learning these two foreign languages. We have also examined and compared students learning motivations and the teaching styles evident in schools in Taiwan and England.

Differences in rote learning as opposed to activity-based learning styles were identified and discussed, followed by important findings on cultural and sociolinguistic bridging, which is pedagogically significant for future foreign language education. Lastly, emerging social issues such as resource divide and social gender identities were discovered in learning these two foreign languages. These issues must arouse our attention at personal, interpersonal and policy level if we wish to encourage students to access them without excluding those who are not provided with appropriate cultural resources. Further synthesis and ways forward in teaching and learning English/Chinese will be discussed in the last chapter of this book.

Notes

(1) The two studies were conducted several years apart, therefore the chronological differences inevitably give rise to a discrepant use of technology in pedagogy. More technology (e.g. electronic whiteboard) was observed to be used in teaching Chinese than the EFL classrooms in Taiwan though 'activity-based' interactional styles in England may also account for more technology-enhanced language teaching activities.
(2) There is critical literature on the issue of PISA. Therefore, caution is needed due to the oversimplified polarisation and claimed effect of rote or non-rote learning styles.
(3) 'No Chinese' policy in EFL language institutes or cram schools has seldom been challenged by Taiwanese parents. However, once children are caught speaking the mother tongue (i.e. Chinese) in class, they sometimes end up being reprimanded, which gives rise to the issue of language identity crisis – speaking English is superior to speaking Chinese.

8 Conclusion

> The journey into a strange language can be hard work at times, like all worthwhile journeys, but the challenge is a necessary part of education. A nation whose school system failed to equip its young people with first hand experience of other cultures, through their languages, would be like a ship navigating in a multicultural ocean without charts, sextant or compass.
>
> (Hawkins, 1999: 272)

In an era of rapid globalisation, learning foreign languages such as English and Chinese is indeed as Hawkins (1999) says 'a ship navigating in a multicultural ocean' full of both excitements and challenges. Learning English in Taiwan has become a policy of primary economic concern as its industry has recognised the need to compete within global markets in which trade is carried out chiefly in English. In contrast, learning Chinese in England as a means of strengthening future economic relations with China remains more policy prospect than actuality and there are few signs of fresh impetus towards foreign language learning, particularly in state schools in England. In Taiwan, national, longitudinal achievement data on English language learning have consistently demonstrated a worrying urban–rural divide and resources discrepancy between social groups such as Holo, Mainlanders, Hakka and indigenous people. In England, similar issues of concern have emerged such as the resource divide in learning Chinese between state and independent schools which give rise to students' unequal access to Chinese, and the idea that only intelligent and motivated students can succeed in foreign language learning, especially in a 'difficult' language such as Chinese. These concerns over unequal access to English/Chinese in Taiwan and England have been investigated and discussed because they are important if we wish to achieve educational equality in foreign language education. This chapter draws together and discusses three major areas of concluding remarks with suggestions for future practice in foreign language education: the impacts of globalisation on foreign language education; towards an inclusive pedagogy in teaching English/Chinese; and reflecting on sociocultural and comparative approaches, to research learning and teaching English/Chinese.

Impacts of Globalisation on Foreign Language Education

Today, the global spread and use of English appears to have become the key force contributing to rapid globalisation in the 21st century, although such a rapid globalisation process also impacts on how English is taught, learned and used, which has garnered attention and concern from foreign language educationalists (Godwin-Jones, 2018; Kramsch, 2014). One of the major concerns is the competitive relationship between foreign and national or ethnic languages, giving rise to emerging social inequalities in language learning processes.

For example, in her examination of teaching foreign languages in an era of globalisation, Kramsch (2014) argues that

> ...globalisation has changed the nature of the game and is putting into question the modernist tenets of our profession. ... scholars are concerned that globalisation is bringing about deep changes into our ways of thinking, learning, and knowing that educational institutions are not prepared to deal with. Language and language education are at the forefront of those concerns. (Kramsch, 2014: 297)

Indeed, as evident in our Taiwanese study, the issue that confronts foreign language teachers and policymakers is the competitive relationship between foreign (e.g. English) and heritage languages (e.g. ethnic dialects). As we pointed out in Chapter 1, since English language competence has been reinforced and recognised at official, community and institutional levels as a strategic route to success, it has become a new form of 'high language' (Huang, 1993), muddying the water of local multilingual and intercultural education and provoking further linguistic identity, conflict and competition. Liddicoat (2014) also points out that in East Asia, including Taiwan, language education policies tend to emphasise bilingualism, commonly in the form of a national language plus English as a lingua franca thanks to globalisation. However, there are unfortunate consequences as 'the policy focus on bilingualism at most creates a significant tension in a region where plurilingualism outside the educational system is widespread but largely ignored' (Liddicoat, 2014: 225).Therefore, Kramsch (2014: 297) calls into question whether 'globalisation weakens the exclusive link between one nation–state and one national language' and argues that it is crucial for foreign and heritage language teachers and teachers of English to 'enter into serious dialogue about the future of language in the 21st century'.

Unfortunately, as we argued in Chapter 1, there has been very little recognition of the impact of globalisation on foreign language learning and its associated consequences such as linguistic identity clashes among minority social groups, latent language competitions and emerging social inequality at institutional and policy level in Taiwan. In particular, Taiwan is currently undergoing a lively debate over implementing a bilingual policy (i.e. Chinese and English) aiming to uphold English to a much higher language status predominantly for economic imperatives. We would argue that, through our investigations, the process of rapid globalisation will further exacerbate the situation of unequal access to languages, not only in Taiwan but elsewhere across the world if relevant social, historical and cultural forces outside of language classrooms are ignored at institutional and policy levels.

Furthermore, the process of rapid globalisation has also impacted on the 'why' factors in learning foreign languages, i.e. motivations. Following Heller and Duchêne's (2012) argument in their book *Language in Late Capitalism: Pride and Profit*, Kramsch (2014) points out that in an era of globalisation, the value of learning a foreign language has changed from traditional 'language learning as use value' to 'language learning as exchange value'. She argues that

> With globalisation, this use value is still important but it is framed differently.... show how proper, educated language use, promoted as an object of pride by the modern nation–state, is now being seen as a source of profit in a globalised economy. Knowledge of a FL… is becoming increasingly desirable for its exchange value. (Kramsch, 2014: 301)

With this emergent shift of values in foreign language learning in mind, it is important to recognise that learning Chinese/English is an economically and politically framed practice whereby education for these two languages should not be taught or learned as isolated 'school subjects', but rather as everyday practice for 'exchange value'. In other words, adding 'exchange value' for intercultural purposes in foreign language education has now been seen as a new trend in an era of globalisation in the 21st century.

The new trend in foreign language education is echoed by Lin et al.'s (2018) recent book, *Internationalizing English Language Education in Globalized Taiwan*, whose purpose is to position English as a foreign language (EFL) education at the intersection of globalisation and internationalisation in Taiwan and calls for a need to situate English language teaching in a local–distant contact zone. In this book, for example, Godwin-Jones (2018) points out new approaches to global English instruction:

> Given global movements towards greater use of English in a large variety of areas, English language instruction is booming, with integration into the school curricula at an early age in many countries... there are an increasing number of possibilities for learning English outside of formal educational settings. Those opportunities have expanded exponentially, with options available through online resources, extracurricular activities, work-related training, travel/study abroad, entertainment, and private schools. (Godwin-Jones, 2018: 257)

Those foreign language learning opportunities taking place online, outside of classrooms and abroad coincide with what Kramsch (2014: 301) argues that knowledge of a foreign language is becoming gradually anticipated for its exchange value and is now being seen 'as a source of profit in a globalised economy'. Therefore, in recent years, there have been growing calls for foreign language teachers at the classroom level to implement new curricular goals for developing students' global competence and intercultural understanding. Such a new trend in foreign language education 'may be the right pedagogy for the right time – a time when we are at the crossroad of globalisation and internationalisation' (Lin & Godwin-Jones, 2018: 4–5).

Towards an Inclusive Pedagogy of Cultural and Sociolinguistic Bridging

In Chapters 5 and 7, we have argued for a need to employ new ways of teaching foreign languages because teachers in such contexts whose classroom pedagogy is characterised by cultural/sociolinguistic bridging may effectively achieve intersubjective meanings with their students, in particular with those who are from linguistic minority backgrounds. In recent years, there is growing recognition of linguistic minority students' home languages and cultures, which provides potential resources for education (Gay, 2000; Lin, 2007; Verplaetse & Migliacci, 2008). Teachers who recognise these resources tend to value the cultural and linguistic experiences students bring to the classroom and share 'a commitment to connecting with individual children on a personal level as well as at an instructional level' (Chow & Cummins, 2003: 33). These developments are all entwined with 'inclusive pedagogy' (Verplaetse & Migliacci, 2008), 'culturally responsive teaching'

(Gay, 2000, 2002), 'culturally relevant pedagogy' (Lopez, 2011) and 'culturally responsive pedagogy' as strategies attempting to improve the academic performance of students from multi-ethnic cultural backgrounds. In North America, for example, English language learners (ELLs) are from diverse backgrounds, and it is recognised that their classroom teachers must employ pedagogical approaches that are culturally responsive (Gollnick & Chinn, 2002). The purpose of culturally responsive teaching is to create a safe learning environment that respects students' individual differences while seeking to achieve social equality and justice by emphasising cultural and cross-disciplinary learning (Wlodkowski & Ginsberg, 2000).

From Vygotsky-inspired sociocultural approaches to learning, we can argue that culturally responsive teaching or inclusive pedagogy entails the cognitive function of 'intersubjectivity' (Rogoff, 1990), a phenomenon in which interlocutors share a common focus of attention that forms the basis for communication and allows shared meaning to occur. Following Vygotsky (1987), Rogoff (1990: 70) argues that the connection between the known and the new in human communication presumes intersubjectivity and refers to this as 'bridging'. Through such cultural bridging, teachers may help to disrupt, for example, the seemingly persistent 'urban–rural divide' in EFL learning in Taiwan, allowing ethnic minority groups, such as indigenous students mostly living in rural mountain areas, to overcome difficulties in accessing English. Therefore, the inclusive pedagogy of cultural and sociolinguistic bridging that connects students' familiar home or community cultural and sociolinguistic resources with their school knowledge may lead to the attainment of intersubjective meanings with students and is hypothesised to effectively support English and Chinese learning.

In addition to cognitive functions, the act of 'bridging' also has affective significance in foreign language pedagogy. Daniels (2001: 308) argued that 'a complete analysis of processes of development and learning within pedagogic practice must consider cognitive and affective matters'. He cautions that ignoring the role of sociocultural forces (including values) in the pedagogical process may contribute to an 'invisible line drawn between teacher and the class' (Leontiev, 1981: 66). With this in mind, it is important for future EFL/Chinese as a foreign language (CFL) teachers to employ 'bridging' as a psychological tool and to use inclusive pedagogy not only to change students' higher mental functions but also to prevent any latent clash between teacher and student values that would lead to feelings of exclusion.

The important findings of pedagogical bridging from our two study sites in Taiwan and England can be extrapolated to many other countries; on the one hand, to countries where English is taught as a lingua franca, and Chinese ethnicity predominates such as areas in China; on the other, to accelerate the ostensibly unsuccessful Chinese learning for Anglophone students from countries such as the UK and Australia.

Reflecting on Sociocultural and Comparative Approaches

As noted in Chapter 2, situated learning theory challenges cognitivist theories as failing to either recognise the heterogeneity of knowledge or take into account its situated character. These two separate studies in Taiwan and in England, inspired by Vygotsky's ideas concerning the social formation of the mind, draw on Scribner and Cole's (1981) notion of a 'practice account of literacy' and situated learning models in order to investigate EFL learning in Taiwan and CFL learning in England. These two studies have sought to do so in terms of interconnected planes of analysis, from the global and political, local/regional/ethnic culture and schools as institutions to the individual. As a way of concentrating our argument, I will recapitulate the importance of a neo-Vygotskian, situated, theoretical framework to the studies and estimate their contribution to the research literature on situated learning theory.

Situated learning models

Scribner and Cole's (1981) study has brought us to understand a 'practice account of literacy'. The socially organised practice of literacy reminds us that learning a language is not merely knowing how to use it (e.g. read or write a particular script) but also applying this knowledge in specific, goal-directed activities. This understanding allowed us to recognise the pivotal role of contexts in learning English/Chinese and took our research design outside the classroom and school in order to examine language learning within historical, cultural and institutional settings. Through this lens, the studies in this book were able to reveal the mutual embeddedness of language and culture and the sets of values that make possible students' asymmetrical, everyday access to English/Chinese. However, it has been contended here that we need to explore issues of English/Chinese language learning from even broader perspectives, particularly in an era of rapid globalisation today.

Following Vygotsky's ideas concerning the social formation of the mind, Lave and Wenger (1991) and Wenger (1998) have proposed that learning is not a discrete and isolated activity, but an integral aspect of active participation in broader 'communities of practice' which challenges 'individualistic problem-solving approaches' in school learning. They challenge the individualistic, decontextualised approaches to school learning, generally revealed in this book, which were often coupled with comparatively low, everyday access to out-of-school milieu, apart from cram school attendance (in Taiwan). Such approaches might easily be accepted as explaining why some Taiwanese students fail to learn English well. However, this explanation is oversimplified and cannot explain the complex circumstances of English language learning within Taiwanese society. The studies, from which this book drew, extended this with a further broader level of investigation to consider the global political planes of analysis. Informed by the situated learning models, for example, how the school curriculum in Taiwan and England was reshaped by the government in response to global market pressure was therefore also investigated.

Using sociocultural approaches

A situated learning model has allowed us to understand that learning English/Chinese does not simply take place in isolated classrooms, as cognitivist theories or other conventional language acquisition theories tend to assume, but rather, in complex and dynamic sociocultural processes in which it is embedded in everyday sociocultural, historico-political and economic worlds. Neo-Vygotskian studies have thus taken us further in seeing learning in general, and literacy learning in particular, as situated practice. However, these two studies have shown that a broader scope of investigation invoking multiple, as well as interconnected, planes of analysis is still needed if we are to capture a sufficiently complex picture of language learning, such as a sociocultural approach affords.

Sociocultural theory poses challenges to conventional theories of learning because it questions deeply held, conventional views about individualistic cognition by demonstrating that thinking takes place among people and between people and tools in situated settings (Lin, 2007; Lin & Ivinson, 2012). Sociocultural research requires multiple methods and a multidisciplinary approach involving areas of psychological, sociological, anthropological and linguistic investigation. It overcomes methodological individualism rooted in traditional psychology and recognises the dynamic relations of the human mind, language and culture. It has opened the door for the two studies to search for innovative models in investigating language learning as situated practices in everyday, lived-in worlds, accomplished by viewing English/Chinese learning from the broadest perspective and through various planes of analysis. In the case of the study in Taiwan, such an approach has afforded a viable explanation of the long-standing urban–rural divide in national, annual English achievement among junior high school students and by showing why some students but not others learn the English language relatively well. For the study in England, this approach has also afforded a viable explanation of the way in which state and independent school students, as different social groups, access learning Chinese differently.

Using cross-cultural comparative perspectives

As Philips (1999) pointed out, making a comparison is by nature an intellectual activity and an essential part of the thought processes that enable us to make sense of the world and our experience of it. By making comparisons, we can appropriately defend our position on questions of importance which require the making of judgements. With this in mind, this book not only compared the situations of English/Chinese as foreign languages between Taiwan and England, but it also carried out 'within-group' comparisons between the four schools within Taiwanese society and state/independent schools in England that provide us with a very useful analytical outlook.

In addition, this book has highlighted the importance of history during the course of carrying out the 'three planes of analysis'. A historical perspective is evident in the analysis of the historical situations of the foreign language curriculum in Taiwan and England as the community plane of analysis; in histories of individual teachers' training backgrounds and students' cultural backgrounds which they brought with them into the classroom settings as the interpersonal plane of analysis; in individual students' English/Chinese learning history which shapes their learning trajectories on the personal plane of analysis. The important use of historical analysis can also be nicely captured in Mills' (1959/2000) words when he said:

> Comparative study and historical study are very involved with each other. You cannot understand the underdeveloped, the Communist, the capitalist political economies as they exist in the world today by flat, timeless comparisons. You must expand the temporal reach of your analysis. To understand and to explain the comparative facts as they lie before you today, you must know the historical phases and the historical reasons for varying rates and varying directions of development and lack of development.... Thus the historical viewpoint leads to the comparative study of societies... the mind cannot even formulate the historical and sociological problems of this one social structure without understanding them in contrast and in comparison with other societies. (Mills, 1959/2000: 150–151)

In fact, informed by Wright Mills' words that the 'historical viewpoint leads to the comparative study of societies', this book has tried to outline the historical situations of EFL learning in Taiwan and CFL learning in England at the outset in Chapter 1, aiming to set the stage for a cross-cultural comparison between social and institutional groups within Taiwan and England, and also between the two nations. The historical analysis of the four ethnic groups (i.e. Holo, Hakka, Mainlanders and indigenous people) was foregrounded and compared which helped enhance our analytical thinking and interpretation of students' EFL learning. In a similar vein, before we understand current trends of learning Chinese in England, we have to understand the historical limitation of England in learning foreign languages at the outset. For when we compare, we can become more aware of the historical as intrinsic to what we want to understand and not merely as 'general background' (Mills, 1959/2000).

Closing Remarks

This is probably the first book that introduces the use of sociocultural theory and comparative perspectives to the study of English language learning in Taiwan and Chinese language learning in England where neo-Vygotskian approaches are gaining recognition within the field of language education. It illuminates how different social and institutional groups recognised, accessed and valued English/Chinese language and points to why some groups achieve less well than others in learning these two foreign languages. It suggests that teachers' capacity to share students' native culture and mother tongue in pedagogical practice facilitates intersubjective meanings and thus support learning cognitively and affectively. In the case in England, a state–independent divide suggests a resource divide in the provision of Chinese language education and brings about social inequality in students' everyday access to Chinese. The findings from the fieldwork in Taiwan and England both illuminate why some social or institutional groups are motivated to learn English/Chinese and are able to gain privileged economic positions in job markets. These insights can be used to make recommendations to education practitioners, parents and policymakers in the UK, Taiwan and other countries such as China, Japan, Australia and the USA, who are concerned with improving young people's foreign language capabilities such as English and Chinese languages.

Moreover, in an era of rapid globalisation, learning Chinese in England and learning English in Taiwan are economically and politically framed practices, meaning education for these two languages cannot be treated as isolated school subjects, but rather as intercultural value-added practices. Through this sociocultural and comparative lens, we may speculate that learning English in Taiwan and learning Chinese in England may move towards a 'bigger gulf' between urban/rural and state/independent schools (in Taiwan and England) and social groups (in Taiwan) than we have had for many decades if decontextualised school learning persists. Towards this end, we may be at risk of creating an 'educational apartheid' in secondary schools in the process of learning English or Chinese, invoking renewed forms of social inequality within classroom settings and beyond.

Appendix

Transcription Conventions (modified from Silverman, 1993)

Speakers
T   Teacher
S   Student (**Ss** indicates more than one students)
         (**S1–5** indicates different single student)

1. [ ]   Square brackets indicate overlapping talk.
2. [...]   Indicates gaps between talks.
3. =   Equal signs at the end of one line and the beginning of the next indicate no pause between the two lines.
4. (1.0)   Numbers in parentheses indicate a tiny pause.
5. (.)   A full stop in parentheses indicates a tiny pause.
6. ___   Underscoring shows stress on a word through a change in the speaker's pitch and/or amplitude.
7. ::   Colons indicate that the preceding sound is lengthened.
            More colons show a greater degree of prolongation.
8. (( ))   Double brackets indicate the author's own descriptions.
9. ?   Change in intonation indicating a question.

References

Abreu, G. de (1995) Understanding how children experience the relationship between home and school mathematics. *Mind, Culture and Activity: An International Journal* 2 (2), 119–142.
Alexander, R.J. (1999) Comparing classrooms and schools. In R.J. Alexander, P. Broadfoot and P. David (eds) *Learning from Comparing: New Directions in Comparative Educational Research, Vol. 1: Contexts, Classrooms and Outcomes* (pp. 109–111). Oxford: Symposium Books.
Alexander, R.J. (2000) *Culture and Pedagogy: International Comparisons in Primary Education.* Oxford: Blackwell.
Apple, M.W. (1988) Social crisis and curriculum accords. *Educational Theory* 38 (2), 191–201.
Asian Studies Association of Australia – ASAA (2009) Asian languages enrolments in Australian higher education 2008–2009. University of Melbourne.
Auld, E. and Morris, P. (2014) Comparative education, the 'New Paradigm' and policy borrowing: Constructing knowledge for educational reform. *Comparative Education* 50 (2), 129–155.
Ball, S.J. (2012) The reluctant state and the beginning of the end of state education. *Journal of Educational Administration and History* 44 (2), 89–103.
Bartram, B. (2006) An examination of perceptions of parental influence on attitudes to language learning. *Educational Research* 48 (2), 211–221.
BBC News (2014a) Confucius Institute: The hard side of China's 'soft power'. See https://www.bbc.com/news/world-asia-china-30567743 (accessed 25 March 2018).
BBC News (2014b) Mandarin: Confucius Institute aims to boost numbers. See https://www.bbc.com/news/education-27731680 (accessed 7 October 2018).
BBC News (2015) Nuclear security fears, migrant flights and an EU 'U-turn'. See http://www.bbc.co.uk/news/blogs-the-papers-34546512 (accessed 20 October 2015).
Bernstein, B. (1990) *Class, Codes and Control. Vol. 4, The Structuring of Pedagogic Discourse.* London: Routledge.
Bourdieu, P. (1986) The forms of capital. In J. Richardson (ed.) *Handbook of Theory and Research for the Sociology of Education* (pp. 241–258). Westport, CT: Greenwood.
Bray, M. (2014) Actors and purposes in comparative education. In M. Bray, B. Adamson and M. Manson (eds) *Comparative Education Research: Approaches and Methods* (2nd edn; pp. 19–46). Cham: Springer International Publishing.
Bray, M., Adamson, B. and Manson, M. (eds) (2014) *Comparative Education Research: Approaches and Methods* (2nd edn). Cham: Springer International Publishing.
British Council (2013) *Languages for the Future: Which Languages the UK Needs Most and Why.* London: British Council.
British Council (2014) *Language Trends 2013/14: The State of Language Learning in Primary and Secondary Schools in England.* London: British Council.

British Council (2016) *Language Trends 2015/16: The State of Language Learning in Primary and Secondary Schools in England*. London: British Council.
Broadfoot, P. (1999) Not so much a context. More a way of life? Comparative education in the 1990s. In R.J. Alexander, P. Broadfoot and P. David (eds) *Learning from Comparing: New Directions in Comparative Educational Research, Vol. 1: Contexts, Classrooms and Outcomes* (pp. 21–32). Oxford: Symposium Books.
Bullock, A. (1975) *A Language for Life*. London: Her Majesty's Stationery Office.
Cazden, C.B. (1988) *Classroom Discourse: The Language of Teaching and Learning*. Portsmouth, NH: Heinemann.
Chiang, B. (ed.) (2004) *The Report of Indigenous Cultural Customs: Paiwan Tribe* (Vol. 5). Taipei: Institute of Ethnology, Academia Sinica. [In Chinese.]
Chomsky, N. (1968) *Language and Mind*. New York: Harcourt Brace Jovanovich, Inc.
Chomsky, N. (2000) *New Horizons in the Study of Language and Mind*. Cambridge: Cambridge University Press.
Chow, P. and Cummins, J. (2003) Valuing multilingual and multicultural approaches to learning. In S.R. Schecter and J. Cummins (eds) *Multilingual Education in Practice: Using Diversity as a Resource* (pp. 32–61). Portsmouth, NH: Heinemann.
CiLT (2006) *Language Trends 2006: Languages in Key Stage 4*. London: CiLT, The National Centre for Languages.
CiLT (2007) *Mandarin Language Learning: Research Study*. London: CiLT, The National Centre for Languages.
Clegg, J. (2003) *Chinese Studies in UK Schools*. Ormskirk: Edge Hill College of Higher Education.
Cole, M. (1996) *Cultural Psychology: A Once and Future Discipline*. Cambridge, MA: Harvard University Press.
Cole, M., Engeström Y. and Vasquez, O. (1997) *Mind, Culture, and Society: Seminal Papers from Laboratory of Comparative Human Cognition*. Cambridge: Cambridge University Press.
Constable, N. (ed.) (1996) *Guest People: Hakka Identity in China and Abroad*. London: University of Washington Press.
Coombs, P.H. (1985) *The World Crisis in Education: The View from the Eighties*. Oxford: Oxford University Press.
Crossley, M. and Jarvis, P. (2000) Introduction: Continuity and change in comparative and international education. *Comparative Education* 36 (3), 261–265.
Crystal, D. (2010) *English as a Global Language* (2nd edn). Cambridge: Cambridge University Press.
Daniels, H. (ed.) (1993) *Charting the Agenda: Educational Activity after Vygotsky*. London: Routledge.
Daniels, H. (2001) *Vygotsky and Pedagogy*. London: RoutledgeFalmer.
DfES (2002) Languages for all: Languages for life – A strategy for England. See https://www.languagescompany.com/wp-content/uploads/the-national-languages-strategy-for-england-1.pdf (accessed 4 May 2016).
EDT (2016) *Language Trends 2015/16: The State of Language Learning in Primary and Secondary Schools in England*. Reading: The Education Development Trust.
Ehrenberg, R.G., Brewer, D.J., Gamoran, A. and Willms, J.D. (2001) *The Class Size Controversy*. Cornell, NY: Cornell University.
Exley, S. and Ball, S.J. (2014) Neo-liberalism and English education. In D.A. Turner and H. Yolcu (eds) *Neo-Liberal Educational Reforms: A Critical Analysis* (pp. 13–31). London: Routledge.
Fishman, J. (1989) *Language and Ethnicity in Minority Sociolinguistic Perspective*. Philadelphia, PA: Multilingual Matters.
Friedman, T.L. (2005) *The World is Flat: A Brief History of the Twenty-First Century*. New York: Farrar, Straus and Giroux.

Gay, G. (2000) *Culturally Responsive Teaching: Theory, Research, and Practice*. New York: Teachers College Press.
Gay, G. (2002) Preparing for culturally responsive teaching. *Journal of Teacher Education* 53 (2), 106–116.
Giddens, A. (2006) *Sociology* (5th edn). Cambridge: Polity.
Giles, H. and Johnson, P. (1981) The role of language in ethnic group relations. In J.C. Turner and H. Giles (eds) *Intergroup Behaviour* (pp. 199–243). Oxford: Blackwell.
Godwin-Jones, R. (2018) Afterword – Reflections on global English instruction: New roles and Approaches. In W.C. Lin, I.J. Weng and R. Godwin-Jones (eds) *Internationalizing English Language Education in Globalized Taiwan* (pp. 247–266). Taipei: Tung Hua.
Gollnick, D.M. and Chinn, P.C. (2002) *Multicultural Education in a Pluralistic Society* (6th edn). New York: Merrill.
Graddol, D. (2006) *English Next: Why Global English may Mean the End of 'English as a Foreign Language'*. London: The British Council.
Graves, W. (1987) Film reviews. *American Anthropologist* 89 (1), 263–264.
Greenhalgh, S. (1984) Networks and their nodes: Urban society on Taiwan. *China Quarterly* 99, 529–552.
Hall, E.T. (1994) *West of the Thirties: Discoveries Among the Navajo and Hopi*. New York: Doubleday.
Hanban (2018) 2016–17 Annual Report. See https://confucius.missouri.edu/2016-17-annual-report/ (accessed 21 October 2018).
Hawkins, E.W. (1987) *Modern Languages in the Curriculum*. Cambridge: Cambridge University Press.
Hawkins, E.W. (1999) *Listening to Lorca: A Journey into Language*. London: CILT.
He, W.W. and Jiao, D. (2010) Curriculum design and special features of 'computer Chinese' and Chinese for tomorrow. In J.G. Chen, C. Wang and J.F. Cai (eds) *Teaching and Learning Chinese* (pp. 217–236). Charlotte, NC: IAP.
Heller, M. and Duchêne, A. (2012) *Language in Late Capitalism: Pride and Profit*. London: Routledge.
Holland, D., Lachicotte, W., Skinner, D. and Cain, C. (1998) *Identity and Agency in Cultural Worlds*. Cambridge, MA: Harvard University Press.
Hu, Tai-li (Director/Producer) (1984) The Return of the Gods and Ancestors: The Five Year Ceremony [Video Recording]. Taiwan.
Huang, T.L. (1993) *The Pedagogic Innovation and Enrichment of EFL*. Taipei: Crane. [In Chinese.]
Huang, S.F. (2000) Language, identity and conflict: A Taiwanese study. *International Journal of Sociology of Language* 143, 139–149.
Hymes, D.H. (1972) On communication competence. In J.B. Pride and J. Holmes (eds) *Sociolinguistics. Selected Readings* (pp. 269–293). New York: Penguin.
Incorporated Association of Assistant Masters in Secondary Schools (1967) *The Teaching of History*. Cambridge: Cambridge University Press.
IMF News (2016) IMF adds Chinese Renminbi to Special Drawing Rights basket. See http://www.imf.org/en/news/articles/2016/09/29/am16-na093016imf-adds-chinese-renminbi-to-special-drawing-rights-basket (accessed 30 September 2016).
Ivinson, G. and Murphy, P. (2007) *Rethinking Single-Sex Teaching*. New York: Open University Press.
Jones, N. (2007) Assessment and the national languages strategy. *Cambridge Journal of Education* 37 (1), 17–33.
Kandel, I.L. (1933) *Studies in Comparative Education*. Boston, MA: Houghton Mifflin.
Kazamias, A.M. and Schwartz, K.A. (1977) Introduction. *Comparative Education Review* Special Issue on 'The State of The Art' 21 (2&3), 151–152.
Kember, D. (1996) The intention to both memories and understand: Another approach to learning? *Higher Education* 31 (3), 341–354.

Kleine, P.F. (1982) Teaching styles. In H.E. Mitzel (ed.) *The Encyclopedia of Educational Research* (5th edn). London: Collier Macmillan.
Kramsch, C. (2014) Teaching foreign languages in an era of globalization: Introduction. *The Modern Language Journal* 98 (2), 295–494.
Kozulin, A. (1990) *Vygotsky's Psychology: A Biography of Ideas*. Cambridge, MA: Harvard University Press.
Lave, J. (1988) *Cognition in Practice: Mind, Mathematics and Culture in Everyday Life*. Cambridge: Cambridge University.
Lave, J. (1996) The practice of learning. In S. Chaiklin and J. Lave (eds) *Understanding Practice: Perspectives on Activity and Context* (pp. 3–32). Cambridge: Cambridge University Press.
Lave, J. and Wenger, E. (1991) *Situated Learning: Legitimate Peripheral Participation*. Cambridge: Cambridge University Press.
Law, N. (2007) Comparing pedagogical innovations. In M. Bray, B. Adamson and M. Mason (eds) *Comparative Education Research: Approaches and Methods* (pp. 315–337). Hong Kong: Springer and HKU.
Lawton, D. (1975) *Class, Culture and the Curriculum*. London: Routledge.
Leontiev, A.A. (1981) *Psychology and the Language Learning Process*. Oxford: Pergamon Press.
Liddicoat, A.J. (2014) Pragmatics and intercultural mediation in intercultural language learning. *Intercultural Pragmatics* 11 (2), 259–277.
Lin, W.C. (2007) Culture, ethnicity and English language learning: A socio-cultural study of secondary schools in Taiwan. Unpublished doctoral dissertation, Cardiff University.
Lin, W.C. (2012a) Choosing between methodologies: An inquiry into English learning processes in a Taiwanese indigenous school. *English Teaching: Practice and Critique* 11 (1), 43–59.
Lin, W.C. (2012b) Language competition and challenges in pluralingual education: The case of a Hakka school in Taiwan. Contribution to Plurilingual and Intercultural Education, a special issue guest-edited by Mike Byram, Mike Fleming and Irene Pieper. *L1-Educational Studies in Language and Literature* 12, 1–19.
Lin, W.C. and Ivinson, G. (2012) Ethnic cultural legacies and EFL learning: A sociocultural study in Taiwan. In E. Hjörne, D. van der Aalsvoort and G. de Abreu (eds) *Learning, Social Interaction and Diversity: Exploring School Practices* (pp. 69–84). Rotterdam: Sense Publishers.
Lin, W.C. and Byram, M. (2016) Introduction. In W.C. Lin and M. Byram (eds) *New Approaches to English Language and Education in Taiwan: Cultural and Intercultural Perspectives* (pp. xvii–xxv). Taiwan: Tunghua Publishers.
Lin, W.C. and Godwin-Jones, R. (2018) Introduction and overview. In W.C. Lin, I.J. Weng and R. Godwin-Jones (eds) *Internationalizing English Language Education in Globalized Taiwan* (pp. 1–9). Taipei: Tung Hua.
Lopez, A. (2011) Culturally relevant pedagogy and critical literacy in diverse English classrooms: A case study of a secondary English teacher's activism and agency. *English Teaching: Practice and Critique* 10 (4), 75–93.
Mason, M. (2007) Comparing cultures. In M. Bray, B. Adamson and M. Mason (eds) *Comparative Education Research: Approaches and Methods* (pp. 165–196). Hong Kong: The University of Hong Kong.
Mehan, H. (1979) *Learning Lessons: Social Organization in the Classroom*. Cambridge, MA: Harvard University Press.
Meyer, H.-D. and Benavot, A. (eds) (2013) *PISA, Power and Policy: The Emergence of Global Educational Governance*. Oxford: Symposium Books.
Mills, C.W. (1959/2000) *The Sociological Imagination*. Oxford: Oxford University Press.
Ministry of Foreign Affairs, Taiwan (2019). About Taiwan: People. See https://www.taiwan.gov.tw/content_2.php (accessed 20 May 2019).

MOE Taiwan (2004) Recruitment of Teachers of Foreign Nationality. See https://english.moe.gov.tw/cp-32-14625-0025C-1.html (accessed 5 May 2004).
MOE Taiwan (2006) *2006 Education in Taiwan*. Taiwan: Ministry of Education.
MOE Taiwan (2015) General guidelines of Grade 1–9 Curriculum of elementary and junior high school education. See http://english.moe.gov.tw/public/Attachment/66618445071.doc (accessed 2 April 2015).
MOE Taiwan (2019) *12-Year Basic Education Curricula* (in Chinese). See https://depart.moe.edu.tw/ED7600/ (accessed 17 June 2019).
Murphy, S. (1999) Young children's behavior in interactive tasks: The effects of popularity on communication and task performance. Unpublished doctoral dissertation. Open University.
Murphy, P. and Elwood, J. (1998) Gendered learning inside and outside school: Influences on achievement. In D. Epstein, J. Elwood, V. Hey and J. Maw (eds) *Failing Boys? Issues in Gender and Achievement* (pp. 162–182). Buckingham: Open University.
Orton, J. (2008) *The Current State of Chinese Language Education in Australia Schools* (3rd edn). Melbourne: The University of Melbourne.
Pedder, D. (2006) Organizational conditions that foster successful classroom promotion of learning How to Learn. *Research Papers in Education* 21 (2), 171–200.
Pennycook, A. (2010) *Language as Local Practice*. New York: Routledge.
Pereyra, M.A., Kotthof, H.-G. and Cowen, R. (eds) (2011) *PISA Under Examination: Changing Knowledge, Changing Tests, and Changing Schools*. Rotterdam: Sense.
Philips, D. (1999) On comparing. In R.J. Alexander, P. Broadfoot and P. David (eds) *Learning from Comparing: New Directions in Comparative Educational Research, Vol. 1: Contexts, Classrooms and Outcomes* (pp. 15–20). Oxford: Symposium Books.
QCA (1998) *Maintaining Breadth and Balance at Key Stages 1 and 2*. London: QCA.
Rogoff, B. (1990) *Apprenticeship in Thinking: Cognitive Development in Social Context*. Oxford: Oxford University Press.
Rogoff, B. (1995) Observing sociocultural activity on three planes: Participatory appropriation, guided participation, and apprenticeship. In J.V. Wertsch, P. del Rio and A. Alvarez (eds) *Sociocultural Studies of Mind* (pp. 139–164). Cambridge: Cambridge University Press.
Rogoff, B. (2003) *The Cultural Nature of Human Development*. Oxford: Oxford University Press.
Rogoff, B. and Lave, J. (eds) (1984) *Everyday Cognition: Development in Social Context*. Cambridge, MA: Harvard University Press.
Sadler, M. (1900/1964) In G. Bereday, Documents: Sir Michael Sadler's 'Study of Foreign Systems of Education'. *Comparative Education Review* 7 (3), 307–314.
Salomon, G. (1993) *Distributed Cognitions: Psychological and Educational Considerations*. Cambridge: Cambridge University Press.
Sandel, T.L. (2003) Linguistic capital in Taiwan: The KMT's Mandarin language policy and its perceived impact on language practices of bilingual Mandarin and Tai-gi speakers. *Language in Society* 32, 523–551.
Scribner, S. and Cole, M. (1981) *The Psychology of Literacy*. Cambridge, MA: Harvard University Press.
Shea, C. (2008) Cross-linguistic similarity in foreign language learning (review). *The Canadian Modern Language Review* 64 (4), 700–702.
Shweder, R.A. (1990) Cultural psychology: What is it? In J.W. Stigler, R.A. Shweder and G. Herdt (eds) *Cultural Psychology: Essay on Comparative Human Development* (pp. 1–43). New York: Cambridge University Press.
Silverman, D. (1993) *Interpreting Qualitative Data: Methods for Analysing Talk, Text and Interaction*. London: Sage.
Singh, M. and Ballantyne, C. (2014) Making Chinese learnable for beginning second language learners? In N. Murray and A. Scarino (eds) *Dynamic Ecologies: A Relational*

Perspective on Languages Education in the Asia-Pacific Region (pp. 199–216). Dordrecht: Springer.

Singh, M. and Han, J. (2014) Making Chinese learnable: Strategies for the retention of language learners. In F. Dervin (ed.) *Chinese Educational Migration and Student-Teacher Mobilities: Experiencing Otherness* (pp. 166–190). London: Palgrave Macmillan.

Stafford, A. (1995) Roland Barthes, 1947–1960: Journalism, Sociology and the Popular Theatre. PhD thesis, University of Nottingham.

Starr, D. (2009) Chinese language education in Europe: The Confucius Institutes. *European Journal of Education* 44 (1), 65–82.

Sunderland, J. (1994) *Exploring Gender: Questions and Implications for English Language Education*. Hemel Hempstead: Prentice Hall.

Thompson, S.E. (1984) Taiwan: Rural society. *China Quarterly* 99, 553–568.

Tinsley, T. and Board, K. (2014) *The Teaching of Chinese in the UK: Research Report.* See https://www.britishcouncil.org/sites/default/files/alcantara_full_report_jun15.pdf (accessed 10 April 2018).

Tomasello, M. (2003) *Constructing a Language: A Usage-Based Theory of Language Acquisition*. Cambridge, MA: Harvard University Press.

Verplaetse, L.S. and Migliacci, N. (2008) Inclusive pedagogy: An introduction. In L.S. Verplaetse and N. Migliacci (eds) *Inclusive Pedagogy for English Language Learners: A Handbook of Research-Informed Practice* (pp. 3–13). New York: Lawrence Erlbaum Associates.

Vygotsky, L.S. (1981) The genesis of higher mental functions. In J.V. Wertsch (ed. and trans.) *The Concept of Activity in Soviet Psychology* (pp. 144–188). Armonk, NY: Sharpe.

Vygotsky, L.S. (1987) Thinking and speech. In R.W. Rieber and A.S. Carton (eds) *The Collected Works of L. S. Vygotsky* (N. Minick, trans.) (pp. 38–285). New York: Plenum Press.

Wang, P. (2009) The provision of Mandarin Chinese in the UK secondary schools: What's in the way? *European Journal of Education* 44 (1), 83–94. doi: 10.1111/j.1465-3435.2008.01372.

Watkins, D.A. (2007) Comparing ways of learning. In M. Bray, B. Adamson and M. Mason (eds) *Comparative Education Research: Approaches and Methods* (pp. 299–314). Hong Kong: Springer and HKU.

Watkins, D.A. and Biggs, J.B. (2001) *Teaching the Chinese Learner: Psychological and Pedagogical Perspectives*. Hong Kong: Comparative Education Research Centre & Australian Council for Educational Research.

Wenger, E. (1998) *Communities of Practice: Learning, Meaning, and Identity*. Cambridge: Cambridge University Press.

Wertsch, J.V. (1991) *Voices of Mind: A Sociocultural Approach to Mediated Action*. Cambridge: Harvard University Press.

Wertsch, J.V. (1998) *Mind as Action*. New York: Oxford University Press.

Wikeley, F. and Stables, A. (1999) Changes in school students' approaches to subject option choices: A study of pupils in the West of England in 1984 and 1996. *Educational Research* 41 (3), 287–299.

Wilson, D.N. (2003) The future of comparative and international education in a globalised world. In M. Bray (ed.) *Comparative Education: Continuing Traditions, New Challenges, and New Paradigms* (pp. 15–33). Dordrecht: Kluwer.

Wlodkowski, R.J. and Ginsberg, M.B. (2000) *Creating Highly Motivating Classrooms for All Students: Powerful Teaching with Diverse Learners*. San Francisco, CA: Jossey-Bass Inc.

Woods, D.J., Bruner, J.S. and Ross, G. (1976) The role of tutoring in problem solving. *Journal of Child Psychology and Psychiatry* 17 (2), 89–100.

Index

Note: References in *italics* are to figures, those in **bold** to tables.

Abreu, G. de 158
academic implications of this book 26–7
access to Chinese in England 79, 196
    everyday Chinese practices 79–82
    family resources 82–3, **83**, 87–8, **88**
    parental education 83, **84**
    state–independent divide 87–8
access to English in Taiwan 72, 196
    everyday English practices 72–4, **73**
    family resources 74–6, **75**, 87
    impact of historico-cultural legacies 84–5, **85**
    parental education and occupation 76–9, **77**
    urban–rural divide and cultural differences 85–7
Alexander, R.J. 20, 31, 39, 45
Apple, M.W. 46
Asian Studies Association of Australia (ASAA) 53, 186
Auld, E. 19, 20
Australia: language learning 15, 53

Ball, S.J. 50
Ballantyne, C. 15
BBC News 11
Benavot, A. 19
Bernstein, B. 59
Board, K. 14
Bourdieu, P. 15, 71–2, 86
Bray, M. *et al.* 17, 18, 19
Britain *see* United Kingdom
British Council 9, 10, 13, 14, 42, 44, 53, 69, 175

Broadfoot, P. 30
Bullock, A. 43
Byram, M. 175–6

Centre for British Teachers (CfBT) Education Trust 9
CFL (Chinese as a foreign language) 12, *12*
    in England 10, *12*, 12–16, 53, 54, 69–70
Chiang, B. 67
Chinese language classrooms in England
    class timetables 102–4, **103**
    language teachers **106**, 106–11
    material culture 104–6, *105*
    texts and note-taking 111–12
Chinese language learning in England 10, **12**, 12–13, 53, 54, 69–70, 196
    beginning of success 11–13
    emerging issues 13–16
Chinese learning trajectories in England 160–1
    central participants 162–7
    individual cases **161**, 161–2
Chinese Mainlanders *see* Mainlanders
Chomsky, N. 32–3
Chow, P. 199
CiLT 8, 9, 13
    Mandarin Language Learning: Research Study 14
class size 104–5, 115, 185
classroom control 125–7
    in England **118**, 118–19
    in Taiwan **116**, 116–19

classroom life 28, 90
  Chinese language classrooms in
    England 102–12
  comparisons across cultures 112–27
  English language classrooms in Taiwan
    90–101
  chapter summary 127–8
Clegg, J. 13
cognitive psychology 32–8
Cole, M. 35–6, 37, 72, 79, 130, 187, 201
communicative competence 33
communities of practice 35, 37, 129–30,
  201
  CFL learning trajectories in England
    160–7
  English learning trajectories in Taiwan
    130–60
  identity as imagined futures 167–72
  chapter summary 172
comparative education research 1–2
  practitioners, policymakers, academics
    18
  schools in Taiwan and England 21–6
  sociocultural approaches 20–1
  value of 16–20
Confucius Institutes 11–12, **12**, 175
Constable, N. 65
contexts of language learning 28, 39–40
  curricula for foreign language
    education 51–5
  political framing 40–5
  school cultures 45–50
  school visions 55–61, **57, 59**
  social group cultures 64–70
  chapter summary 70
Coombs, P.H. 6, 68, 85
cross-cultural comparisons 28, 173,
  180–3, 203–4
  differences in learning and teaching
    179–87
  emerging social issues 187–94
  similarities in learning and teaching
    174–9
Crossley, M. 17
Crystal, D. 40–1
cultural capital 16, 70–1
  England 86, 87–8
  Taiwan 85–6
cultural development 33–4

cultural psychology 32
cultural/sociolinguistic bridging 125–7,
  185–7, 199–200
culturally responsive pedagogy 200
Cummins, J. 199
curricula for foreign language education
  England 52–5
  Taiwan Grades 1–9 51

Daniels, H. 34, 200
DfES 8
differences in learning and teaching
  motivations and experiences 179–83
  teaching styles 183–7
Duchêne, A. 198

Education Development Trust (EDT) 13
Ehrenberg, R.G. *et al.* 185
elite social status in learning English/
  Chinese? 175–9
Elwood, J. 189
England
  Chinese language learning 10, **12**,
    12–16, 53, 54, 63, 69–70, 102–12
  cultural capital 86, 87–8
  education system 47–50, 69, 87–8
  foreign culture experiences 64
  foreign language learning 8–10, *10*,
    42–5, 52, 53–5, **54, 55**
  Language Trends 2013/14 9–10
  Latin 54
  neo-liberalism 48, 50
  social group culture 68–70
  see also access to Chinese in England
England participant schools
  Bath High School **24**, 25, 60,
    63, 64
  Chinese language teachers **106**,
    106–11
  classroom contexts 104–6, *105*
  classroom control **118**, 118–19
  demographic features 24
  Highland School 24, **24**, 63, 177–8
  King's School **24**, 26, 64, 79–82, **81**,
    83, 87–8, **88**, 102–3, **103**, 162–7,
    180–3
  motivations and experiences in learning
    Chinese **180**, 180–3, **181**
  school visions 58–61, **59**

sociolinguistic bridging 125–7, 186
St Mary's School **24**, 25–6, 79, 176–7, 178
St Peter's School **24**, 24–5, 64, 178
using everyday culture 119–20
English language classrooms in Taiwan 90–1
　class timetables as daily schedules 91–2, **92**
　comparing class timetables 92–3, **93**
　English teachers **96**, 96–100
　material culture 93–6, **94**, *94*
　texts and note-taking 100–1
English language learning in Taiwan
　educational inequality among social groups 4–7
　EFL academic achievement in secondary schools 3–4
　national movement 2–3, 196
English learning trajectories in Taiwan 130
　central participants 137–53
　individual cases 130–7, **131**, **132**, **133**
　peripheral participants **153**, 153–60
everyday practice 71–2
　access to Chinese in England 79–83, **83**, **84**, 87–8, **88**
　access to English in Taiwan 72–9, **73**, **75**, **77**
　impact of historico-cultural legacies 84–5, **85**
　urban–rural divide and cultural differences 85–7
　chapter summary 88–9

Fishman, J. 68
foreign language education 196–7
　curricula 51–5
　England 8–10, *10*, 42–5, 52, 53–5, **54**, **55**
　impacts of globalisation 197–9
　inclusive pedagogy of cultural and sociolinguistic bridging 199–201
　sociocultural and comparative approaches 201–4
　Taiwan 40–2, 51, **51**, **53**, 197
　closing remarks 204–5
Friedman, T.L. 174

Gay, G. 200
GEPT (General English Proficiency Test, Taiwan) 47, 174–5
Giddens, A. 69–70
Giles, H. 6
Global Englishes 47
globalisation 39–40, 174–5, 196
　impacts on foreign language education 197–9
Godwin-Jones, R. 47, 99
Graddol, D. 44
Graves, W. 67
Greenhalgh, S. 5, 64–5, 78, 84
guided participation 89, 90, 98

Hakka language 4, 6, 7, 120, 122–3
Hakka people 4, 5–6, 65–6
　everyday access to English **73**, 74, **75**, **76**, **77**
　historico-cultural legacies 84
　religious beliefs **85**
Hall, E.T. 40
Han, J. 186, 187
Hawkins, E.W. 9, 43, 52, 54, 64, 194
Heller, M. 198
hidden curricula 55
　cram schools in Taiwan **61**, 61–2, 92, 132, 136, 142–3, 189
　foreign culture experiences for the British 64
　foreign English teachers/tutorials in Taiwan 62–3, **63**
　holistic education 59
　moral education 59, 60
　private Chinese tutors in England 63
　school visions 55–61, **57**, **59**
historico-cultural legacies 84–5, 203–4
　resource discrepancy in England 87–8
　urban–rural divide and cultural differences 85–7
holistic education 59
Holland, D. *et al.* 167–8
Holo people 4, 5, 7, 64–5
　everyday access to English 72, **73**, 74, **75**, **75**, 76, **77**, 77–8
　religious beliefs **85**
Hu, Tai-Li 67
Huang, S.F. 6, 7, 197
Hymes, D.H. 33

identity
  as imagined futures 167–72
  and language learning 28
Incorporated Association of Assistant
    Masters in Secondary Schools 42–3
indigenous people 4, 5
  everyday access to English 72, 73, **73**,
    74, 75, **75**, 76–7, **77**, 78, 86
  religious beliefs **85**
individualistic mind 32–3
intercultural communication 47
International Monetary Fund (IMF) 11,
    174
intersubjectivity 124, 125, 152–3, 170–1
Ivinson, G. 193

Jarvis, P. 17
Johnson, P. 6
Johnson, R. 68

Kandel, I.L. 31
Kazamias, A.M. 17
Kleine, P.F. 116
Kramsch, C. 194, 197, 198, 199

Lave, J. 35, 37, 187, 189, 201
Law, N. 90
Lawton, D. 49
Leontiev, A.A. 200
Liddicoat, A.J. 197
Lin, W.C. *et al.* 6, 47, 175–6, 198,
    199
Lopez, A. 200

Mainlanders 4, 5, 65
  everyday access to English 72–3, **73**,
    74, **75**, 75–6, **77**, 77–8, 86, 87
  religious beliefs 84–5, **85**
Mandarin Chinese 4–5, 6
Mason, M. 1, 39, 40, 173
Meyer, H.-D 19
Migliacci, N. 185, 189
Mills, C.W. 1, 16, 27, 203, 204
moral education 59, 60
Morris, P. 19, 20
motivations and experiences 179
  in learning Chinese **180**, 180–3, **181**
  in learning English 179–80, **180**
Murphy, P. 189, 193

Northern Ireland: Erse 8

Organisation for Economic Cooperation
    and Development (OECD)
  PISA study 19
Orton, J. 15, 186

Paiwan ethnic culture 123–4
Paiwan language 60, 124–5
Paiwan tribe 23, 24, 56–7, 61–2, 66–7,
    77, 78–9, 85
pedagogical comparisons 112–13, **114**
  activity-based in England 115–16
  grammar-oriented in Taiwan 113–14
  instruction: using everyday culture
    119–25
  patterns of classroom control **116**,
    116–19
  'sociolinguistic bridging' in England
    125–7
  chapter summary 127–8
Pedder, D. 185
Pennycook, A. 186
Philips, D. 16, 17–18, 203
PISA (Programme for International
    Student Assessment) 19
political and practical implications of this
    book 27–8
political framing of foreign language
    learning
  EFL context in Taiwan 40–2
  foreign language learning in England
    42–5
practice approach to literacy 35–6, 201

resources 188–9
Rogoff, B. 20, 30, 34, 71, 89, 90, 125,
    129, 130, 200
rote learning vs activity-based learning
    183–5

Sadler, M. 19, 31
school cultures 45
  England 47–50, 69, 87–8
  Taiwan 45–7
school visions 55
  comparing school visions 59,
    60–1
  England 58–9, **59**

holistic education 59
moral education 59, 60
Taiwan 55–7, **57**, 59, 60
Schwartz, K.A. 17
Scotland 8
Scribner, S. 35–6, 37, 72, 79, 130, 187, 201
Shea, C. 126
Shweder, R.A. 32
similarities in learning and teaching
elite social status in learning English/Chinese? 175–9
global and political framing 174–5
Singh, M. 15, 186, 187
situated learning theory 35, 37–8, 129, 187, 201–2
see also communities of practice
social capital 86–7
social dimension of human minds 33–5
social gender identities 189–90
boundary crosser 193–4
learning Chinese in England **190**, 190–1
social expectations of gender roles in Taiwan **131**, **192**, 192–3
social group cultures 64
ethnic group cultures in Taiwan 64–8
social group culture in England 68–70
social issues 187–8
resource divide 188–9
social gender identities 189–94
chapter summary 194–5
sociocultural views on language learning 20–1, 26, 28, 30–2, *31*, 202–3
challenge of the individualistic mind 32–3
neo-Vygotskyian studies 35–8
social dimension of human minds 33–5
chapter summary 38
Southern Min language 4
speech 34
Stafford, A. 76, 83
Starr, D. 11
structure of the book 28–9
Sunderland, J. 189–90
Suzhou Link 25, 58, 64

Taiwan
bilingualism 3, 22, 41–2, 60, 141–2, 155–6, 197, 198
Challenge 2008 National Development Plan 3, 41–2
cram schools **61**, 61–2, 92, 132, 136, 142–3, 189
cultural capital 85–6
current issues in learning English 2–7, 196
EFL context 40–2
English language classrooms 90–101
ethnic group cultures 64–8
foreign English teachers/tutorials 62–3, **63**
foreign language curriculum 40–2, 51, **51**, **53**, 197
indigenous people 4, 5
language status 6–7, **7**
multiculturalism 6
national language 6
school systems 46–7
social groups 4–7, *5*
see also access to English in Taiwan
Taiwan participant schools
class timetables 92–3, **93**
classroom contexts 93–6, **94**, *94*
classroom control **116**, 116–19
demographic features *22*
English learning trajectories 130–60, **131**
English teachers **96**, 96–100
Hakka Rural School *22*, 23, 66, 134–6, **135**, 147–9, 156–9, 189
motivations and experiences in learning English 179–80, **180**
Mountainside School *22*, 23–4, **136**, 136–7, 149–53, 159–60
school visions 55–7, **57**, 59, 60
Suburbany School *22*, 22–3, 63, **133**, 133–4, 143–7, 168–9
Urbany School 21, 22, *22*, 56, 96, 131–2, **132**, 138–43, 140–2, 153–6
using everyday culture 119–20, **120**
Taiwanese language 4
teaching styles 183
cultural and sociolinguistic bridging 125–7, 185–7

rote learning vs activity-based learning 183–5
Thompson, S.E. 5, 76, 77
Tinsley, T. 14
Tomasello, M. 33
transcription conventions 206

United Kingdom 68
  Confucius Institutes **12**
  education systems 8
  foreign language learning 8–9
  heritage languages 69

Vai study 35–6
Verplaetse, L.S. 185, 199

Vygotsky, L.S. 26, 30, 33–5, 168, 200

Wales: Welsh 8
Watkins, D.A. 114, 184
Wenger, E. 35, 37, 130, 201
Wertsch, J.V. 61, 100, 129
Wilson, D.N. 18
Wore, J. 44
World Trade Organisation (WTO) 3, 65

Xi Jinping 11

Yang, Chuan-Guang 67–8

For Product Safety Concerns and Information please contact our EU Authorised Representative:

Easy Access System Europe

Mustamäe tee 50

10621 Tallinn

Estonia

gpsr.requests@easproject.com